LETTERS *from a* STOIC

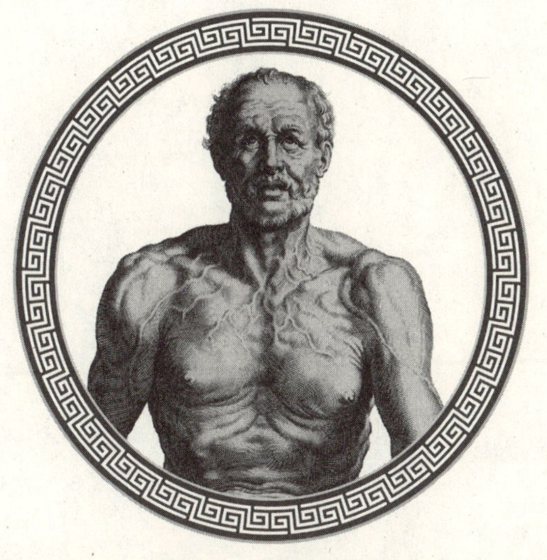

SENECA

Published 2025

FINGERPRINT! CLASSICS
Prakash Books

Fingerprint Publishing
@FingerprintP
@fingerprintpublishingbooks
www.fingerprintpublishing.com

ISBN: 978 93 5856 674 1

"That from which you are running, is within you. Accordingly, reform your own self, get the burden off your own shoulders, and keep within safe limits the cravings which ought to be removed. Wipe out from your soul all trace of sin."

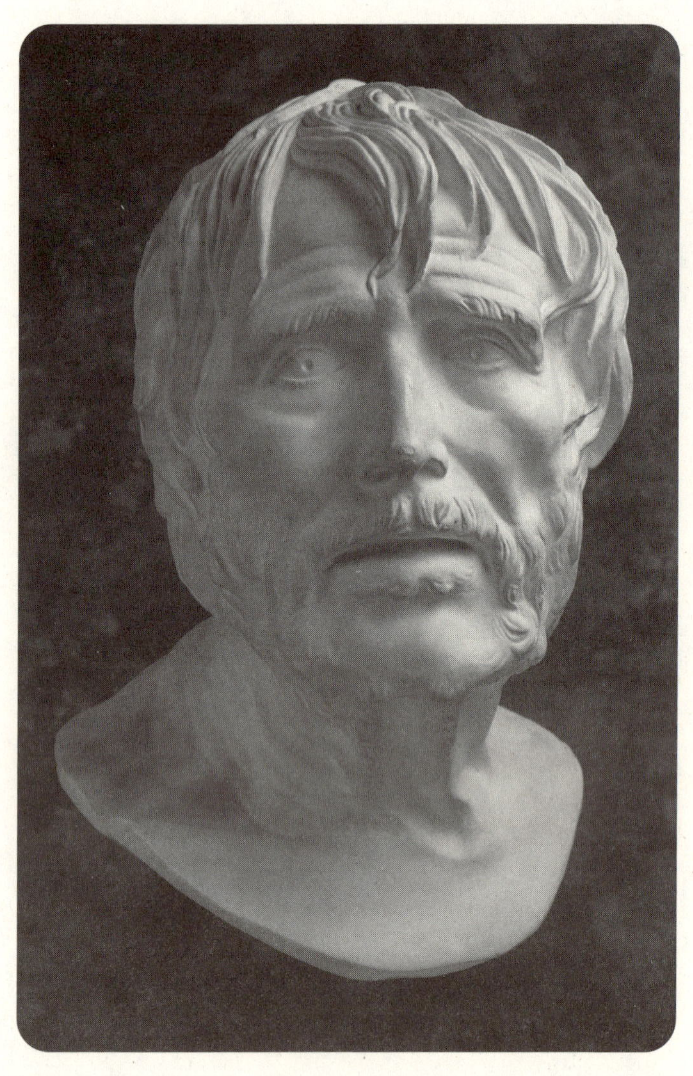

Considered to be the greatest Roman philosopher in history, Lucius Annaeus Seneca (known as Seneca the younger) was born in Cordoba (Spain) in C. 4 BC to Seneca the Elder, a Roman knight who was well-known as a teacher of rhetoric, and Helvia, who was from a prominent Baetician family. He was the second of three brothers. When Seneca was about five years old, he was taken to Rome by his aunt, where he was educated at the School of Sextii, which combined Stoicism with Pythagoreanism. There, he studied philosophy and was trained as an orator.

Seneca had a bout of illness when he was in his twenties. He traveled to Egypt to recover and stayed with his aunt and uncle. For a period of about ten years, his aunt took care of him and nursed him back to health. He then returned to Rome with her in 31 AD and began his political career. Seneca's oratorical skills were unparalleled. It is believed that his success infuriated the then emperor Caligula, who gave him a death sentence. Caligula then recanted this order, as he was made to believe that Seneca will anyway have a short life due to his frequent bouts of illness.

Claudius ascended the throne in 41 AD after Caligula's assassination, and accused Seneca of adultery with his niece. By the order of the Senate, Seneca was exiled. He spent the next eight years of his life on the island of Corsica, where he allegedly wrote *Consolation to Helvia* (to comfort his mother who was grieving over the fate of her son) and *Consolation to Polybius*. With the help of Claudius' wife, Agrippina, Seneca was called back to Rome in 49 AD, and a year later was made tutor to Agrippina's son, the future emperor Nero.

Nero became emperor upon Claudius' death. He trusted his new tutor, who had then turned into a royal adviser and perhaps one of the most powerful men in Rome. The initial years of Nero's reign were peaceful. He relied on Seneca and often sought counsel regarding royal matters. He was, however, very young to have the wisdom to manage a kingdom. Slowly and steadily, Seneca's influence on Nero began to diminish and they became estranged. And then there came a day when Nero's volatile nature reared its head. He staged events to kill his own mother. Seneca's pupil had become a monster. Nero's planned strategy to make his mother's murder look like an accident, didn't work. Even so, Seneca came to his pupil's aid at what he considered to be his duty, and helped as required.

Even after all this, Seneca was embroiled in a conspiracy. He was charged with an attempt to assassinate emperor Nero. He had been marked a traitor and was consequently told to commit suicide.

Seneca obeyed and calmly did as he was commanded. The image of Seneca lying in his bathtub with his veins slashed has been an inspiration to many artists. Unfazed in the face of death, Seneca was a man who practiced what he preached. Philosophers, or even people in general, wonder about how to live well and how to prepare for death. Seneca had answers to both of these questions. In his book *Letters from a Stoic*, he wrote that a life lived virtuously is a life well lived. He wrote that death was inevitable, so there was no merit to worrying about it or fearing it.

The writings of Seneca were revived in the Renaissance. His dramas, all of which were tragedies, inspired the writers of that period and helped formulate the genre of the 'revenge tragedy' that was prominent in the Renaissance and continued flourishing in the Jacobean Era. The philosophical writings made Seneca appear to be a very different man than he was pictured through his dramas. Characters in his plays were driven by the very same emotions he wanted his readers to distance themselves from, as is evidenced from his philosophical treatises.

The chronology of Seneca's works has been a matter of debate since very little information on his life is available. His earliest work is believed to be *Consolation to Marcia.* Around 43 or 44 AD, he wrote *Consolation to Helvia* and *Consolation to Polybius,* when he had been exiled and was living in Corsica. Upon his return to Rome, he composed

Letters from a Stoic, and *Natural Questions* was written in the last few years of his life. The date of composition of Seneca's plays is not clear either. Among the ten plays that he wrote, all of which were widely read during the Renaissance, *Thyestes* is considered his best. *Medea* and *Oedipus* were very popular as well.

Seneca's letters to Lucilius in *Letters from a Stoic* are, in fact, personal essays. These essays advocate Stoicism , a Greek school of thought that held the belief that happiness in life could be attained if one followed reason and a strict moral code. Seneca's writings may be called ancient, but he wrote of things that are still studied and are relevant in modern times. From the importance of friendship to the benefits of living a simple life, Seneca's letters cover everything simply putting across the correct way of life and offering the readers a glimpse into the rich and complicated mind of one of the finest philosophers in history.

CONTENTS

VOLUME-1

VOLUME-2

VOLUME-3

VOLUME 1

LETTER II

ON DISCURSIVENESS IN READING

Judging by what you write me, and by what I hear, I am forming a good opinion regarding your future. You do not run hither and thither and distract yourself by changing your abode; for such restlessness is the sign of a disordered spirit. The primary indication, to my thinking, of a well-ordered mind is a man's ability to remain in one place and linger in his own company. Be careful, however, lest this reading of many authors and books of every sort may tend to make you discursive and unsteady. You must linger among a limited number of master-thinkers, and digest their works, if you would derive ideas which shall win firm hold in your mind. Everywhere means nowhere. When a person spends all his time in foreign travel, he ends by having many acquaintances, but no friends. And the same thing must hold true of men who seek intimate acquaintance with no single author, but visit them all in a hasty and hurried manner. Food does no good and is not assimilated into the body if it leaves the stomach as soon as it is eaten; nothing hinders a cure so much as frequent change of medicine; no wound will heal when one salve is tried after another; a plant which is often moved can never grow strong. There is nothing so efficacious that it can be helpful while it is being shifted about. And in reading of many books is distraction.

Accordingly, since you cannot read all the books which you may possess, it is enough to possess only as many books as you can read. "But," you reply, "I wish to dip first into one book and then into another." I tell you that it is the sign of an overnice appetite to toy with many dishes; for when they are manifold and varied, they cloy but do not nourish. So you should always read standard authors; and when you crave a change, fall back upon those whom you read before. Each day acquire something that will fortify you against poverty, against death, indeed against other misfortunes as well; and after you have run over many thoughts, select one to be thoroughly digested that day. This is my own custom; from the many things which I have read, I claim some one part for myself.

The thought for today is one which I discovered in Epicurus;* for I am wont to cross over even into the enemy's camp,—not as a deserter, but as a scout. He says: "Contented poverty is an honourable estate." Indeed, if it be contented, it is not poverty at all. It is not the man who has too little, but the man who craves more, that is poor. What does it matter how much a man has laid up in his safe, or in his warehouse, how large are his flocks and how fat his dividends, if he covets his neighbour's property, and reckons, not his past gains, but his hopes of gains to come? Do you ask what is the proper limit to wealth? It is, first, to have what is necessary, and, second, to have what is enough. Farewell.

---

* Frag. 475 Usener

LETTER III

ON TRUE AND FALSE FRIENDSHIP

You have sent a letter to me through the hand of a "friend" of yours, as you call him. And in your very next sentence you warn me not to discuss with him all the matters that concern you, saying that even you yourself are not accustomed to do this; in other words, you have in the same letter affirmed and denied that he is your friend. Now if you used this word of ours* in the popular sense, and called him "friend" in the same way in which we speak of all candidates for election as "honourable gentlemen," and as we greet all men whom we meet casually, if their names slip us for the moment, with the salutation "my dear sir,"—so be it. But if you consider any man a friend whom you do not trust as you trust yourself, you are mightily mistaken and you do not sufficiently understand what true friendship means. Indeed, I would have you discuss everything with a friend; but first of all discuss the man himself. When friendship is settled, you must trust; before friendship is formed, you must pass judgment. Those persons indeed put last first and confound their

* i.e., a word which has a special significance to the Stoics; see Ep. xlviii, note.

duties, who, violating the rules of Theophrastus,* judge a man after they have made him their friend, instead of making him their friend after they have judged him. Ponder for a long time whether you shall admit a given person to your friendship; but when you have decided to admit him, welcome him with all your heart and soul. Speak as boldly with him as with yourself. As to yourself, although you should live in such a way that you trust your own self with nothing which you could not entrust even to your enemy, yet, since certain matters occur which convention keeps secret, you should share with a friend at least all your worries and reflections. Regard him as loyal, and you will make him loyal. Some, for example, fearing to be deceived, have taught men to deceive; by their suspicions they have given their friend the right to do wrong. Why need I keep back any words in the presence of my friend? Why should I not regard myself as alone when in his company?

There is a class of men who communicate, to anyone whom they meet, matters which should be revealed to friends alone, and unload upon the chance listener whatever irks them. Others, again, fear to confide in their closest intimates; and if it were possible, they would not trust even themselves, burying their secrets deep in their hearts. But we should do neither. It is equally faulty to trust everyone and to trust no one. Yet the former fault is, I should say, the more ingenuous, the latter the more safe. In like manner you should rebuke these two kinds of men,—both those who always lack repose, and those who are always in repose. For love of bustle is not industry,—it is only the restlessness of a hunted mind. And true repose does not consist in condemning all motion as merely vexation; that kind of repose is slackness and inertia. Therefore, you should note the following saying, taken from my reading in Pomponius:† "Some men shrink into dark corners, to such a degree that they see darkly by day." No, men should combine these tendencies, and he who reposes should act and he who acts should take repose. Discuss the problem with Nature; she will tell you that she has created both day and night. Farewell.

---

* Frag. 74 Wimmer.

† See Index.

LETTER V

ON THE PHILOSOPHER'S MEAN

I commend you and rejoice in the fact that you are persistent in your studies, and that, putting all else aside, you make it each day your endeavour to become a better man. I do not merely exhort you to keep at it; I actually beg you to do so. I warn you, however, not to act after the fashion of those who desire to be conspicuous rather than to improve, by doing things which will rouse comment as regards your dress or general way of living. Repellent attire, unkempt hair, slovenly beard, open scorn of silver dishes, a couch on the bare earth, and any other perverted forms of self-display, are to be avoided. The mere name of philosophy, however quietly pursued, is an object of sufficient scorn; and what would happen if we should begin to separate ourselves from the customs of our fellow-men? Inwardly, we ought to be different in all respects, but our exterior should conform to society. Do not wear too fine, nor yet too frowzy, a toga. One needs no silver plate, encrusted and embossed in solid gold; but we should not believe the lack of silver and gold to be proof of the simple life. Let us try to maintain a higher standard of life than that of the multitude, but not a contrary standard; otherwise, we shall frighten away and repel the very persons whom we are trying to improve. We also bring it about that they are unwilling to imitate us in anything, because they are afraid lest they might be compelled to imitate us in everything.

The first thing which philosophy undertakes to give is fellow-feeling with all men; in other words, sympathy and sociability. We part company with our promise if we are unlike other men. We must see to it that the means by which we wish to draw admiration be not absurd and odious. Our motto,* as you know, is "Live according to Nature"; but it is quite contrary to nature to torture the body, to hate unlaboured elegance, to be dirty on purpose, to eat food that is not only plain, but disgusting and forbidding. Just as it is a sign of luxury to seek out dainties, so it is madness to avoid that which is customary and can be purchased at no great price. Philosophy calls for plain living, but not for penance; and we may perfectly well be plain and neat at the same time. This is the mean of which I approve; our life should observe a happy medium between the ways of a sage and the ways of the world at large; all men should admire it, but they should understand it also.

"Well then, shall we act like other men? Shall there be no distinction between ourselves and the world?" Yes, a very great one; let men find that we are unlike the common herd, if they look closely. If they visit us at home, they should admire us, rather than our household appointments. He is a great man who uses earthenware dishes as if they were silver; but he is equally great who uses silver as if it were earthenware. It is the sign of an unstable mind not to be able to endure riches.

But I wish to share with you today's profit also. I find in the writings of our† Hecato that the limiting of desires helps also to cure

---

* i.e., of the Stoic school.

† Frag. 25 Fowler.

fears: "Cease to hope," he says, "and you will cease to fear." "But how," you will reply, "can things so different go side by side?" In this way, my dear Lucilius: though they do seem at variance, yet they are really united. Just as the same chain fastens the prisoner and the soldier who guards him, so hope and fear, dissimilar as they are, keep step together; fear follows hope. I am not surprised that they proceed in this way; each alike belongs to a mind that is in suspense, a mind that is fretted by looking forward to the future. But the chief cause of both these ills is that we do not adapt ourselves to the present, but send our thoughts a long way ahead. And so foresight, the noblest blessing of the human race, becomes perverted. Beasts avoid the dangers which they see, and when they have escaped them are free from care; but we men torment ourselves over that which is to come as well as over that which is past. Many of our blessings bring bane to us; for memory recalls the tortures of fear, while foresight anticipates them. The present alone can make no man wretched. Farewell.

LETTER VI

ON SHARING KNOWLEDGE

I feel, my dear Lucilius, that I am being not only reformed, but transformed. I do not yet, however, assure myself, or indulge the hope, that there are no elements left in me which need to be changed. Of course there are many that should be made more compact, or made thinner, or be brought into greater prominence. And indeed this very fact is proof that my spirit is altered into something better,—that it can see its own faults, of which it was previously ignorant. In certain cases sick men are congratulated because they themselves have perceived that they are sick.

I therefore wish to impart to you this sudden change in myself; I should then begin to place a surer trust in our friendship,—the true friendship which hope and fear and self-interest cannot sever, the friendship in which and for the sake of which men meet death. I can show you many who have lacked, not a friend, but a friendship; this, however, cannot possibly happen when souls are drawn together by identical inclinations into an alliance of honourable desires. And why can it not happen? Because in such cases men know that they have all things in common, especially their troubles.

You cannot conceive what distinct progress I notice that each day brings to me. And when you say: "Give me also a share in these gifts which you have found so helpful," I reply that I am anxious to heap all these privileges upon you, and that I am glad to learn in order that I may teach. Nothing will ever please me, no matter how excellent or beneficial, if I must retain the knowledge of it to myself. And if wisdom were given me under the express condition that it must be kept hidden and not uttered, I should refuse it. No good thing is pleasant to possess, without friends to share it.

I shall therefore send to you the actual books; and in order that you may not waste time in searching here and there for profitable topics, I shall mark certain passages, so that you can turn at once to those which I approve and admire. Of course, however, the living voice and the intimacy of a common life will help you more than the written word. You must go to the scene of action, first, because men put more faith in their eyes than in their ears,* and second, because the way is long if one follows precepts, but short and helpful, if one follows patterns. Cleanthes could not have been the express image of Zeno, if he had merely heard his lectures; he shared in his life, saw into his hidden purposes, and watched him to see whether he lived according to his own rules. Plato, Aristotle, and the whole throng of sages who were destined to go each his different way, derived more benefit from the character than from the words of Socrates. It was not the class-room of Epicurus, but living together under the same roof, that made great men of Metrodorus, Hermarchus, and Polyaenus. Therefore I summon you, not merely that you may derive benefit, but that you may confer benefit; for we can assist each other greatly.

Meanwhile, I owe you my little daily contribution; you shall be told what pleased me today in the writings of Hecato;† it is these

---

* Cf. Herodotus, i. 8 ὦτα τυγχάνει ἀνθρώποισι ἐόντα ἀπιστότερα ὀφθαλμῶν.

† Frag. 26 Fowler.

words: "What progress, you ask, have I made? I have begun to be a friend to myself." That was indeed a great benefit; such a person can never be alone. You may be sure that such a man is a friend to all mankind. Farewell.

LETTER VII

ON CROWDS

Do you ask me what you should regard as especially to be avoided? I say, crowds; for as yet you cannot trust yourself to them with safety. I shall admit my own weakness, at any rate; for I never bring back home the same character that I took abroad with me. Something of that which I have forced to be calm within me is disturbed; some of the foes that I have routed return again. Just as the sick man, who has been weak for a long time, is in such a condition that he cannot be taken out of the house without suffering a relapse, so we ourselves are affected when our souls are recovering from a lingering disease. To consort with the crowd is harmful; there is no person who does not make some vice attractive to us, or stamp it upon us, or taint us unconsciously therewith. Certainly, the greater the mob with which we mingle, the greater the danger.

But nothing is so damaging to good character as the habit of lounging at the games; for then it is that vice steals subtly upon one through the avenue of pleasure. What do you think I mean? I mean that I come home more greedy, more ambitious, more voluptuous, and even more cruel and inhuman,—because I have been among human beings. By chance I attended a mid-day exhibition, expecting some fun, wit, and relaxation,—an exhibition at which men's eyes have respite from the slaughter of their fellow-men. But it was quite the reverse. The previous combats were the essence of compassion; but now all the trifling is put aside and it is pure murder.* The men have no defensive armour. They are exposed to blows at all points, and no one ever strikes in vain. Many persons prefer this programme to the usual pairs and to the bouts "by request." Of course they do; there is no helmet or shield to deflect the weapon. What is the need of defensive armour, or of skill? All these mean delaying death. In the morning they throw men to the lions and the bears; at noon, they throw them to the spectators. The spectators demand that the slayer shall face the man who is to slay him in his turn; and they always reserve the latest conqueror for another butchering. The outcome of every fight is death, and the means are fire and sword. This sort of thing goes on while the arena is empty. You may retort: "But he was a highway robber; he killed a man!" And what of it? Granted that, as a murderer, he deserved this punishment, what crime have you committed, poor fellow, that you should deserve to sit and see this show? In the morning they cried "Kill him! Lash him! Burn him! Why does he meet the sword in so cowardly a way? Why does he strike so feebly? Why doesn't he die game? Whip him to meet his wounds! Let them receive blow for blow, with chests bare and exposed to the stroke!" And when the games stop for the intermission, they announce: "A little throat-cutting in the meantime, so that there may still be something going on!"

Come now; do you† not understand even this truth, that a bad example reacts on the agent? Thank the immortal gods that you are

* During the luncheon interval condemned criminals were often driven into the arena and compelled to fight, for the amusement of those spectators who remained throughout the day.

† The remark is addressed to the brutalized spectators.

teaching cruelty to a person who cannot learn to be cruel. The young character, which cannot hold fast to righteousness, must be rescued from the mob; it is too easy to side with the majority. Even Socrates, Cato, and Laelius might have been shaken in their moral strength by a crowd that was unlike them; so true it is that none of us, no matter how much he cultivates his abilities, can withstand the shock of faults that approach, as it were, with so great a retinue. Much harm is done by a single case of indulgence or greed; the familiar friend, if he be luxurious, weakens and softens us imperceptibly; the neighbour, if he be rich, rouses our covetousness; the companion, if he be slanderous, rubs off some of his rust upon us, even though we be spotless and sincere. What then do you think the effect will be on character, when the world at large assaults it! You must either imitate or loathe the world.

But both courses are to be avoided; you should not copy the bad simply because they are many, nor should you hate the many because they are unlike you. Withdraw into yourself, as far as you can. Associate with those who will make a better man of you. Welcome those whom you yourself can improve. The process is mutual; for men learn while they teach. There is no reason why pride in advertising your abilities should lure you into publicity, so that you should desire to recite or harangue before the general public. Of course I should be willing for you to do so if you had a stock-in-trade that suited such a mob; as it is, there is not a man of them who can understand you. One or two individuals will perhaps come in your way, but even these will have to be moulded and trained by you so that they will understand you. You may say: "For what purpose did I learn all these things?" But you need not fear that you have wasted your efforts; it was for yourself that you learned them.

In order, however, that I may not today have learned exclusively for myself, I shall share with you three excellent sayings, of the same general purport, which have come to my attention. This letter will give you one of them as payment of my debt; the other two you may accept as a contribution in advance. Democritus* says: "One man means as much to me as a multitude, and a multitude only as much as one man." The following also was nobly spoken by someone or other, for it is doubtful who the author was; they asked him what was the object of all this study applied to an art that would reach but very few. He replied: "I am content with few, content with one, content with none at all." The third saying—and a noteworthy one, too—is by Epicurus,† written to one of the partners of his studies: "I write this not for the many, but for you; each of us is enough of an audience for the other." Lay these words to heart, Lucilius, that you may scorn the pleasure which comes from the applause of the majority. Many men praise you; but have you any reason for being pleased with yourself, if you are a person whom the many can understand? Your good qualities should face inwards. Farewell.

---

* Frag. 302[a] Diels[2].

† Frag. 208 Usener.

LETTER

VIII

ON THE PHILOSOPHER'S SECLUSION

"Do you bid me," you say, "shun the throng, and withdraw from men, and be content with my own conscience? Where are the counsels of your school, which order a man to die in the midst of active work?" As to the course* which I seem to you to be urging on you now and then, my object in shutting myself up and locking the door is to be able to help a greater number. I never spend a day in idleness; I appropriate even a part of the night for study. I do not allow time for sleep but yield to it when I must, and when my eyes are wearied with waking and ready to fall shut, I keep them at their task. I have withdrawn not only from men, but from affairs, especially from my own affairs; I am working for later generations, writing down some ideas that may be of assistance to them. There are certain wholesome counsels, which may be compared to prescriptions of useful drugs; these I am putting

* As contrasted with the general Stoic doctrine of taking part in the world's work.

into writing; for I have found them helpful in ministering to my own sores, which, if not wholly cured, have at any rate ceased to spread.

I point other men to the right path, which I have found late in life, when wearied with wandering. I cry out to them: "Avoid whatever pleases the throng: avoid the gifts of Chance! Halt before every good which Chance brings to you, in a spirit of doubt and fear; for it is the dumb animals and fish that are deceived by tempting hopes. Do you call these things the 'gifts' of Fortune? They are snares. And any man among you who wishes to live a life of safety will avoid, to the utmost of his power, these limed twigs of her favour, by which we mortals, most wretched in this respect also, are deceived; for we think that we hold them in our grasp, but they hold us in theirs. Such a career leads us into precipitous ways, and life on such heights ends in a fall. Moreover, we cannot even stand up against prosperity when she begins to drive us to leeward; nor can we go down, either, 'with the ship at least on her course,' or once for all;[*] Fortune does not capsize us,—she plunges our bows under[†] and dashes us on the rocks.

"Hold fast, then, to this sound and wholesome rule of life; that you indulge the body only so far as is needful for good health. The body should be treated more rigorously, that it may not be disobedient to the mind. Eat merely to relieve your hunger; drink merely to quench your thirst; dress merely to keep out the cold; house yourself merely as a protection against personal discomfort. It matters little whether the house be built of turf, or of variously coloured imported marble; understand that a man is sheltered just as well by a thatch as by a roof of gold. Despise everything that useless toil creates as an ornament and an object of beauty. And reflect that nothing except the soul is worthy of wonder; for to the soul, if it be great, naught is great."[‡]

When I commune in such terms with myself and with future generations, do you not think that I am doing more good than when I appear as counsel in court, or stamp my seal upon a will, or lend my

* See Ep. lxxxv. 33 for the famous saying of the Rhodian pilot.

† *cernulat*, equivalent to Greek ἀναχαιτίζω, of a horse which throws a rider over its head.

‡ Cf. the Stoic precept *nil admirandum*.

assistance in the senate, by word or action, to a candidate? Believe me, those who seem to be busied with nothing are busied with the greater tasks; they are dealing at the same time with things mortal and things immortal.

But I must stop, and pay my customary contribution, to balance this letter. The payment shall not be made from my own property; for I am still conning Epicurus.* I read today, in his works, the following sentence: "If you would enjoy real freedom, you must be the slave of Philosophy." The man who submits and surrenders himself to her is not kept waiting; he is emancipated† on the spot. For the very service of Philosophy is freedom.

It is likely that you will ask me why I quote so many of Epicurus's noble words instead of words taken from our own school. But is there any reason why you should regard them as sayings of Epicurus and not common property? How many poets give forth ideas that have been uttered, or may be uttered, by philosophers! I need not touch upon the tragedians and our writers of national drama;‡ for these last are also somewhat serious, and stand half-way between comedy and tragedy. What a quantity of sagacious verses lie buried in the mime! How many of Publilius's lines are worthy of being spoken by buskin-clad actors, as well as by wearers of the slipper!§ I shall quote one verse of his, which concerns philosophy, and particularly that phase of it which we were discussing a moment ago, wherein he says that the gifts of Chance are not to be regarded as part of our possessions:

Still alien is whatever you have gained
By coveting.¶

* Frag. 199 Usener.

† Literally "spun around" by the master and dismissed to freedom. Cf. Persius, v. 75f.

‡ *Fabulae togatae* were plays which dealt with Roman subject matter, as contrasted with adaptations from the Greek, called *palliatae*. The term, in the widest sense includes both comedy and tragedy.

§ i.e., comedians or mimes.

¶ *Syri Sententiae*, p. 309 Ribbeck^2.

I recall that you yourself expressed this idea much more happily and concisely:

What Chance has made yours is not really yours.*

And a third, spoken by you still more happily, shall not be omitted:

The good that could be given, can be removed.†

I shall not charge this up to the expense account, because I have given it to you from your own stock. Farewell.

---

* *Com. Rom. Frag.* p. 394 Ribbeck^2.

† *ibidem.*

LETTER IX

ON PHILOSOPHY AND FRIENDSHIP

You desire to know whether Epicurus is right when, in one of his letters,[*] he rebukes those who hold that the wise man is self-sufficient and for that reason does not stand in need of friendships. This is the objection raised by Epicurus against Stilbo and those who believe[†] that the Supreme Good is a soul which is insensible to feeling.

We are bound to meet with a double meaning if we try to express the Greek term "lack of feeling" summarily, in a single word, rendering it by the Latin word *impatientia*. For it may be understood in the meaning the opposite to that which we wish it to have. What we mean to express is, a soul which rejects any sensation of evil; but people will interpret the idea as that of a soul which can endure no evil. Consider, therefore, whether it is not better to say "a soul that cannot be harmed," or "a soul entirely beyond the realm of suffering." There is

* Frag. 174 Usener.

† i.e., the Cynics.

this difference between ourselves and the other school:[*] our ideal wise man feels his troubles, but overcomes them; their wise man does not even feel them. But we and they alike hold this idea,—that the wise man is self-sufficient. Nevertheless, he desires friends, neighbours, and associates, no matter how much he is sufficient unto himself. And mark how self-sufficient he is; for on occasion he can be content with a part of himself. If he lose a hand through disease or war, or if some accident puts out one or both of his eyes, he will be satisfied with what is left, taking as much pleasure in his impaired and maimed body as he took when it was sound. But while he does not pine for these parts if they are missing, he prefers not to lose them. In this sense the wise man is self-sufficient, that he can do without friends, not that he desires to do without them. When I say "can," I mean this: he endures the loss of a friend with equanimity.

But he need never lack friends, for it lies in his own control how soon he shall make good a loss. Just as Phidias, if he lose a statue, can straightway carve another, even so our master in the art of making friendships can fill the place of a friend he has lost. If you ask how one can make oneself a friend quickly, I will tell you, provided we are agreed that I may pay my debt[†] at once and square the account, so far as this letter is concerned. Hecato,[‡] says: "I can show you a philtre, compounded without drugs, herbs, or any witch's incantation: 'If you would be loved, love.'" Now there is great pleasure, not only in maintaining old and established friendships, but also in beginning and acquiring new ones. There is the same difference between winning a new friend and having already won him, as there is between the farmer who sows and the farmer who reaps. The philosopher Attalus used to say: "It is more pleasant to make than to keep a friend, as it is more pleasant to the artist to paint than to have finished painting." When one is busy and absorbed in one's work, the very absorption affords great delight; but when

* i.e., the Cynics.

† i.e., the *diurna mercedula*; see Ep. vi, 7.

‡ Frag. 27 Fowler.

one has withdrawn one's hand from the completed masterpiece, the pleasure is not so keen. Henceforth it is the fruits of his art that he enjoys; it was the art itself that he enjoyed while he was painting. In the case of our children, their young manhood yields the more abundant fruits, but their infancy was sweeter.

Let us now return to the question. The wise man, I say, self-sufficient though he be, nevertheless desires friends if only for the purpose of practising friendship, in order that his noble qualities may not lie dormant. Not, however, for the purpose mentioned by Epicurus* in the letter quoted above: "That there may be someone to sit by him when he is ill, to help him when he is in prison or in want;" but that he may have someone by whose sick-bed he himself may sit, someone a prisoner in hostile hands whom he himself may set free. He who regards himself only, and enters upon friendships for this reason, reckons wrongly. The end will be like the beginning: he has made friends with one who might assist him out of bondage; at the first rattle of the chain such a friend will desert him. These are the so-called "fair-weather" friendships; one who is chosen for the sake of utility will be satisfactory only so long as he is useful. Hence prosperous men are blockaded by troops of friends; but those who have failed stand amid vast loneliness, their friends fleeing from the very crisis which is to test their worth. Hence, also, we notice those many shameful cases of persons who, through fear, desert or betray. The beginning and the end cannot but harmonize. He who begins to be your friend because it pays will also cease because it pays. A man will be attracted by some reward offered in exchange for his friendship, if he be attracted by aught in friendship other than friendship itself.

For what purpose, then, do I make a man my friend? In order to have someone for whom I may die, whom I may follow into exile, against whose death I may stake my own life, and pay the pledge, too. The friendship which you portray is a bargain and not a friendship; it

* Frag. 175 Usener.

regards convenience only, and looks to the results. Beyond question the feeling of a lover has in it something akin to friendship; one might call it friendship run mad. But, though this is true, does anyone love for the sake of gain, or promotion, or renown? Pure* love, careless of all other things, kindles the soul with desire for the beautiful object, not without the hope of a return of the affection. What then? Can a cause which is more honourable produce a passion that is base? You may retort: "We are not now discussing the question whether friendship is to be cultivated for its own sake." On the contrary, nothing more urgently requires demonstration; for if friendship is to be sought for its own sake, he may seek it who is self-sufficient. "How, then," you ask, "does he seek it?" Precisely as he seeks an object of great beauty, not attracted to it by desire for gain, nor yet frightened by the instability of Fortune. One who seeks friendship for favourable occasions, strips it of all its nobility.

"The wise man is self-sufficient." This phrase, my dear Lucilius, is incorrectly explained by many; for they withdraw the wise man from the world, and force him to dwell within his own skin. But we must mark with care what this sentence signifies and how far it applies; the wise man is sufficient unto himself for a happy existence, but not for mere existence. For he needs many helps towards mere existence; but for a happy existence he needs only a sound and upright soul, one that despises Fortune.

I should like also to state to you one of the distinctions of Chrysippus,† who declares that the wise man is in want of nothing, and yet needs many things.‡ "On the other hand," he says, "nothing is needed by the fool, for he does not understand how to use anything, but he is in want of everything." The wise man needs hands, eyes, and many things that are necessary for his daily use; but he is in want of nothing. For want implies a necessity, and nothing is

* "Pure love," i.e., love in its essence, unalloyed with other emotions.

† Cf. his *Frag. moral.* 674 von Arnim.

‡ The distinction is based upon the meaning of *egere*, "to be in want of" something indispensible, and *opus esse*, "to have need of" something which one can do without.

necessary to the wise man. Therefore, although he is self-sufficient, yet he has need of friends. He craves as many friends as possible, not, however, that he may live happily; for he will live happily even without friends. The Supreme Good calls for no practical aids from outside; it is developed at home, and arises entirely within itself. If the good seeks any portion of itself from without, it begins to be subject to the play of Fortune.

People may say: "But what sort of existence will the wise man have, if he be left friendless when thrown into prison, or when stranded in some foreign nation, or when delayed on a long voyage, or when cast upon a lonely shore?" His life will be like that of Jupiter, who, amid the dissolution of the world, when the gods are confounded together and Nature rests for a space from her work, can retire into himself and give himself over to his own thoughts.* In some such way as this the sage will act; he will retreat into himself, and live with himself. As long as he is allowed to order his affairs according to his judgment, he is self-sufficient—and marries a wife; he is self-sufficient—and brings up children; he is self-sufficient—and yet could not live if he had to live without the society of man. Natural promptings, and not his own selfish needs, draw him into friendships. For just as other things have for us an inherent attractiveness, so has friendship. As we hate solitude and crave society, as nature draws men to each other, so in this matter also there is an attraction which makes us desirous of friendship. Nevertheless, though the sage may love his friends dearly, often comparing them with himself, and putting them ahead of himself, yet all the good will be limited to his own being, and he will speak the words which were spoken by the very Stilbo† whom Epicurus criticizes in his letter. For Stilbo, after his country was captured and his children and his wife lost, as he emerged from the general desolation alone and yet happy, spoke as follows to Demetrius, called Sacker of Cities because of the destruction

* This refers to the Stoic conflagration: after certain cycles their world was destroyed by fire. Cf. E. V. Arnold, *Roman Stoicism*, pp. 192 f.; cf. also Chrysippus, Frag. phys. 1065 von Arnim.

† *Gnomologici Vaticani* 515[a] Sternberg.

he brought upon them, in answer to the question whether he had lost anything: "I have all my goods with me!" There is a brave and stout-hearted man for you! The enemy conquered, but Stilbo conquered his conqueror. "I have lost nothing!" Aye, he forced Demetrius to wonder whether he himself had conquered after all. "My goods are all with me!" In other words, he deemed nothing that might be taken from him to be a good.

We marvel at certain animals because they can pass through fire and suffer no bodily harm; but how much more marvellous is a man who has marched forth unhurt and unscathed through fire and sword and devastation! Do you understand now how much easier it is to conquer a whole tribe than to conquer one *man*? This saying of Stilbo makes common ground with Stoicism; the Stoic also can carry his goods unimpaired through cities that have been burned to ashes; for he is self-sufficient. Such are the bounds which he sets to his own happiness.

But you must not think that our school alone can utter noble words; Epicurus himself, the reviler of Stilbo, spoke similar language;[*] put it down to my credit, though I have already wiped out my debt for the present day.[†] He says: "Whoever does not regard what he has as most ample wealth, is unhappy, though he be master of the whole world." Or, if the following seems to you a more suitable phrase,—for we must try to render the meaning and not the mere words: "A man may rule the world and still be unhappy, if he does not feel that he is supremely happy." In order, however, that you may know that these sentiments are universal,[‡] suggested, of course, by Nature, you will find in one of the comic poets this verse:

Unblest is he who thinks himself unblest.[§]

---

* Frag. 474 Usener.

† Cf. above § 6.

‡ i.e., not confined to the Stoics, etc.

§ Author unknown; perhaps, as Buecheler thinks, adapted from the Greek.

For what does your condition matter, if it is bad in your own eyes? You may say: "What then? If yonder man, rich by base means, and yonder man, lord of many but slave of more, shall call themselves happy, will their own opinion make them happy?" It matters not what one says, but what one feels; also, not how one feels on one particular day, but how one feels at all times. There is no reason, however, why you should fear that this great privilege will fall into unworthy hands; only the wise man is pleased with his own. Folly is ever troubled with weariness of itself. Farewell.

LETTER XI

ON THE BLUSH OF MODESTY

Your friend and I have had a conversation. He is a man of ability; his very first words showed what spirit and understanding he possesses, and what progress he has already made. He gave me a foretaste, and he will not fail to answer thereto. For he spoke not from forethought, but was suddenly caught off his guard. When he tried to collect himself, he could scarcely banish that hue of modesty, which is a good sign in a young man; the blush that spread over his face seemed so to rise from the depths. And I feel sure that his habit of blushing will stay with him after he has strengthened his character, stripped off all his faults, and become wise. For by no wisdom can natural weaknesses of the body be removed. That which is implanted and inborn can be toned down by training, but not overcome. The steadiest speaker, when before the public, often breaks into a perspiration, as if he had wearied or over-heated himself; some tremble in the knees when they rise to speak; I know of some whose teeth chatter, whose tongues falter, whose lips quiver. Training and experience can never shake off this habit; nature exerts her own power and through such a weakness makes her presence known even to the strongest. I know that the blush, too, is a habit of this sort, spreading suddenly over the faces of the most dignified men. It is, indeed more prevalent in youth, because of the warmer blood and the sensitive countenance; nevertheless, both seasoned men and aged men are affected by it. Some are most dangerous when they redden, as if they were letting all their sense of shame escape. Sulla, when the blood mantled his cheeks, was in his fiercest mood. Pompey had the most sensitive cast of countenance; he always blushed in the presence of a gathering, and especially at a public assembly. Fabianus also, I remember, reddened when he appeared as a witness before the senate; and his embarrassment became him to a remarkable degree. Such a habit is not due to mental weakness, but to the novelty of a situation; an inexperienced person is not necessarily confused, but is usually affected, because he slips into this habit by natural tendency of the body. Just as certain men are full-blooded, so others are of a quick and mobile blood, that rushes to the face at once.

As I remarked, Wisdom can never remove this habit; for if she could rub out all our faults, she would be mistress of the universe. Whatever is assigned to us by the terms of our birth and the blend in our constitutions, will stick with us, no matter how hard or how long the soul may have tried to master itself. And we cannot forbid these feelings any more than we can summon them. Actors in the theatre, who imitate the emotions, who portray fear and nervousness, who depict sorrow, imitate bashfulness by hanging their heads, lowering their voices, and keeping their eyes fixed and rooted upon the ground. They cannot, however, muster a blush; for the blush cannot be prevented or acquired. Wisdom will not assure us of a remedy, or give us help against it; it comes or goes unbidden, and is a law unto itself.

But my letter calls for its closing sentence. Hear and take to heart this useful and wholesome motto:* "Cherish some man of high

---

* Epicurus, Frag. 210 Usener.

character, and keep him ever before your eyes, living as if he were watching you, and ordering all your actions as if he beheld them." Such, my dear Lucilius, is the counsel of Epicurus;* he has quite properly given us a guardian and an attendant. We can get rid of most sins, if we have a witness who stands near us when we are likely to go wrong. The soul should have someone whom it can respect,—one by whose authority it may make even its inner shrine more hallowed.† Happy is the man who can make others better, not merely when he is in their company, but even when he is in their thoughts! And happy also is he who can so revere a man as to calm and regulate himself by calling him to mind! One who can so revere another, will soon be himself worthy of reverence. Choose therefore a Cato; or, if Cato seems too severe a model, choose some Laelius, a gentler spirit. Choose a master whose life, conversation, and soul-expressing face have satisfied you; picture him always to yourself as your protector or your pattern. For we must indeed have someone according to whom we may regulate our characters; you can never straighten that which is crooked unless you use a ruler. Farewell.

---

* Frag. 210 Usener.

† The figure is taken from the ἄδυτον, the Holy of Holies in a temple. Cf. Vergil, *Aeneid*, vi. 10 *secreta Sibyllas*.

LETTER

XII

ON OLD AGE

Wherever I turn, I see evidences of my advancing years. I visited lately my country-place, and protested against the money which was spent on the tumble-down building. My bailiff maintained that the flaws were not due to his own carelessness; "he was doing everything possible, but the house was old." And this was the house which grew under my own hands! What has the future in store for me, if stones of my own age are already crumbling? I was angry, and I embraced the first opportunity to vent my spleen in the bailiff's presence. "It is clear," I cried, "that these plane-trees are neglected; they have no leaves. Their branches are so gnarled and shrivelled; the boles are so rough and unkempt! This would not happen, if someone loosened the earth at their feet, and watered them." The bailiff swore by my protecting deity that "he was doing everything possible, and never relaxed his efforts, but those trees were old." Between you and me, I had planted those trees myself, I had seen them in their first leaf. Then I turned to the door and asked: "Who is that broken-down dotard? You have done well to place him at the entrance; for he is outward bound.[*] Where did you get him? What pleasure did it give you to take up for burial some other man's dead?"[†] But the slave said: "Don't you know me, sir? I am Felicio; you used to bring me little images.[‡] My father was Philositus the steward, and I am your pet slave." "The man is clean crazy," I remarked. "Has my pet slave become a little boy again? But it is quite possible; his teeth are just dropping out."[§]

I owe it to my country-place that my old age became apparent whithersoever I turned. Let us cherish and love old age; for it is full of pleasure if one knows how to use it. Fruits are most welcome when almost over; youth is most charming at its close; the last drink delights the toper,—the glass which souses him and puts the finishing touch on his drunkenness. Each pleasure reserves to the end the greatest delights which it contains. Life is most delightful when it is on the downward slope, but has not yet reached the abrupt decline. And I myself believe that the period which stands, so to speak, on the edge of the roof, possesses pleasures of its own. Or else the very fact of our not wanting pleasures has taken the place of the pleasures themselves. How comforting it is to have tired out one's appetites, and to have done with them! "But," you say, "it is a nuisance to be looking death in the face!" Death, however, should be looked in the face by young and old alike. We are not summoned according to our rating on the censor's list.[¶] Moreover, no one is so old that it would be improper for him to hope for another day of existence. And one day, mind you, is a stage on life's journey.

Our span of life is divided into parts; it consists of large circles enclosing smaller. One circle embraces and bounds the rest; it reaches

---

* A jesting allusion to the Roman funeral; the corpse's feet pointing towards the door.

† His former owner should have kept him and buried him.

‡ Small figures, generally of terra-cotta, were frequently given to children as presents at the Saturnalia. Cf. Macrobius, i. 11. 49 *sigila . . . pro se atque suis piaculum.*

§ i.e., the old slave resembles a child in that he is losing his teeth (but for the second time).

¶ i.e., *seniores*, as contrasted with *iuniores.*

from birth to the last day of existence. The next circle limits the period of our young manhood. The third confines all of childhood in its circumference. Again, there is, in a class by itself, the year; it contains within itself all the divisions of time by the multiplication of which we get the total of life. The month is bounded by a narrower ring. The smallest circle of all is the day; but even a day has its beginning and its ending, its sunrise and its sunset. Hence Heraclitus, whose obscure style gave him his surname,* remarked: "One day is equal to every day." Different persons have interpreted the saying in different ways. Some hold that days are equal in number of hours, and this is true; for if by "day" we mean twenty-four hours' time, all days must be equal, inasmuch as the night acquires what the day loses. But others maintain that one day is equal to all days through resemblance, because the very longest space of time possesses no element which cannot be found in a single day,—namely, light and darkness,—and even to eternity day makes these alternations† more numerous, not different when it is shorter and different again when it is longer. Hence, every day ought to be regulated as if it closed the series, as if it rounded out and completed our existence.

Pacuvius, who by long occupancy made Syria his own,‡ used to hold a regular burial sacrifice in his own honour, with wine and the usual funeral feasting, and then would have himself carried from the dining room to his chamber, while eunuchs applauded and sang in Greek to a musical accompaniment: "He has lived his life, he has lived his life!" Thus Pacuvius had himself carried out to burial every day. Let us, however, do from a good motive what he used to do from a debased motive; let us go to our sleep with joy and gladness; let us say:

---

* ὁ σκοτεινός, "the Obscure," Frag. 106 Diels².

† i.e., of light and darkness.

‡ *Usus* was the mere enjoyment of a piece of property; *dominium* was the exclusive right to its control. Possession for one, or two, years conferred ownership. See Leage, *Roman Private Law*, pp. 133, 152, and 164. Although Pacuvius was governor so long that the province seemed to belong to him, yet he knew he might die any day.

I have lived; the course which Fortune set for me
Is finished.*

And if God is pleased to add another day, we should welcome it with glad hearts. That man is happiest, and is secure in his own possession of himself, who can await the morrow without apprehension. When a man has said: "I have lived!", every morning he arises he receives a bonus.

But now I ought to close my letter. "What?" you say; "shall it come to me without any little offering?" Be not afraid; it brings something,—nay, more than something, a great deal. For what is more noble than the following saying† of which I make this letter the bearer: "It is wrong to live under constraint; but no man is constrained to live under constraint." Of course not. On all sides lie many short and simple paths to freedom; and let us thank God that no man can be kept in life. We may spurn the very constraints that hold us. "Epicurus," you reply, "uttered these words; what are you doing with another's property?" Any truth, I maintain, is my own property. And I shall continue to heap quotations from Epicurus upon you, so that all persons who swear by the words of another, and put a value upon the speaker and not upon the thing spoken, may understand that the best ideas are common property. Farewell.

---

* Vergil, *Aeneid*, iv. 653.

† Epicurus, Sprüche, 9 Wokte.

LETTER XV

ON BRAWN AND BRAINS

The old Romans had a custom which survived even into my lifetime. They would add to the opening words of a letter: "If you are well, it is well; I also am well." Persons like ourselves would do well to say: "If you are studying philosophy, it is well." For this is just what "being well" means. Without philosophy the mind is sickly, and the body, too, though it may be very powerful, is strong only as that of a madman or a lunatic is strong. This, then, is the sort of health you should primarily cultivate; the other kind of health comes second, and will involve little effort, if you wish to be well physically. It is indeed foolish, my dear Lucilius, and very unsuitable for a cultivated man, to work hard over developing the muscles and broadening the shoulders and strengthening the lungs. For although your heavy feeding produce good results and your sinews grow solid, you can never be a match, either in strength or in weight, for a first-class bull. Besides, by overloading the body with food you strangle the soul and render it less active. Accordingly, limit the flesh as much as possible, and allow free play to the spirit. Many inconveniences beset those who devote themselves to such pursuits. In the first place, they have their exercises, at which they must work and waste their life-force and render it less fit to bear a strain or the severer studies. Second, their keen edge is dulled by heavy eating. Besides, they must take orders from slaves of the vilest stamp,—men who alternate between the oil-flask* and the flagon, whose day passes satisfactorily if they have got up a good perspiration and quaffed, to make good what they have lost in sweat, huge draughts of liquor which will sink deeper because of their fasting. Drinking and sweating,—it's the life of a dyspeptic!†

Now there are short and simple exercises which tire the body rapidly, and so save our time; and time is something of which we ought to keep strict account. These exercises are running, brandishing weights, and jumping,—high-jumping or broad-jumping, or the kind which I may call, "the Priest's dance,"‡ or, in slighting terms, "the clothes-cleaner's jump."§ Select for practice any one of these, and you will find it plain and easy. But whatever you do, come back soon from body to mind. The mind must be exercised both day and night, for it is nourished by moderate labour; and this form of exercise need not be hampered by cold or hot weather, or even by old age. Cultivate that good which improves with the years. Of course I do not command you to be always bending over your books and your writing materials; the mind must have a change,—but a change of such a kind that it is not unnerved, but merely unbent. Riding in a litter shakes up the body, and does not interfere with study; one may read, dictate, converse, or listen to another; nor does walking prevent any of these things.

You need not scorn voice-culture; but I forbid you to practise raising and lowering your voice by scales and specific intonations.

---

* i.e., the prize-ring; the contestants were rubbed with oil before the fight began.

† *Cardiacus* meant, according to Pliny, *N. H.* xxiii. 1. 24, a sort of dyspepsia accompanied by fever and perspiration. Compare the man in Juvenal v. 32, who will not send a spoonful of wine to a friend ill of this complaint.

‡ Named from the Salii, or leaping priests of Mars.

§ The fuller, or washerman, cleansed the clothes by leaping and stamping upon them in the tub.

What if you should next propose to take lessons in walking! If you consult the sort of person whom starvation has taught new tricks, you will have someone to regulate your steps, watch every mouthful as you eat, and go to such lengths as you yourself, by enduring him and believing in him, have encouraged his effrontery to go. "What, then?" you will ask; "is my voice to begin at the outset with shouting and straining the lungs to the utmost?" No; the natural thing is that it be aroused to such a pitch by easy stages, just as persons who are wrangling begin with ordinary conversational tones and then pass to shouting at the top of their lungs. No speaker cries "Help me, citizens!" at the outset of his speech. Therefore, whenever your spirit's impulse prompts you, raise a hubbub, now in louder now in milder tones, according as your voice, as well as your spirit, shall suggest to you, when you are moved to such a performance. Then let your voice, when you rein it in and call it back to earth, come down gently, not collapse; it should trail off in tones half way between high and low, and should not abruptly drop from its raving in the uncouth manner of countrymen. For our purpose is, not to give the voice exercise, but to make it give us exercise.

You see, I have relieved you of no slight bother; and I shall throw in a little complementary present,—it is Greek, too. Here is the proverb; it is an excellent one: "The fool's life is empty of gratitude and full of fears; its course lies wholly toward the future." "Who uttered these words?" you say. The same writer whom I mentioned before.* And what sort of life do you think is meant by the fool's life? That of Baba and Isio?† No; he means our own, for we are plunged by our blind desires into ventures which will harm us, but certainly will never satisfy us; for if we could be satisfied with anything, we should have been satisfied long ago; nor do we reflect how pleasant it is to demand nothing, how noble it is to be contented and not to be dependent upon Fortune. Therefore continually remind yourself,

* Epicurus, Frag. 491 Usener.

† Court fools of the period.

Lucilius, how many ambitions you have attained. When you see many ahead of you, think how many are behind! If you would thank the gods, and be grateful for your past life, you should contemplate how many men you have outstripped. But what have you to do with the others? You have outstripped yourself.

Fix a limit which you will not even desire to pass, should you have the power. At last, then, away with all these treacherous goods! They look better to those who hope for them than to those who have attained them. If there were anything substantial in them, they would sooner or later satisfy you; as it is, they merely rouse the drinkers' thirst. Away with fripperies which only serve for show! As to what the future's uncertain lot has in store, why should I demand of Fortune that she give, rather than demand of myself that I should not crave? And why should l crave? Shall I heap up my winnings, and forget that man's lot is unsubstantial? For what end should I toil? Lo, today is the last; if not, it is near the last. Farewell.

LETTER XVI

ON PHILOSOPHY, THE GUIDE OF LIFE

It is clear to you, I am sure, Lucilius, that no man can live a happy life, or even a supportable life, without the study of wisdom; you know also that a happy life is reached when our wisdom is brought to completion, but that life is at least endurable even when our wisdom is only begun. This idea, however, clear though it is, must be strengthened and implanted more deeply by daily reflection; it is more important for you to keep the resolutions you have already made than to go on and make noble ones. You must persevere, must develop new strength by continuous study, until that which is only a good inclination becomes a good settled purpose. Hence you no longer need to come to me with much talk and protestations; I know that you have made great progress. I understand the feelings which prompt your words; they are not feigned or specious words. Nevertheless I shall tell you what I think,—that at present I have hopes for you, but not yet perfect trust. And I wish that you would adopt the same attitude towards yourself; there is no reason why you should put confidence in yourself too quickly and readily. Examine yourself; scrutinize and observe yourself in divers ways; but mark, before all else, whether it is in philosophy or merely in life itself* that you have made progress. Philosophy is no trick to catch the public; it is not devised for show. It is a matter, not of words, but of facts. It is not pursued in order that the day may yield some amusement before it is spent, or that our leisure may be relieved of a tedium that irks us. It moulds and constructs the soul; it orders our life, guides our conduct, shows us what we should do and what we should leave undone; it sits at the helm and directs our course as we waver amid uncertainties. Without it, no one can live fearlessly or in peace of mind. Countless things that happen every hour call for advice; and such advice is to be sought in philosophy.

Perhaps someone will say: "How can philosophy help me, if Fate exists? Of what avail is philosophy, if God rules the universe? Of what avail is it, if Chance governs everything? For not only is it impossible to change things that are determined, but it is also impossible to plan beforehand against what is undetermined; either God has forestalled my plans, and decided what I am to do, or else Fortune gives no free play to my plans." Whether the truth, Lucilius, lies in one or in all of these views, we must be philosophers; whether Fate binds us down by an inexorable law, or whether God as arbiter of the universe has arranged everything, or whether Chance drives and tosses human affairs without method, philosophy ought to be our defence. She will encourage us to obey God cheerfully, but Fortune defiantly; she will teach us to follow God and endure Chance. But it is not my purpose now to be led into a discussion as to what is within our own control,—if foreknowledge is supreme, or if a chain of fated events drags us along in its clutches, or if the sudden and the unexpected play the tyrant over us; I return now to my warning and my exhortation, that you should not allow the impulse of your spirit to weaken and grow cold. Hold fast to it and establish it firmly, in order that what is now impulse may become a habit of the mind.

---

* i.e., have merely advanced in years.

If I know you well, you have already been trying to find out, from the very beginning of my letter, what little contribution it brings to you. Sift the letter, and you will find it. You need not wonder at any genius of mine; for as yet I am lavish only with other men's property.—But why did I say "other men"? Whatever is well said by anyone is mine.—This also is a saying of Epicurus:* "If you live according to nature, you will never be poor; if you live according to opinion, you will never be rich." Nature's wants are slight; the demands of opinion are boundless. Suppose that the property of many millionaires is heaped up in your possession. Assume that fortune carries you far beyond the limits of a private income, decks you with gold, clothes you in purple, and brings you to such a degree of luxury and wealth that you can bury the earth under your marble floors; that you may not only possess, but tread upon, riches. Add statues, paintings, and whatever any art has devised for the satisfaction of luxury; you will only learn from such things to crave still greater.

Natural desires are limited; but those which spring from false opinion can have no stopping-point. The false has no limits. When you are travelling on a road, there must be an end; but when astray, your wanderings are limitless. Recall your steps, therefore, from idle things, and when you would know whether that which you seek is based upon a natural or upon a misleading desire, consider whether it can stop at any definite point. If you find, after having travelled far, that there is a more distant goal always in view, you may be sure that this condition is contrary to nature. Farewell.

---

* Frag. 201 Usener.

LETTER XVIII

ON FESTIVALS AND FASTING

It is the month of December, and yet the city is at this very moment in a sweat. Licence is given to the general merrymaking. Everything resounds with mighty preparations,—as if the Saturnalia differed at all from the usual business day! So true it is that the difference is nil, that I regard as correct the remark of the man who said: "Once December was a month; now it is a year."*

If I had you with me, I should be glad to consult you and find out what you think should be done,—whether we ought to make no change in our daily routine, or whether, in order not to be out of sympathy with the ways of the public, we should dine in gayer fashion and doff the toga.† As it is now, we Romans have changed our dress for the sake of pleasure and holiday-making, though in former times that was only customary when the State was disturbed and had fallen on evil days. I am sure

* i.e., the whole year is a Saturnalia.

† For a dinner dress.

that, if I know you aright, playing the part of an umpire you would have wished that we should be neither like the liberty-capped* throng in all ways, nor in all ways unlike them; unless, perhaps, this is just the season when we ought to lay down the law to the soul, and bid it be alone in refraining from pleasures just when the whole mob has let itself go in pleasures; for this is the surest proof which a man can get of his own constancy, if he neither seeks the things which are seductive and allure him to luxury, nor is led into them. It shows much more courage to remain dry and sober when the mob is drunk and vomiting; but it shows greater self-control to refuse to withdraw oneself and to do what the crowd does, but in a different way,—thus neither making oneself conspicuous nor becoming one of the crowd. For one may keep holiday without extravagance.

I am so firmly determined, however, to test the constancy of your mind that, drawing from the teachings of great men, I shall give you also a lesson: Set aside a certain number of days, during which you shall be content with the scantiest and cheapest fare, with coarse and rough dress, saying to yourself the while: "Is this the condition that I feared?" It is precisely in times of immunity from care that the soul should toughen itself beforehand for occasions of greater stress, and it is while Fortune is kind that it should fortify itself against her violence. In days of peace the soldier performs manœuvres, throws up earthworks with no enemy in sight, and wearies himself by gratuitous toil, in order that he may be equal to unavoidable toil. If you would not have a man flinch when the crisis comes, train him before it comes. Such is the course which those men† have followed who, in their imitation of poverty, have every month come almost to want, that they might never recoil from what they had so often rehearsed.

* The *pilleus* was worn by newly freed slaves and by the Roman populace on festal occasions.

† The Epicurians. Cf. § 9 and Epicurus, Frag. 158. Usener.

You need not suppose that I mean meals like Timon's, or "paupers' huts,"* or any other device which luxurious millionaires use to beguile the tedium of their lives. Let the pallet be a real one, and the coarse cloak; let the bread be hard and grimy. Endure all this for three or four days at a time, sometimes for more, so that it may be a test of yourself instead of a mere hobby. Then, I assure you, my dear Lucilius, you will leap for joy when filled with a pennyworth of food, and you will understand that a man's peace of mind does not depend upon Fortune; for, even when angry she grants enough for our needs.

There is no reason, however, why you should think that you are doing anything great; for you will merely be doing what many thousands of slaves and many thousands of poor men are doing every day. But you may credit yourself with this item,—that you will not be doing it under compulsion, and that it will be as easy for you to endure it permanently as to make the experiment from time to time. Let us practise our strokes on the "dummy";† let us become intimate with poverty, so that Fortune may not catch us off our guard. We shall be rich with all the more comfort, if we once learn how far poverty is from being a burden.

Even Epicurus, the teacher of pleasure, used to observe stated intervals, during which he satisfied his hunger in niggardly fashion; he wished to see whether he thereby fell short of full and complete happiness, and, if so, by what amount he fell short, and whether this amount was worth purchasing at the price of great effort. At any rate, he makes such a statement in the well known letter written to Polyaenus in the archonship of Charinus.‡ Indeed, he boasts that he himself lived on less than a penny, but that Metrodorus, whose progress was not yet so great, needed a whole penny. Do you think that there can be fullness on such fare? Yes, and there is pleasure

---

* Cf. Ep. c. 6 and Martial, iii. 48.

† The post which gladiators used when preparing themselves for combats in the arena.

‡ Usually identified with Chaerimus, 307-8 B.C. But Wilhelm, *Öster Jahreshefte*, V.136, has shown that there is probably no confusion of names. A Charinus was archon at Athens in 290-89; see Johnson, *Class. Phil.* ix. p. 256.

also,—not that shifty and fleeting pleasure which needs a fillip now and then, but a pleasure that is steadfast and sure. For though water, barley-meal, and crusts of barley-bread, are not a cheerful diet, yet it is the highest kind of pleasure to be able to derive pleasure from this sort of food, and to have reduced one's needs to that modicum which no unfairness of Fortune can snatch away. Even prison fare is more generous; and those who have been set apart for capital punishment are not so meanly fed by the man who is to execute them. Therefore, what a noble soul must one have, to descend of one's own free will to a diet which even those who have been sentenced to death have not to fear! This is indeed forestalling the spear-thrusts of Fortune.

So begin, my dear Lucilius, to follow the custom of these men, and set apart certain days on which you shall withdraw from your business and make yourself at home with the scantiest fare. Establish business relations with poverty.

> Dare, O my friend, to scorn the sight of wealth,
> And mould thyself to kinship with thy God.*

For he alone is in kinship with God who has scorned wealth. Of course I do not forbid you to possess it, but I would have you reach the point at which you possess it dauntlessly; this can be accomplished only by persuading yourself that you can live happily without it as well as with it, and by regarding riches always as likely to elude you.

But now I must begin to fold up my letter. "Settle your debts first," you cry. Here is a draft on Epicurus; he will pay down the sum: "Ungoverned anger begets madness."† You cannot help knowing the truth of these words, since you have had not only slaves, but also enemies. But indeed this emotion blazes out against all sorts of persons; it springs from love as much as from hate, and shows itself not less in serious matters than in jest and sport. And it makes no

* Vergil, *Aeneid*, viii. 364 f.

† Frag. 484 Usener.

difference how important the provocation may be, but into what kind of soul it penetrates. Similarly with fire; it does not matter how great is the flame, but what it falls upon. For solid timbers have repelled a very great fire; conversely, dry and easily inflammable stuff nourishes the slightest spark into a conflagration. So it is with anger, my dear Lucilius; the outcome of a mighty anger is madness, and hence anger should be avoided, not merely that we may escape excess, but that we may have a healthy mind. Farewell.

LETTER XXVI

ON OLD AGE AND DEATH

I was just lately telling you that I was within sight of old age.* I am now afraid that I have left old age behind me. For some other word would now apply to my years, or at any rate to my body; since old age means a time of life that is weary rather than crushed. You may rate me in the worn-out class,—of those who are nearing the end.

Nevertheless, I offer thanks to myself, with you as witness; for I feel that age has done no damage to my mind, though I feel its effects on my constitution. Only my vices, and the outward aids to these vices, have reached senility; my mind is strong and rejoices that it has but slight connexion with the body. It has laid aside the greater part of its load. It is alert; it takes issue with me on the subject of old age; it declares that old age is its time of bloom. Let me take it at its word, and let it make the most of the advantages it possesses. The mind bids me do some

* See the twelfth letter. Seneca was by this time at least sixty-five years old, and probably older.

thinking and consider how much of this peace of spirit and moderation of character I owe to wisdom and how much to my time of life; it bids me distinguish carefully what I cannot do and what I do not want to do . . . .* For why should one complain or regard it as a disadvantage, if powers which ought to come to an end have failed? "But," you say, "it is the greatest possible disadvantage to be worn out and to die off, or rather, if I may speak literally, to melt away! For we are not suddenly smitten and laid low; we are worn away, and every day reduces our powers to a certain extent."

But is there any better end to it all than to glide off to one's proper haven, when nature slips the cable? Not that there is anything painful in a shock and a sudden departure from existence; it is merely because this other way of departure is easy,—a gradual withdrawal. I, at any rate, as if the test were at hand and the day were come which is to pronounce its decision concerning all the years of my life, watch over myself and commune thus with myself: "The showing which we have made up to the present time, in word or deed, counts for nothing. All this is but a trifling and deceitful pledge of our spirit, and is wrapped in much charlatanism. I shall leave it to Death to determine what progress I have made. Therefore with no faint heart I am making ready for the day when, putting aside all stage artifice and actor's rouge, I am to pass judgment upon myself,—whether I am merely declaiming brave sentiments, or whether I really feel them; whether all the bold threats I have uttered against fortune are a pretence and a farce. Put aside the opinion of the world; it is always wavering and always takes both sides. Put aside the studies which you have pursued throughout your life; Death will deliver the final judgment in your case. This is what I mean: your debates and learned talks, your maxims gathered from the teachings of the wise, your cultured conversation,—all these afford no proof of the real strength of your soul. Even the most timid man can deliver a bold speech. What you have done in the past will be manifest

* This passage is hopelessly corrupt. The course of the argument requires something like this: For it is just as much to my advantage not to be able to do what I do not want to do, as it is to be able to do whatever gives me pleasure.

only at the time when you draw your last breath. I accept the terms; I do not shrink from the decision." This is what I say to myself, but I would have you think that I have said it to you also. You are younger; but what does that matter? There is no fixed count of our years. You do not know where death awaits you; so be ready for it everywhere.

I was just intending to stop, and my hand was making ready for the closing sentence; but the rites are still to be performed and the travelling money for the letter disbursed. And just assume that I am not telling where I intend to borrow the necessary sum; you know upon whose coffers I depend. Wait for me but a moment, and I will pay you from my own account;* meanwhile, Epicurus will oblige me with these words:† "Think on death," or rather, if you prefer the phrase, on "migration to heaven." The meaning is clear,—that it is a wonderful thing to learn thoroughly how to die. You may deem it superfluous to learn a text that can be used only once; but that is just the reason why we ought to think on a thing. When we can never prove whether we really know a thing, we must always be learning it. "Think on death." In saying this, he bids us think on freedom. He who has learned to die has unlearned slavery; he is above any external power, or, at any rate, he is beyond it. What terrors have prisons and bonds and bars for him? His way out is clear. There is only one chain which binds us to life, and that is the love of life. The chain may not be cast off, but it may be rubbed away, so that, when necessity shall demand, nothing may retard or hinder us from being ready to do at once that which at some time we are bound to do. Farewell.

---

* i.e., the money will be brought from home,—the saying will be one of Seneca's own.

† Epicurus, Frag. 205 Usener.

LETTER

XXVII

ON THE GOOD WHICH ABIDES

"What," say you, "are you giving me advice? Indeed, have you already advised yourself, already corrected your own faults? Is this the reason why you have leisure to reform other men?" No, I am not so shameless as to undertake to cure my fellow-men when I am ill myself. I am, however, discussing with you troubles which concern us both, and sharing the remedy with you, just as if we were lying ill in the same hospital. Listen to me, therefore, as you would if I were talking to myself. I am admitting you to my inmost thoughts, and am having it out with myself, merely making use of you as my pretext. I keep crying out to myself: "Count your years, and you will be ashamed to desire and pursue the same things you desired in your boyhood days. Of this one thing make sure against your dying day,—let your faults die before you die. Away with those disordered pleasures, which must be dearly paid for; it is not only those which are to come that harm me, but also those which have come and gone. Just as crimes, even if they have not been detected when they were committed, do not allow anxiety to end with them; so with guilty pleasures, regret remains even after the pleasures are over. They are not substantial, they are not trustworthy; even if they do not harm us, they are fleeting. Cast about rather for some good which will abide. But there can be no such good except as the soul discovers it for itself within itself. Virtue alone affords everlasting and peace-giving joy; even if some obstacle arise, it is but like an intervening cloud, which floats beneath the sun but never prevails against it."

When will it be your lot to attain this joy? Thus far, you have indeed not been sluggish, but you must quicken your pace. Much toil remains; to confront it, you must yourself lavish all your waking hours, and all your efforts, if you wish the result to be accomplished. This matter cannot be delegated to someone else. The other kind of literary activity* admits of outside assistance. Within our own time there was a certain rich man named Calvisius Sabinus; he had the bank-account and the brains of a freedman.† I never saw a man whose good fortune was a greater offence against propriety. His memory was so faulty that he would sometimes forget the name of Ulysses, or Achilles, or Priam,—names which we know as well as we know those of our own attendants. No major-domo in his dotage, who cannot give men their right names, but is compelled to invent names for them,—no such man, I say, calls off the names‡ of his master's tribesmen so atrociously as Sabinus used to call off the Trojan and Achaean heroes. But none the less did he desire to appear learned. So he devised this short cut to learning: he paid fabulous prices for slaves,—one to know Homer by heart and another to know Hesiod; he also delegated a special slave to each of the nine lyric poets. You need not wonder that he paid high prices for these slaves; if he did not find them ready to hand he had them made to order. After collecting this

* i.e., ordinary studies, or literature, as contrasted with philosophy.

† Compare with the following the vulgarities of Trimalchio in the Satire of Petronius, and the bad taste of Nasidienus in Horace (*Sat.* ii. 8).

‡ At the *salutatio*, or morning call. The position of *nomenclator*, "caller-of-names," was originally devoted more strictly to political purposes. Here it is primarily social.

retinue, he began to make life miserable for his guests; he would keep these fellows at the foot of his couch, and ask them from time to time for verses which he might repeat, and then frequently break down in the middle of a word. Satellius Quadratus, a feeder, and consequently a fawner, upon addle-pated millionaires, and also (for this quality goes with the other two) a flouter of them, suggested to Sabinus that he should have philologists to gather up the bits.* Sabinus remarked that each slave cost him one hundred thousand sesterces; Satellius replied: "You might have bought as many book-cases for a smaller sum." But Sabinus held to the opinion that what any member of his household knew, he himself knew also. This same Satellius began to advise Sabinus to take wrestling lessons,—sickly, pale, and thin as he was, Sabinus answered: "How can I? I can scarcely stay alive now." "Don't say that, I implore you," replied the other, "consider how many perfectly healthy slaves you have!" No man is able to borrow or buy a sound mind; in fact, as it seems to me, even though sound minds were for sale, they would not find buyers. Depraved minds, however, are bought and sold every day.

But let me pay off my debt and say farewell: "Real wealth is poverty adjusted to the law of Nature."† Epicurus has this saying in various ways and contexts; but it can never be repeated too often, since it can never be learned too well. For some persons the remedy should be merely prescribed; in the case of others, it should be forced down their throats. Farewell.

* i.e., all the ideas that dropped out of the head of Sabinus. The slave who picked up the crumbs was called *analecta.*

† Epicurus, Frag. 477 Usener.

LETTER

XXVIII

ON TRAVEL AS A CURE FOR DISCONTENT

Do you suppose that you alone have had this experience? Are you surprised, as if it were a novelty, that after such long travel and so many changes of scene you have not been able to shake off the gloom and heaviness of your mind? You need a change of soul rather than a change of climate.* Though you may cross vast spaces of sea, and though, as our Vergil† remarks,

> Lands and cities are left astern,

your faults will follow you whithersoever you travel. Socrates made the same remark to one who complained; he said: "Why do you wonder that globe-trotting does not help you, seeing that you always take yourself with you? The reason which set you wandering is ever at your heels." What pleasure is there in

* Cf. Horace, *Ep.* i. 11, 27 *caelum non animum mutant qui trans mare currunt.*

† *Aeneid*, iii. 72.

seeing new lands? Or in surveying cities and spots of interest? All your bustle is useless. Do you ask why such flight does not help you? It is because you flee along with yourself. You must lay aside the burdens of the mind; until you do this, no place will satisfy you. Reflect that your present behaviour is like that of the prophetess whom Vergil describes:[*] she is excited and goaded into fury, and contains within herself much inspiration that is not her own:

The priestess raves, if haply she may shake
The great god from her heart.

You wander hither and yon, to rid yourself of the burden that rests upon you, though it becomes more troublesome by reason of your very restlessness, just as in a ship the cargo when stationary makes no trouble, but when it shifts to this side or that, it causes the vessel to heel more quickly in the direction where it has settled. Anything you do tells against you, and you hurt yourself by your very unrest; for you are shaking up a sick man.

That trouble once removed, all change of scene will become pleasant; though you may be driven to the uttermost ends of the earth, in whatever corner of a savage land you may find yourself, that place, however forbidding, will be to you a hospitable abode. The person you are matters more than the place to which you go; for that reason we should not make the mind a bondsman to any one place. Live in this belief: "I am not born for any one corner of the universe; this whole world is my country." If you saw this fact clearly, you would not be surprised at getting no benefit from the fresh scenes to which you roam each time through weariness of the old scenes. For the first would have pleased you in each case, had you believed it wholly yours.[†] As it is, however, you are not journeying; you are drifting and being driven, only exchanging one place for another,

---

* *Aeneid*, vi. 78 f.

† i.e., had you been able to say *patria mea totus mundus est.*

although that which you seek,—to live well,—is found everywhere.[*] Can there be any spot so full of confusion as the Forum? Yet you can live quietly even there, if necessary. Of course, if one were allowed to make one's own arrangements, I should flee far from the very sight and neighbourhood of the Forum. For just as pestilential places assail even the strongest constitution, so there are some places which are also unwholesome for a healthy mind which is not yet quite sound, though recovering from its ailment. I disagree with those who strike out into the midst of the billows and, welcoming a stormy existence, wrestle daily in hardihood of soul with life's problems. The wise man will endure all that, but will not choose it; he will prefer to be at peace rather than at war. It helps little to have cast out your own faults if you must quarrel with those of others. Says one: "There were thirty tyrants surrounding Socrates, and yet they could not break his spirit"; but what does it matter how many masters a man has? "Slavery" has no plural; and he who has scorned it is free,—no matter amid how large a mob of over-lords he stands.

It is time to stop, but not before I have paid duty. "The knowledge of sin is the beginning of salvation." This saying of Epicurus[†] seems to me to be a noble one. For he who does not know that he has sinned does not desire correction; you must discover yourself in the wrong before you can reform yourself. Some boast of their faults. Do you think that the man has any thought of mending his ways who counts over his vices as if they were virtues? Therefore, as far as possible, prove yourself guilty, hunt up charges against yourself; play the part, first of accuser, then of judge, last of intercessor. At times be harsh with yourself.[‡] Farewell.

* Cf. Horace, *Ep.* i. 11, 28—*navibus atque Quadrigis petimus bene vivere; quod petis, hic est.*

† Frag. 522 Usener.

‡ i.e., refuse your own intercession.

LETTER XXXIII

ON THE FUTILITY OF LEARNING MAXIMS

You wish me to close these letters also, as I closed my former letters, with certain utterances taken from the chiefs of our school. But they did not interest themselves in choice extracts; the whole texture of their work is full of strength. There is unevenness, you know, when some objects rise conspicuous above others. A single tree is not remarkable if the whole forest rises to the same height. Poetry is crammed with utterances of this sort, and so is history. For this reason I would not have you think that these utterances belong to Epicurus: they are common property and are emphatically our own.* They are, however, more noteworthy in Epicurus, because they appear at infrequent intervals and when you do not expect them, and because it is surprising that brave words should be spoken at any time by a man who made a practice of being effeminate. For that is what most persons maintain. In my own opinion, however, Epicurus is really a

* Stoic as well as Epicurean.

brave man, even though he did wear long sleeves.* Fortitude, energy, and readiness for battle are to be found among the Persians,† just as much as among men who have girded themselves up high.

Therefore, you need not call upon me for extracts and quotations; such thoughts as one may extract here and there in the works of other philosophers run through the whole body of our writings. Hence we have no "show-window goods," nor do we deceive the purchaser in such a way that, if he enters our shop, he will find nothing except that which is displayed in the window. We allow the purchasers themselves to get their samples from anywhere they please. Suppose we should desire to sort out each separate motto from the general stock; to whom shall we credit them? To Zeno, Cleanthes, Chrysippus, Panaetius, or Posidonius? We Stoics are not subjects of a despot: each of us lays claim to his own freedom. With them,‡ on the other hand, whatever Hermarchus says, or Metrodorus, is ascribed to one source. In that brotherhood, everything that any man utters is spoken under the leadership and commanding authority§ of one alone. We cannot, I maintain, no matter how we try, pick out anything from so great a multitude of things equally good.

Only the poor man counts his flock.¶

Wherever you direct your gaze, you will meet with something that might stand out from the rest, if the context in which you read it were not equally notable.

---

* Contrasted with *alte cinctos*. The sleeveless and "girt-up" tunic is the sign of energy; cf. Horace, *Sat.* i. 5. 5, and Suetonius, *Caligula*, 52: the effeminate Caligula would "appear in public with a long-sleeved tunic and bracelets."

† Who wore sleeves.

‡ i.e., the Epicureans.

§ For the phrase *ductu et auspiciis* see Plautus, *Amph.* i. 1. 41 *ut gesserit rem publicam ductu imperio auspicio suo*; and Horace, *Od.* i. 7. 27 *Teucro duce et auspice Teucro*. The original significance of the phrase refers to the right of the commander-in-chief to take the auspices.

¶ Ovid, *Metamorphosis*, xiii. 824.

For this reason, give over hoping that you can skim, by means of epitomes, the wisdom of distinguished men. Look into their wisdom as a whole; study it as a whole. They are working out a plan and weaving together, line upon line, a masterpiece, from which nothing can be taken away without injury to the whole. Examine the separate parts, if you like, provided you examine them as parts of the man himself. She is not a beautiful woman whose ankle or arm is praised, but she whose general appearance makes you forget to admire her single attributes.

If you insist, however, I shall not be niggardly with you, but lavish; for there is a huge multitude of these passages; they are scattered about in profusion,—they do not need to be gathered together, but merely to be picked up. They do not drip forth occasionally; they flow continuously. They are unbroken and are closely connected. Doubtless they would be of much benefit to those who are still novices and worshipping outside the shrine; for single maxims sink in more easily when they are marked off and bounded like a line of verse. That is why we give to children a proverb, or that which the Greeks call *Chria*,* to be learned by heart; that sort of thing can be comprehended by the young mind, which cannot as yet hold more. For a man, however, whose progress is definite, to chase after choice extracts and to prop his weakness by the best known and the briefest sayings and to depend upon his memory, is disgraceful; it is time for him to lean on himself. He should make such maxims and not memorize them. For it is disgraceful even for an old man, or one who has sighted old age, to have a note-book knowledge. "This is what Zeno said." But what have you yourself said? "This is the opinion of Cleanthes." But what is your own opinion? How long shall you march under another man's orders? Take command, and utter some word which posterity will remember. Put forth something from your own stock. For this reason I hold that there is nothing of eminence in all such men as these, who never create

* Either "maxims" or "outlines," "themes." For a discussion of them see Quintilian, *Inst. Orat.* i. 9. 3 ff.

anything themselves, but always lurk in the shadow of others, playing the rôle of interpreters, never daring to put once into practice what they have been so long in learning. They have exercised their memories on other men's material. But it is one thing to remember, another to know. Remembering is merely safeguarding something entrusted to the memory; knowing, however, means making everything your own; it means not depending upon the copy and not all the time glancing back at the master. "Thus said Zeno, thus said Cleanthes, indeed!" Let there be a difference between yourself and your book! How long shall you be a learner? From now on be a teacher as well! "But why," one asks,* "should I have to continue hearing lectures on what I can read?" "The living voice," one replies, "is a great help." Perhaps, but not the voice which merely makes itself the mouthpiece of another's words, and only performs the duty of a reporter.

Consider this fact also. Those who have never attained their mental independence begin, in the first place, by following the leader in cases where everyone has deserted the leader; then, in the second place, they follow him in matters where the truth is still being investigated. However, the truth will never be discovered if we rest contented with discoveries already made. Besides, he who follows another not only discovers nothing but is not even investigating. What then? Shall I not follow in the footsteps of my predecessors? I shall indeed use the old road, but if I find one that makes a shorter cut and is smoother to travel, I shall open the new road. Men who have made these discoveries before us are not our masters, but our guides. Truth lies open for all; it has not yet been monopolized. And there is plenty of it left even for posterity to discover. Farewell.

* The objector is the assumed auditor. The answer to the objection gives the usual view as to the power of the living voice; to this Seneca assents, provided that the voice has a message of its own.

LETTER XXXVIII

ON QUIET CONVERSATION

You are right when you urge that we increase our mutual traffic in letters. But the greatest benefit is to be derived from conversation, because it creeps by degrees into the soul. Lectures prepared beforehand and spouted in the presence of a throng have in them more noise but less intimacy. Philosophy is good advice; and no one can give advice at the top of his lungs. Of course we must sometimes also make use of these harangues, if I may so call them, when a doubting member needs to be spurred on; but when the aim is to make a man learn, and not merely to make him wish to learn, we must have recourse to the low-toned words of conversation. They enter more easily, and stick in the memory; for we do not need many words, but, rather, effective words.

Words should be scattered like seed; no matter how small the seed may be, if it has once found favourable ground, it unfolds its strength and from an insignificant thing spreads to its greatest growth. Reason grows in the same way; it is not large to the outward view, but increases as it does its work. Few words are spoken; but if the mind has truly caught them, they come into their strength and spring up. Yes, precepts and seeds have the same quality; they produce much, and yet they are slight things. Only, as I said, let a favourable mind receive and assimilate them. Then of itself the mind also will produce bounteously in its turn, giving back more than it has received. Farewell.

LETTER XL

ON THE PROPER STYLE FOR A PHILOSOPHER'S DISCOURSE

I thank you for writing to me so often; for you are revealing your real self to me in the only way you can. I never receive a letter from you without being in your company forthwith. If the pictures of our absent friends are pleasing to us, though they only refresh the memory and lighten our longing by a solace that is unreal and unsubstantial, how much more pleasant is a letter, which brings us real traces, real evidences, of an absent friend! For that which is sweetest when we meet face to face is afforded by the impress of a friend's hand upon his letter,—recognition.

You write me that you heard a lecture by the philosopher Serapio,* when he landed at your present place of residence. "He is wont," you say, "to wrench up his words with a mighty rush, and he does not let them flow forth one by one, but makes

* This person cannot be identified.

them crowd and dash upon each other.* For the words come in such quantity that a single voice is inadequate to utter them." I do not approve of this in a philosopher; his speech, like his life, should be composed; and nothing that rushes headlong and is hurried is well ordered. That is why, in Homer, the rapid style, which sweeps down without a break like a snow-squall, is assigned to the younger speaker; from the old man eloquence flows gently, sweeter than honey.†

Therefore, mark my words; that forceful manner of speech, rapid and copious, is more suited to a mountebank than to a man who is discussing and teaching an important and serious subject. But I object just as strongly that he should drip out his words as that he should go at top speed; he should neither keep the ear on the stretch, nor deafen it. For that poverty-stricken and thin-spun style also makes the audience less attentive because they are weary of its stammering slowness; nevertheless, the word which has been long awaited sinks in more easily than the word which flits past us on the wing. Finally, people speak of "handing down" precepts to their pupils; but one is not "handing down" that which eludes the grasp. Besides, speech that deals with the truth should be unadorned and plain. This popular style has nothing to do with the truth; its aim is to impress the common herd, to ravish heedless ears by its speed; it does not offer itself for discussion, but snatches itself away from discussion. But how can that speech govern others which cannot itself be governed? May I not also remark that all speech which is employed for the purpose of healing our minds, ought to sink into us? Remedies do not avail unless they remain in the system.

Besides, this sort of speech contains a great deal of sheer emptiness; it has more sound than power. My terrors should be quieted, my irritations soothed, my illusions shaken off, my indulgences checked, my greed rebuked. And which of these cures can be brought about in

---

* The explanation of Professor Summers seems sound, that the metaphor is taken from a mountain-torrent. Compare the description of Cratinus' style in Aristophanes, *Ach.* 526, or that of Pindar in Horace, *Od.* iv. 2. 5 ff.

† *Iliad*, iii. 222 (Odysseus), and i. 249 (Nestor).

a hurry? What physician can heal his patient on a flying visit? May I add that such a jargon of confused and ill-chosen words cannot afford pleasure, either? No; but just as you are well satisfied, in the majority of cases, to have seen through tricks which you did not think could possibly be done*, so in the case of these word-gymnasts,—to have heard them once is amply sufficient. For what can a man desire to learn or to imitate in them? What is he to think of their souls, when their speech is sent into the charge in utter disorder, and cannot be kept in hand? Just as, when you run down hill, you cannot stop at the point where you had decided to stop, but your steps are carried along by the momentum of your body and are borne beyond the place where you wished to halt; so this speed of speech has no control over itself, nor is it seemly for philosophy; since philosophy should carefully place her words, not fling them out, and should proceed step by step.

"What then?" you say; "should not philosophy sometimes take a loftier tone?" Of course she should; but dignity of character should be preserved, and this is stripped away by such violent and excessive force. Let philosophy possess great forces, but kept well under control; let her stream flow unceasingly, but never become a torrent. And I should hardly allow even to an orator a rapidity of speech like this, which cannot be called back, which goes lawlessly ahead; for how could it be followed by jurors, who are often inexperienced and untrained? Even when the orator is carried away by his desire to show off his powers, or by uncontrollable emotion, even then he should not quicken his pace and heap up words to an extent greater than the ear can endure.

You will be acting rightly, therefore, if you do not regard those men who seek how much they may say, rather than how they shall say it, and if for yourself you choose, provided a choice must be made,

* Seneca's phrase, *quae fieri posse non crederes*, has been interpreted as a definition of παϱάδοξα. It is more probable, however, that he is comparing with the juggler's tricks the verbal performances of certain lecturers, whose jargon one marvels at but does not care to hear again.

to speak as Publius Vinicius the stammerer does. When Asellius was asked how Vinicius spoke, he replied: "Gradually"! (It was a remark of Geminus Varius, by the way: "I don't see how you can call that man 'eloquent'; why, he can't get out three words together.") Why, then, should you not choose to speak as Vinicius does? Though of course some wag may cross your path, like the person who said, when Vinicius was dragging out his words one by one, as if he were dictating and not speaking. "Say, haven't you anything to say?" And yet that were the better choice, for the rapidity of Quintus Haterius, the most famous orator of his age, is, in my opinion, to be avoided by a man of sense. Haterius never hesitated, never paused; he made only one start, and only one stop.

However, I suppose that certain styles of speech are more or less suitable to nations also; in a Greek you can put up with the unrestrained style, but we Romans, even when writing, have become accustomed to separate our words.* And our compatriot Cicero, with whom Roman oratory sprang into prominence, was also a slow pacer.† The Roman language is more inclined to take stock of itself, to weigh, and to offer something worth weighing. Fabianus, a man noteworthy because of his life, his knowledge, and, less important than either of these, his eloquence also, used to discuss a subject with dispatch rather than with haste; hence you might call it ease rather than speed. I approve this quality in the wise man; but I do not demand it; only let his speech proceed unhampered, though I prefer that it should be deliberately uttered rather than spouted.

However, I have this further reason for frightening you away from the latter malady, namely, that you could only be successful in practising this style by losing your sense of modesty; you would have to rub all shame from your countenance,‡ and refuse to hear yourself

* The Greek texts were still written without separation of the words, in contrast with the Roman.

† *Gradarius* may be contrasted with *tolutarius*, "trotter." The word might also mean one who walks with dignified step, as in a religious procession.

‡ Cf. Martial, xi. 27. 7 *aut cum perfricuit frontem posuitque pudorem*. After a violent rubbing,

speak. For that heedless flow will carry with it many expressions which you would wish to criticize. And, I repeat, you could not attain it and at the same time preserve your sense of shame. Moreover, you would need to practise every day, and transfer your attention from subject matter to words. But words, even if they came to you readily and flowed without any exertion on your part, yet would have to be kept under control. For just as a less ostentatious gait becomes a philosopher, so does a restrained style of speech, far removed from boldness. Therefore, the ultimate kernel of my remarks is this: I bid you be slow of speech. Farewell.

---

the face would not show blushes.

LETTER XLI

ON THE GOD WITHIN US

You are doing an excellent thing, one which will be wholesome for you, if, as you write me, you are persisting in your effort to attain sound understanding; it is foolish to pray for this when you can acquire it from yourself. We do not need to uplift our hands towards heaven, or to beg the keeper of a temple to let us approach his idol's ear, as if in this way our prayers were more likely to be heard. God is near you, he is with you, he is within you. This is what I mean, Lucilius: a holy spirit indwells within us, one who marks our good and bad deeds, and is our guardian. As we treat this spirit, so are we treated by it. Indeed, no man can be good without the help of God. Can one rise superior to fortune unless God helps him to rise? He it is that gives noble and upright counsel. In each good man

A god doth dwell, but what god know we not.*

---

* Vergil, *Aeneid*, viii. 352, *Hoc nemus, hunc, inquit, frondoso vertice collem, Quis deus incertum est, habitat deus*, and cf. Quintillian, i. 10. 88, where he is speaking of Ennius, whom "*sicut sacros vetustate lucos adoremus, in quibus grandia et antiqua robora iam non tantum habent speciem quantem religionem.*"

If ever you have come upon a grove that is full of ancient trees which have grown to an unusual height, shutting out a view of the sky by a veil of pleached and intertwining branches, then the loftiness of the forest, the seclusion of the spot, and your marvel at the thick unbroken shade in the midst of the open spaces, will prove to you the presence of deity. Or if a cave, made by the deep crumbling of the rocks, holds up a mountain on its arch, a place not built with hands but hollowed out into such spaciousness by natural causes, your soul will be deeply moved by a certain intimation of the existence of God. We worship the sources of mighty rivers; we erect altars at places where great streams burst suddenly from hidden sources; we adore springs of hot water as divine, and consecrate certain pools because of their dark waters or their immeasurable depth. If you see a man who is unterrified in the midst of dangers, untouched by desires, happy in adversity, peaceful amid the storm, who looks down upon men from a higher plane, and views the gods on a footing of equality, will not a feeling of reverence for him steal over you? Will you not say: "This quality is too great and too lofty to be regarded as resembling this petty body in which it dwells? A divine power has descended upon that man." When a soul rises superior to other souls, when it is under control, when it passes through every experience as if it were of small account, when it smiles at our fears and at our prayers, it is stirred by a force from heaven. A thing like this cannot stand upright unless it be propped by the divine. Therefore, a greater part of it abides in that place from whence it came down to earth. Just as the rays of the sun do indeed touch the earth, but still abide at the source from which they are sent; even so the great and hallowed soul, which has come down in order that we may have a nearer knowledge of divinity, does indeed associate with us, but still cleaves to its origin; on that source it depends, thither it turns its gaze and strives to go, and it concerns itself with our doings only as a being superior to ourselves.

What, then, is such a soul? One which is resplendent with no external good, but only with its own. For what is more foolish than to praise in a man the qualities which come from without? And what is more insane than to marvel at characteristics which may at the next instant be passed on to someone else? A golden bit does not make a better horse. The lion with gilded mane, in process of being trained and forced by weariness to endure the decoration, is sent into the arena in quite a different way from the wild lion whose spirit is unbroken; the latter, indeed, bold in his attack, as nature wished him to be, impressive because of his wild appearance,—and it is his glory that none can look upon him without fear,—is favoured* in preference to the other lion, that languid and gilded brute.

No man ought to glory except in that which is his own. We praise a vine if it makes the shoots teem with increase, if by its weight it bends to the ground the very poles which hold its fruit; would any man prefer to this vine one from which golden grapes and golden leaves hang down? In a vine the virtue peculiarly its own is fertility; in man also we should praise that which is his own. Suppose that he has a retinue of comely slaves and a beautiful house, that his farm is large and large his income; none of these things is in the man himself; they are all on the outside. Praise the quality in him which cannot be given or snatched away, that which is the peculiar property of the man. Do you ask what this is? It is soul, and reason brought to perfection in the soul. For man is a reasoning animal. Therefore, man's highest good is attained, if he has fulfilled the good for which nature designed him at birth. And what is it which this reason demands of him? The easiest thing in the world,—to live in accordance with his own nature. But this is turned into a hard task by the general madness of mankind; we push one another into vice. And how can a man be recalled to salvation, when he has none to restrain him, and all mankind to urge him on? Farewell.

* The spectators of the fight, which is to take place between the two lions, applaud the wild lion and bet on him.

LETTER XLVI

ON A NEW BOOK BY LUCILIUS

I received the book of yours which you promised me. I opened it hastily with the idea of glancing over it at leisure; for I meant only to taste the volume. But by its own charm the book coaxed me into traversing it more at length. You may understand from this fact how eloquent it was; for it seemed to be written in the smooth style,* and yet did not resemble your handiwork or mine, but at first sight might have been ascribed to Titus Livius or to Epicurus. Moreover, I was so impressed and carried along by its charm that I finished it without any postponement. The sunlight called to me, hunger warned, and clouds were lowering; but I absorbed the book from beginning to end.

I was not merely pleased; I rejoiced. So full of wit and spirit it was! I should have added "force," had the book contained moments of repose, or had it risen to energy only at intervals. But I found that there was no burst of force, but an even flow,

* Possibly *levis* in the sense of *light*, referring to size.

a style that was vigorous and chaste. Nevertheless I noticed from time to time your sweetness, and here and there that mildness of yours. Your style is lofty and noble; I want you to keep to this manner and this direction. Your subject also contributed something; for this reason you should choose productive topics, which will lay hold of the mind and arouse it.

I shall discuss the book more fully after a second perusal; meantime, my judgment is somewhat unsettled, just as if I had heard it read aloud, and had not read it myself. You must allow me to examine it also. You need not be afraid; you shall hear the truth. Lucky fellow, to offer a man no opportunity to tell you lies at such long range! Unless perhaps, even now, when excuses for lying are taken away, custom serves as an excuse for our telling each other lies! Farewell.

LETTER

XLVII

ON MASTER AND SLAVE

I am glad to learn, through those who come from you, that you live on friendly terms with your slaves. This befits a sensible and well-educated man like yourself. "They are slaves," people declare.* Nay, rather they are men. "Slaves!" No, comrades. "Slaves!" No, they are unpretentious friends. "Slaves!" No, they are our fellow-slaves, if one reflects that Fortune has equal rights over slaves and free men alike.

That is why I smile at those who think it degrading for a man to dine with his slave. But why should they think it degrading? It is only because purse-proud etiquette surrounds a householder at his dinner with a mob of standing slaves. The master eats more than he can hold, and with monstrous greed loads his belly until it is stretched and at length ceases to do the work of a belly; so that he is at greater pains to discharge all the food than he was to stuff it down. All this time the poor slaves may not move

* Much of the following is quoted by Macrobius, *Sat.* i. 11. 7 ff., in the passage beginning *vis tu cogitare eos, quos ios tuum vocas, isdem seminibus ortos eodem frui caelo*, etc.

their lips, even to speak. The slightest murmur is repressed by the rod; even a chance sound,—a cough, a sneeze, or a hiccup,—is visited with the lash. There is a grievous penalty for the slightest breach of silence. All night long they must stand about, hungry and dumb.

The result of it all is that these slaves, who may not talk in their master's presence, talk about their master. But the slaves of former days, who were permitted to converse not only in their master's presence, but actually with him, whose mouths were not stitched up tight, were ready to bare their necks for their master, to bring upon their own heads any danger that threatened him; they spoke at the feast, but kept silence during torture. Finally, the saying, in allusion to this same high-handed treatment, becomes current: "As many enemies as you have slaves." They are not enemies when we acquire them; we make them enemies.

I shall pass over other cruel and inhuman conduct towards them; for we maltreat them, not as if they were men, but as if they were beasts of burden. When we recline at a banquet, one slave mops up the disgorged food, another crouches beneath the table and gathers up the left-overs of the tipsy guests. Another carves the priceless game birds; with unerring strokes and skilled hand he cuts choice morsels along the breast or the rump. Hapless fellow, to live only for the purpose of cutting fat capons correctly,—unless, indeed, the other man is still more unhappy than he, who teaches this art for pleasure's sake, rather than he who learns it because he must. Another, who serves the wine, must dress like a woman and wrestle with his advancing years; he cannot get away from his boyhood; he is dragged back to it; and though he has already acquired a soldier's figure, he is kept beardless by having his hair smoothed away or plucked out by the roots, and he must remain awake throughout the night, dividing his time between his master's drunkenness and his lust; in the chamber he must be a man, at the feast a boy.* Another, whose duty it is to put a

* *Glabri*, *delicati*, or *exoleti* were favourite slaves, kept artifically youthful by Romans of the more dissolute class. Cf. Catullus, lxi. 142, and Seneca, *De Brevitate Vitae*, 12. 5 (a passage closely resembling the description given above by Seneca), where the master prides himself upon the elegant appearance and graceful gestures of these favourites.

valuation on the guests, must stick to his task, poor fellow, and watch to see whose flattery and whose immodesty, whether of appetite or of language, is to get them an invitation for tomorrow. Think also of the poor purveyors of food, who note their masters' tastes with delicate skill, who know what special flavours will sharpen their appetite, what will please their eyes, what new combinations will rouse their cloyed stomachs, what food will excite their loathing through sheer satiety, and what will stir them to hunger on that particular day. With slaves like these the master cannot bear to dine; he would think it beneath his dignity to associate with his slave at the same table! Heaven forfend!

But how many masters is he creating in these very men! I have seen standing in the line, before the door of Callistus, the former master,* of Callistus; I have seen the master himself shut out while others were welcomed,—the master who once fastened the "For Sale" ticket on Callistus and put him in the market along with the good-for-nothing slaves. But he has been paid off by that slave who was shuffled into the first lot of those on whom the crier practises his lungs; the slave, too, in his turn has cut *his* name from the list and in his turn has adjudged him unfit to enter his house. The master sold Callistus, but how much has Callistus made his master pay for!

Kindly remember that he whom you call your slave sprang from the same stock, is smiled upon by the same skies, and on equal terms with yourself breathes, lives, and dies. It is just as possible for you to see in him a free-born man as for him to see in you a slave. As a result of the massacres in Marius's† day, many a man of distinguished birth, who was taking the first steps toward senatorial rank by service in the army, was humbled by fortune, one becoming a shepherd, another a caretaker of a country cottage. Despise, then, if you dare, those to whose estate you may at any time descend, even when you are despising them.

---

* The master of Callistus, before he became the favourite of Caligula, is unknown.

† There is some doubt whether we should not read Variana, as Lipsius suggests. This method of qualifying for senator suits the Empire better than the Republic. Variana would refer to the defeat of Varus in Germany, A.D. 9.

I do not wish to involve myself in too large a question, and to discuss the treatment of slaves, towards whom we Romans are excessively haughty, cruel, and insulting. But this is the kernel of my advice: Treat your inferiors as you would be treated by your betters. And as often as you reflect how much power you have over a slave, remember that your master has just as much power over you. "But I have no master," you say. You are still young; perhaps you will have one. Do you not know at what age Hecuba entered captivity, or Croesus, or the mother of Darius, or Plato, or Diogenes?*

Associate with your slave on kindly, even on affable, terms; let him talk with you, plan with you, live with you. I know that at this point all the exquisites will cry out against me in a body; they will say: "There is nothing more debasing, more disgraceful, than this." But these are the very persons whom I sometimes surprise kissing the hands of other men's slaves. Do you not see even this,—how our ancestors removed from masters everything invidious, and from slaves everything insulting? They called the master "father of the household," and the slaves "members of the household," a custom which still holds in the mime. They established a holiday on which masters and slaves should eat together,—not as the only day for this custom, but as obligatory on that day in any case. They allowed the slaves to attain honours in the household and to pronounce judgment;† they held that a household was a miniature commonwealth.

"Do you mean to say," comes the retort, "that I must seat all my slaves at my own table?" No, not any more than that you should invite all free men to it. You are mistaken if you think that I would bar from my table certain slaves whose duties are more humble, as, for example, yonder muleteer or yonder herdsman; I propose to value

* Plato was about forty years old when he visited Sicily, whence he was afterwards deported by Dionysius the Elder. He was sold into slavery at Aegina and ransomed by a man from Cyrene. Diogenes, while travelling from Athens to Aegina, is said to have been captured by pirates and sold in Crete, where he was purchased by a certain Corinthian and given his freedom.

† i.e., as the praetor himself was normally accustomed to do.

them according to their character, and not according to their duties. Each man acquires his character for himself, but accident assigns his duties. Invite some to your table because they deserve the honour, and others that they may come to deserve it. For if there is any slavish quality in them as the result of their low associations, it will be shaken off by intercourse with men of gentler breeding. You need not, my dear Lucilius, hunt for friends only in the forum or in the Senate-house; if you are careful and attentive, you will find them at home also. Good material often stands idle for want of an artist; make the experiment, and you will find it so. As he is a fool who, when purchasing a horse, does not consider the animal's points, but merely his saddle and bridle; so he is doubly a fool who values a man from his clothes or from his rank, which indeed is only a robe that clothes us.

"He is a slave." His soul, however, may be that of a freeman. "He is a slave." But shall that stand in his way? Show me a man who is not a slave; one is a slave to lust, another to greed, another to ambition, and all men are slaves to fear. I will name you an ex-consul who is slave to an old hag, a millionaire who is slave to a serving-maid; I will show you youths of the noblest birth in serfdom to pantomime players! No servitude is more disgraceful than that which is self-imposed.

You should therefore not be deterred by these finicky persons from showing yourself to your slaves as an affable person and not proudly superior to them; they ought to respect you rather than fear you. Some may maintain that I am now offering the liberty-cap to slaves in general and toppling down lords from their high estate, because I bid slaves respect their masters instead of fearing them. They say: "This is what he plainly means: slaves are to pay respect as if they were clients or early-morning callers!" Anyone who holds this opinion forgets that what is enough for a god cannot be too little for a master. Respect means love, and love and fear cannot be mingled. So I hold that you are entirely right in not wishing to be feared by your slaves, and in lashing them merely with the tongue; only dumb animals need the thong.

That which annoys us does not necessarily injure us; but we are driven into wild rage by our luxurious lives, so that whatever does not answer our whims arouses our anger. We don the temper of kings. For they, too, forgetful alike of their own strength and of other men's weakness, grow white-hot with rage, as if they had received an injury, when they are entirely protected from danger of such injury by their exalted station. They are not unaware that this is true, but by finding fault they seize upon opportunities to do harm; they insist that they have received injuries, in order that they may inflict them.

I do not wish to delay you longer; for you need no exhortation. This, among other things, is a mark of good character: it forms its own judgments and abides by them; but badness is fickle and frequently changing, not for the better, but for something different. Farewell.

LETTER

XLVIII

ON QUIBBLING AS UNWORTHY OF THE PHILOSOPHER

In answer to the letter which you wrote me while travelling,—a letter as long as the journey itself,—I shall reply later. I ought to go into retirement, and consider what sort of advice I should give you. For you yourself, who consult me, also reflected for a long time whether to do so; how much more, then, should I myself reflect, since more deliberation is necessary in settling than in propounding a problem! And this is particularly true when one thing is advantageous to you and another to me. Am I speaking again in the guise of an Epicurean?* But the fact is, the same thing is advantageous

* The Epicureans, who reduced all goods to "utilities," could not regard a friend's advantage as identical to one's own advantage. And yet they laid great stress upon friendship as one of the chief sources of pleasure. For an attempt to reconcile these two positions see Cicero, *De Finibus*, i. 65 ff. Seneca has inadvertantly used a phrase that implies a difference between a friend's interest and one's own. This leads him to reassert the Stoic view of friendship, which adopted as its motto κοινὰ τὰ τῶν φίλων.

to me which is advantageous to you; for I am not your friend unless whatever is at issue concerning you is my concern also. Friendship produces between us a partnership in all our interests. There is no such thing as good or bad fortune for the individual; we live in common. And no one can live happily who has regard to himself alone and transforms everything into a question of his own utility; you must live for your neighbour, if you would live for yourself. This fellowship, maintained with scrupulous care, which makes us mingle as men with our fellow-men and holds that the human race have certain rights in common, is also of great help in cherishing the more intimate fellowship which is based on friendship, concerning which I began to speak above. For he that has much in common with a fellow-man will have all things in common with a friend.

And on this point, my excellent Lucilius, I should like to have those subtle dialecticians of yours advise me how I ought to help a friend, or how a fellow-man, rather than tell me in how many ways the word "friend" is used, and how many meanings the word "man" possesses. Lo, Wisdom and Folly are taking opposite sides. Which shall I join? Which party would you have me follow? On that side, "man" is the equivalent of "friend"; on the other side, "friend" is not the equivalent of "man." The one wants a friend for his own advantage; the other wants to make himself an advantage to his friend.* What *you* have to offer me is nothing but distortion of words and splitting of syllables. It is clear that unless I can devise some very tricky premises and by false deductions tack on to them a fallacy which springs from the truth, I shall not be able to distinguish between what is desirable and what is to be avoided! I am ashamed! Old men as we are, dealing with a problem so serious, we make play of it!

* The sides are given in the reverse order in the two clauses: to the Stoic the terms "friend" and "man" are co-extensive; he is the friend of everybody, and his motive in friendship is to be of service; the Epicurean, however, narrows the definition of "friend" and regards him merely as an instrument to his own happiness.

"'Mouse' is a syllable.* Now a mouse eats cheese; therefore, a syllable eats cheese." Suppose now that I cannot solve this problem; see what peril hangs over my head as a result of such ignorance! What a scrape I shall be in! Without doubt I must beware, or some day I shall be catching syllables in a mousetrap, or, if I grow careless, a book may devour my cheese! Unless, perhaps, the following syllogism is shrewder still: "'Mouse' is a syllable. Now a syllable does not eat cheese. Therefore a mouse does not eat cheese." What childish nonsense! Do we knit our brows over this sort of problem? Do we let our beards grow long for this reason? Is this the matter which we teach with sour and pale faces?

Would you really know what philosophy offers to humanity? Philosophy offers counsel. Death calls away one man, and poverty chafes another; a third is worried either by his neighbour's wealth or by his own. So-and-so is afraid of bad luck; another desires to get away from his own good fortune. Some are ill-treated by men, others by the gods. Why, then, do you frame for me such games as these? It is no occasion for jest; you are retained as counsel for unhappy mankind. You have promised to help those in peril by sea, those in captivity, the sick and the needy, and those whose heads are under the poised axe. Whither are you straying? What are you doing?

This friend, in whose company you are jesting, is in fear. Help him, and take the noose from about his neck. Men are stretching out imploring hands to you on all sides; lives ruined and in danger of ruin are begging for some assistance; men's hopes, men's resources, depend upon you. They ask that you deliver them from all their restlessness, that you reveal to them, scattered and wandering as they are, the clear light of truth. Tell them what nature has made necessary, and what superfluous; tell them how simple are the laws that she has laid down, how pleasant and unimpeded life is for those who follow these laws, but how bitter and perplexed it is for those who have put their trust in opinion rather than in nature.

* In this paragraph Seneca exposes the folly of trying to prove a truth by means of logical tricks, and offers a caricature of those which were current among the philosophers whom he derides.

I should deem your games of logic to be of some avail in relieving men's burdens, if you could first show me what part of these burdens they will relieve. What among these games of yours banishes lust? Or controls it? Would that I could say that they were merely of no profit! They are positively harmful. I can make it perfectly clear to you whenever you wish, that a noble spirit when involved in such subtleties is impaired and weakened. I am ashamed to say what weapons they supply to men who are destined to go to war with fortune, and how poorly they equip them! Is this the path to the greatest good? Is philosophy to proceed by such claptrap* and by quibbles which would be a disgrace and a reproach even for expounders† of the law? For what else is it that you men are doing, when you deliberately ensnare the person to whom you are putting questions, than making it appear that the man has lost his case on a technical error?‡ But just as the judge can reinstate those who have lost a suit in this way, so philosophy has reinstated these victims of quibbling to their former condition. Why do you men abandon your mighty promises, and, after having assured me in high-sounding language that you will permit the glitter of gold to dazzle my eyesight no more than the gleam of the sword, and that I shall, with mighty steadfastness, spurn both that which all men crave and that which all men fear, why do you descend to the ABC's of scholastic pedants? What is your answer?

Is this the path to heaven?§

---

* Literally, "or if or if not," words constantly employed by the logicians in legal instruments. For the latter cf. Cicero, *Pro Caecina*, 23. 65 *tum illud, quod dicitur, "sive nive" irrident, tum aucupia verborum et litterarum tendiculas in invidiam vocant.*

† Literally, "to those who sit studying the praetor's edicts." The *album* is the bulletin-board, on which the edicts of the praetor were posted, giving the formulae and stipulations for legal processes of various kinds.

‡ In certain actions the praetor appointed a judge and established a formula, indicating the plaintiff's claim and the judge's duty. If the statement was false, or the claim excessive, the plaintiff lost his case; under certain conditions (see last sentence of Seneca § 11) the defendant could claim annulment of the formula and have the case tried again. Such cases were not lost on their merits, and for that reason the lawyer who purposely took such an advantage was doing a contemptible thing.

§ Vergil, *Aeneid*, ix. 641.

For that is exactly what philosophy promises to me, that I shall be made equal to God. For this I have been summoned, for this purpose have I come. Philosophy, keep your promise!

Therefore, my dear Lucilius, withdraw yourself as far as possible from these exceptions and objections of so-called philosophers. Frankness, and simplicity beseem true goodness. Even if there were many years left to you, you would have had to spend them frugally in order to have enough for the necessary things; but as it is, when your time is so scant, what madness it is to learn superfluous things! Farewell.

LETTER LIII

ON THE FAULTS OF THE SPIRIT

You can persuade me into almost anything now, for I was recently persuaded to travel by water. We cast off when the sea was lazily smooth; the sky, to be sure, was heavy with nasty clouds, such as usually break into rain or squalls. Still, I thought that the few miles between Puteoli and your dear Parthenope* might be run off in quick time, despite the uncertain and lowering sky. So, in order to get away more quickly, I made straight out to sea for Nesis,† with the purpose of cutting across all the inlets. But when we were so far out that it made little difference to me whether I returned or kept on, the calm weather, which had enticed me, came to naught. The

* The poetical name for Naples; perhaps it was once a town near by which gave a sort of romantic second title to the larger city. Professor Summers thinks that this poetical name, together with *tua*, indicates a reference to a passage from the verse of Lucilius. Perhaps, however, *tua* means nothing more than "the place which you love so well," being in the neighbourhood of Pompeii, the birthplace of Lucilius.

† An islet near the mouth of the bay wherein Baiae was situated. Puteoli was on the opposite side of the bay from Baiae.

storm had not yet begun, but the ground-swell was on, and the waves kept steadily coming faster. I began to ask the pilot to put me ashore somewhere; he replied that the coast was rough and a bad place to land, and that in a storm he feared a lee shore more than anything else. But I was suffering too grievously to think of the danger, since a sluggish seasickness which brought no relief was racking me, the sort that upsets the liver without clearing it. Therefore I laid down the law to my pilot, forcing him to make for the shore, willy-nilly. When we drew near, I did not wait for things to be done in accordance with Vergil's orders, until

Prow faced seawards[*]

or

Anchor plunged from bow;[†]

I remembered my profession[‡] as a veteran devotee of cold water, and, clad as I was in my cloak, let myself down into the sea, just as a cold-water bather should. What do you think my feelings were, scrambling over the rocks, searching out the path, or making one for myself? I understood that sailors have good reason to fear the land. It is hard to believe what I endured when I could not endure myself; you may be sure that the reason why Ulysses was shipwrecked on every possible occasion was not so much because the sea-god was angry with him from his birth; he was simply subject to seasickness. And in the future I also, if I must go anywhere by sea, shall only reach my destination in the twentieth year.[§]

* *Aeneid*, vi. 3. This was the usual method of mooring a ship in ancient times.

† *Aeneid*, iii. 277.

‡ Compare Ep. lxxxiii. 5.

§ Ulysses took ten years on his journey, because of sea-sickness; Seneca will need twice as many.

When I finally calmed my stomach (for you know that one does not escape seasickness by escaping from the sea) and refreshed my body with a rubdown, I began to reflect how completely we forget or ignore our failings, even those that affect the body, which are continually reminding us of their existence,—not to mention those which are more serious in proportion as they are more hidden. A slight ague deceives us; but when it has increased and a genuine fever has begun to burn, it forces even a hardy man, who can endure much suffering, to admit that he is ill. There is pain in the foot, and a tingling sensation in the joints; but we still hide the complaint and announce that we have sprained a joint, or else are tired from over-exercise. Then the ailment, uncertain at first, must be given a name; and when it begins to swell the ankles also, and has made both our feet "right" feet,* we are bound to confess that we have the gout. The opposite holds true of diseases of the soul; the worse one is, the less one perceives it. You need not be surprised, my beloved Lucilius. For he whose sleep is light pursues visions during slumber, and sometimes, though asleep, is conscious that he is asleep; but sound slumber annihilates our very dreams and sinks the spirit down so deep that it has no perception of self. Why will no man confess his faults? Because he is still in their grasp; only he who is awake can recount his dream, and similarly a confession of sin is a proof of sound mind.

Let us, therefore, rouse ourselves, that we may be able to correct our mistakes. Philosophy, however, is the only power that can stir us, the only power that can shake off our deep slumber. Devote yourself wholly to philosophy. You are worthy of her; she is worthy of you; greet one another with a loving embrace. Say farewell to all other interests with courage and frankness. Do not study philosophy merely during your spare time.†

If you were ill, you would stop caring for your personal concerns, and forget your business duties; you would not think highly enough

---

* That is, they are so swollen that left and right look alike.

† Literally "on sufferance," whenever other matters permit. Cf. Pliny, *Ep.* vii. 30 *precario studeo*,—"subject to interruption from others."

of any client to take active charge of his case during a slight abatement of your sufferings. You would try your hardest to be rid of the illness as soon as possible. What, then? Shall you not do the same thing now? Throw aside all hindrances and give up your time to getting a sound mind; for no man can attain it if he is engrossed in other matters. Philosophy wields her own authority; she appoints her own time and does not allow it to be appointed for her. She is not a thing to be followed at odd times, but a subject for daily practice; she is mistress, and she commands our attendance. Alexander, when a certain state promised him a part of its territory and half its entire property, replied: "I invaded Asia with the intention, not of accepting what you might give, but of allowing you to keep what I might leave." Philosophy likewise keeps saying to all occupations: "I do not intend to accept the time which you have left over, but I shall allow you to keep what I myself shall leave."

Turn to her, therefore, with all your soul, sit at her feet, cherish her; a great distance will then begin to separate you from other men. You will be far ahead of all mortals, and even the gods will not be far ahead of you. Do you ask what will be the difference between yourself and the gods? They will live longer. But, by my faith, it is the sign of a great artist to have confined a full likeness to the limits of a miniature. The wise man's life spreads out to him over as large a surface as does all eternity to a god. There is one point in which the sage has an advantage over the god; for a god is freed from terrors by the bounty of nature, the wise man by his own bounty. What a wonderful privilege, to have the weaknesses of a man and the serenity of a god! The power of philosophy to blunt the blows of chance is beyond belief. No missile can settle in her body; she is well-protected and impenetrable. She spoils the force of some missiles and wards them off with the loose folds of her gown, as if they had no power to harm; others she dashes aside, and hurls them back with such force that they recoil upon the sender. Farewell.

LETTER LIV

ON ASTHMA AND DEATH

My ill-health had allowed me a long furlough, when suddenly it resumed the attack. "What kind of ill-health?" you say. And you surely have a right to ask; for it is true that no kind is unknown to me. But I have been consigned, so to speak, to one special ailment. I do not know why I should call it by its Greek name;* for it is well enough described as "shortness of breath." Its attack is of very brief duration, like that of a squall at sea; it usually ends within an hour. Who indeed could breathe his last for long? I have passed through all the ills and dangers of the flesh; but nothing seems to me more troublesome than this. And naturally so; for anything else may be called illness; but this is a sort of continued "last gasp."† Hence physicians call it "practising how to die." For some day the breath will succeed in doing what it

* i.e., asthma. Seneca thinks that the Latin name is good enough.

† Celcus (iv. 8) gives this disease as the second of those which deal with the respiratory organs; *cum vehementior est, ut spirare aeger sine sono et anhelatione non possit.*

has so often essayed. Do you think I am writing this letter in a merry spirit, just because I have escaped? It would be absurd to take delight in such supposed restoration to health, as it would be for a defendant to imagine that he had won his case when he had succeeded in postponing his trial. Yet in the midst of my difficult breathing I never ceased to rest secure in cheerful and brave thoughts.

"What?" I say to myself; "does death so often test me? Let it do so; I myself have for a long time tested death." "When?" you ask. Before I was born. Death is non-existence, and I know already what that means. What was before me will happen again after me. If there is any suffering in this state, there must have been such suffering also in the past, before we entered the light of day. As a matter of fact, however, we felt no discomfort then. And I ask you, would you not say that one was the greatest of fools who believed that a lamp was worse off when it was extinguished than before it was lighted? We mortals also are lighted and extinguished; the period of suffering comes in between, but on either side there is a deep peace. For, unless I am very much mistaken, my dear Lucilius, we go astray in thinking that death only follows, when in reality it has both preceded us and will in turn follow us. Whatever condition existed before our birth, is death. For what does it matter whether you do not begin at all, or whether you leave off, inasmuch as the result of both these states is non-existence?

I have never ceased to encourage myself with cheering counsels of this kind, silently, of course, since I had not the power to speak; then little by little this shortness of breath, already reduced to a sort of panting, came on at greater intervals, and then slowed down and finally stopped. Even by this time, although the gasping has ceased, the breath does not come and go normally; I still feel a sort of hesitation and delay in breathing. Let it be as it pleases, provided there be no sigh from the soul.* Accept this assurance from me: I shall never be

---

* i.e., that the sigh be physical,—an asthmatic gasp,—and not caused by anguish of the soul.

frightened when the last hour comes; I am already prepared and do not plan a whole day ahead. But do you praise* and imitate the man whom it does not irk to die, though he takes pleasure in living. For what virtue is there in going away when you are thrust out? And yet there is virtue even in this: I am indeed thrust out, but it is as if I were going away willingly. For that reason the wise man can never be thrust out, because that would mean removal from a place which he was unwilling to leave; and the wise man does nothing unwillingly. He escapes necessity, because he wills to do what necessity is about to force upon him. Farewell.

* The argument is: I am ready to die, but do not praise me on that account; reserve your praise for him who is not loth to die, though (unlike me) he finds it a pleasure to live (because he is in good health). Yes, for there is no more virtue in accepting death when one hates life, than there is in leaving a place when one is ejected.

LETTER

LV

ON VATIA'S VILLA

I have just returned from a ride in my litter; and I am as weary as if I had walked the distance, instead of being seated. Even to be carried for any length of time is hard work, perhaps all the more so because it is an unnatural exercise; for Nature gave us legs with which to do our own walking, and eyes with which to do our own seeing. Our luxuries have condemned us to weakness; we have ceased to be able to do that which we have long declined to do. Nevertheless, I found it necessary to give my body a shaking up, in order that the bile which had gathered in my throat, if that was my trouble, might be shaken out, or, if the very breath within me had become, for some reason, too thick, that the jolting, which I have felt was a good thing for me, might make it thinner. So I insisted on being carried longer than usual, along an attractive beach, which bends between Cumae and Servilius Vatia's country-house,[*] shut in by the sea on one side and the lake on the other, just like a narrow path. It was packed firm under foot, because of a recent storm; since, as you know, the waves, when they beat upon the beach hard and fast, level it out; but a continuous period of fair weather loosens it, when the sand, which is kept firm by the water, loses its moisture.

As my habit is, I began to look about for something there that might be of service to me, when my eyes fell upon the villa which had once belonged to Vatia. So this was the place where that famous praetorian millionaire passed his old age! He was famed for nothing else than his life of leisure, and he was regarded as lucky only for that reason. For whenever men were ruined by their friendship with Asinius Gallus[†] whenever others were ruined by their hatred of Sejanus, and later[‡] by their intimacy with him,—for it was no more dangerous to have offended him than to have loved him,—people used to cry out: "O Vatia, you alone know how to live!" But what he knew was how to hide, not how to live; and it makes a great deal of difference whether your life be one of leisure or one of idleness. So I never drove past his country-place during Vatia's lifetime without saying to myself: "Here lies Vatia!"

But, my dear Lucilius, philosophy is a thing of holiness, something to be worshipped, so much so that the very counterfeit pleases. For the mass of mankind consider that a person is at leisure who has withdrawn from society, is free from care, self-sufficient, and lives for himself; but these privileges can be the reward only of the wise man. Does he who is a victim of anxiety know how to live for

---

* Cumae was on the coast about six miles north of Cape Misenum. Lake Acheron (see § 6) was a salt-water pool between those two points, separated from the sea by a sandbar; it lay near Lake Avernus and probably derived its name from that fact. The Vatia mentioned here is unknown; he must not be confused with Isauricus.

† Son of Asinius Pollio; his frankness got him into trouble and he died of starvation in a dungeon in A.D. 33. Tacitus, *Ann.* i. 32. 2, quotes Augustus, discussing his own successor, as saying of Gallus *avidus et minor*. Sejanus was overthrown and executed in A.D. 31.

‡ i.e., after his fall.

himself? What? Does he even know (and that is of first importance) how to live at all? For the man who has fled from affairs and from men, who has been banished to seclusion by the unhappiness which his own desires have brought upon him, who cannot see his neighbour more happy than himself, who through fear has taken to concealment, like a frightened and sluggish animal,—this person is not living for himself; he is living for his belly, his sleep, and his lust,—and that is the most shameful thing in the world. He who lives for no one does not necessarily live for himself. Nevertheless, there is so much in steadfastness and adherence to one's purpose that even sluggishness, if stubbornly maintained, assumes an air of authority* with us.

I could not describe the villa accurately; for I am familiar only with the front of the house, and with the parts which are in public view and can be seen by the mere passer-by. There are two grottoes, which cost a great deal of labour, as big as the most spacious hall, made by hand. One of these does not admit the rays of the sun, while the other keeps them until the sun sets. There is also a stream running through a grove of plane-trees, which draws for its supply both on the sea and on Lake Acheron; it intersects the grove just like a race-way,† and is large enough to support fish, although its waters are continually being drawn off. When the sea is calm, however, they do not use the stream, only touching the well-stocked waters when the storms give the fishermen a forced holiday. But the most convenient thing about the villa is the fact that Baiae is next door, it is free from all the inconveniences of that resort, and yet enjoys its pleasures. I myself understand these attractions, and I believe that it is a villa suited to every season of the year. It fronts the west wind, which it intercepts in such a way that Baiae is denied it. So it seems that Vatia was no fool when he selected this place as the best in which to spend his leisure when it was already unfruitful and decrepit.

* i.e., imposes on us.

† Literally, "like a Euripus," referring to the narrow strait which divides Euboea from Boeotia at Chalcis. Its current is swift.

The place where one lives, however, can contribute little towards tranquillity; it is the mind which must make everything agreeable to itself. I have seen men despondent in a gay and lovely villa, and I have seen them to all appearance full of business in the midst of a solitude. For this reason you should not refuse to believe that your life is well-placed merely because you are not now in Campania. But why are you not there? Just let your thoughts travel, even to this place. You may hold converse with your friends when they are absent, and indeed as often as you wish and for as long as you wish. For we enjoy this, the greatest of pleasures, all the more when we are absent from one another. For the presence of friends makes us fastidious; and because we can at any time talk or sit together, when once we have parted we give not a thought to those whom we have just beheld. And we ought to bear the absence of friends cheerfully, just because everyone is bound to be often absent from his friends even when they are present. Include among such cases, in the first place, the nights spent apart, then the different engagements which each of two friends has, then the private studies of each and their excursions into the country, and you will see that foreign travel does not rob us of much. A friend should be retained in the spirit; such a friend can never be absent. He can see every day whomsoever he desires to see.

I would therefore have you share your studies with me, your meals, and your walks. We should be living within too narrow limits if anything were barred to our thoughts. I see you, my dear Lucilius, and at this very moment I hear you; I am with you to such an extent that I hesitate whether I should not begin to write you notes instead of letters. Farewell.

LETTER

LVI

ON QUIET AND STUDY

Beshrew me if I think anything more requisite than silence for a man who secludes himself in order to study! Imagine what a variety of noises reverberates about my ears! I have lodgings right over a bathing establishment. So picture to yourself the assortment of sounds, which are strong enough to make me hate my very powers of hearing! When your strenuous gentleman, for example, is exercising himself by flourishing leaden weights; when he is working hard, or else pretends to be working hard, I can hear him grunt; and whenever he releases his imprisoned breath, I can hear him panting in wheezy and high-pitched tones. Or perhaps I notice some lazy fellow, content with a cheap rubdown, and hear the crack of the pummelling hand on his shoulder, varying in sound according as the hand is laid on flat or hollow. Then, perhaps, a professional* comes along, shouting out the score;

---

* *Pilicrepus* probably means "ball-counter,"—one who keeps a record of the strokes. Compare our "billiard-marker."

that is the finishing touch. Add to this the arresting of an occasional roysterer or pickpocket, the racket of the man who always likes to hear his own voice in the bathroom,[*] or the enthusiast who plunges into the swimming-tank with unconscionable noise and splashing. Besides all those whose voices, if nothing else, are good, imagine the hair-plucker with his penetrating, shrill voice,—for purposes of advertisement,—continually giving it vent and never holding his tongue except when he is plucking the armpits and making his victim yell instead. Then the cake-seller with his varied cries, the sausageman, the confectioner, and all the vendors of food hawking their wares, each with his own distinctive intonation.

So you say: "What iron nerves or deadened ears, you must have, if your mind can hold out amid so many noises, so various and so discordant, when our friend Chrysippus[†] is brought to his death by the continual good-morrows that greet him!" But I assure you that this racket means no more to me than the sound of waves or falling water; although you will remind me that a certain tribe once moved their city merely because they could not endure the din of a Nile cataract.[‡] Words seem to distract me more than noises; for words demand attention, but noises merely fill the ears and beat upon them. Among the sounds that din round me without distracting, I include passing carriages, a machinist in the same block, a saw-sharpener near by, or some fellow who is demonstrating with little pipes and flutes at the Trickling Fountain,[§] shouting rather than singing.

---

* This was especially true of poets, cf. Horace, *Sat.* i. 4. 76 *suave locus voci resonat conclusus*, and Martial, iii. 44.

† It is nowhere else related of the famous Stoic philosopher Chrysippus that he objected to the salutations of his friends; and, besides, the morning salutation was a Roman, not a Greek, custom. Lipsius, therefore, was probably right when he proposed to read here, for Chrysippus, Crispus, one of Seneca's friends; cf. *Epigr.* 6.

‡ The same story is told in *Naturalis Quaestiones*, iv. 2. 5.

§ A cone-shaped fountain, resembling a turning-post (*meta*) in the circus, from which the water spouted through many jets; hence the "sweating" (*sudans*). Its remains may still be seen now not far from the Colosseum on the Velia.

Furthermore, an intermittent noise upsets me more than a steady one. But by this time I have toughened my nerves against all that sort of thing, so that I can endure even a boatswain marking the time in high-pitched tones for his crew. For I force my mind to concentrate, and keep it from straying to things outside itself; all outdoors may be bedlam, provided that there is no disturbance within, provided that fear is not wrangling with desire in my breast, provided that meanness and lavishness are not at odds, one harassing the other. For of what benefit is a quiet neighbourhood, if our emotions are in an uproar?

'Twas night, and all the world was lulled to rest.*

This is not true; for no real rest can be found when reason has not done the lulling. Night brings our troubles to the light, rather than banishes them; it merely changes the form of our worries. For even when we seek slumber, our sleepless moments are as harassing as the daytime. Real tranquillity is the state reached by an unperverted mind when it is relaxed. Think of the unfortunate man who courts sleep by surrendering his spacious mansion to silence, who, that his ear may be disturbed by no sound, bids the whole retinue of his slaves be quiet and that whoever approaches him shall walk on tiptoe; he tosses from this side to that and seeks a fitful slumber amid his frettings! He complains that he has heard sounds, when he has not heard them at all. The reason, you ask? His soul is in an uproar; it must be soothed, and its rebellious murmuring checked. You need not suppose that the soul is at peace when the body is still. Sometimes quiet means disquiet.

We must therefore rouse ourselves to action and busy ourselves with interests that are good, as often as we are in the grasp of an uncontrollable sluggishness. Great generals, when they see that their men are mutinous, check them by some sort of labour or keep them busy with small forays. The much occupied man has no time for wantonness, and it is an obvious commonplace that the evils of

---

* A fragment from the Argonautica of Varro Atacinus.

leisure can be shaken off by hard work. Although people may often have thought that I sought seclusion because I was disgusted with politics and regretted my hapless and thankless position,* yet, in the retreat to which apprehension and weariness have driven me, my ambition sometimes develops afresh. For it is not because my ambition was rooted out that it has abated, but because it was wearied or perhaps even put out of temper by the failure of its plans. And so with luxury, also, which sometimes seems to have departed, and then when we have made a profession of frugality, begins to fret us and, amid our economies, seeks the pleasures which we have merely left but not condemned. Indeed, the more stealthily it comes, the greater is its force. For all unconcealed vices are less serious; a disease also is farther on the road to being cured when it breaks forth from concealment and manifests its power. So with greed, ambition, and the other evils of the mind,—you may be sure that they do most harm when they are hidden behind a pretence of soundness.

Men think that we are in retirement, and yet we are not. For if we have sincerely retired, and have sounded the signal for retreat, and have scorned outward attractions, then, as I remarked above,† no outward thing will distract us; no music of men or of birds‡ can interrupt good thoughts, when they have once become steadfast and sure. The mind which starts at words or at chance sounds is unstable and has not yet withdrawn into itself; it contains within itself an element of anxiety and rooted fear, and this makes one a prey to care, as our Vergil says:

> I, whom of yore no dart could cause to flee,
> Nor Greeks, with crowded lines of infantry.
> Now shake at every sound, and fear the air,
> Both for my child and for the load I bear.§

---

* See Introduction, page viii.

† § 4 of this letter.

‡ An allusion to the Sirens and Ulysses, cf. § 15 below.

§ Aeneas is escaping from Troy, *Aeneid*, ii. 726 ff.

This man in his first state is wise; he blenches neither at the brandished spear, nor at the clashing armour of the serried foe, nor at the din of the stricken city. This man in his second state lacks knowledge fearing for his own concerns, he pales at every sound; any cry is taken for the battle-shout and overthrows him; the slightest disturbance renders him breathless with fear. It is the load that makes him afraid.* Select anyone you please from among your favourites of Fortune, trailing their many responsibilities, carrying their many burdens, and you will behold a picture of Vergil's hero, "fearing both for his child and for the load he bears."

You may therefore be sure that you are at peace with yourself, when no noise reaches you, when no word shakes you out of yourself, whether it be of flattery or of threat, or merely an empty sound buzzing about you with unmeaning din. "What then?" you say, "is it not sometimes a simpler matter just to avoid the uproar?" I admit this. Accordingly, I shall change from my present quarters. I merely wished to test myself and to give myself practice. Why need I be tormented any longer, when Ulysses found so simple a cure for his comrades† even against the songs of the Sirens? Farewell.

---

* Aeneas carries Anchises; the rich man carries his burden of wealth.

† Not merely by stopping their ears with wax, but also by bidding them row past the Sirens as quickly as possible. *Odyssey*, xii. 182.

LETTER LXIII

ON GRIEF FOR LOST FRIENDS

I am grieved to hear that your friend Flaccus is dead, but I would not have you sorrow more than is fitting. That you should not mourn at all I shall hardly dare to insist; and yet I know that it is the better way. But what man will ever be so blessed with that ideal steadfastness of soul, unless he has already risen far above the reach of Fortune? Even such a man will be stung by an event like this, but it will be only a sting. We, however, may be forgiven for bursting into tears, if only our tears have not flowed to excess, and if we have checked them by our own efforts. Let not the eyes be dry when we have lost a friend, nor let them overflow. We may weep, but we must not wail.

Do you think that the law which I lay down for you is harsh, when the greatest of Greek poets has extended the privilege of weeping to one day only, in the lines where he tells us that even Niobe took thought of food?* Do you wish to know the reason

---

* Homer, *Iliad*, xix. 229 and xxiv. 602.

for lamentations and excessive weeping? It is because we seek the proofs of our bereavement in our tears, and do not give way to sorrow, but merely parade it. No man goes into mourning for his own sake. Shame on our ill-timed folly! There is an element of self-seeking even in our sorrow.

"What," you say, "am I to forget my friend?" It is surely a short-lived memory that you vouchsafe to him, if it is to endure only as long as your grief; presently that brow of yours will be smoothed out in laughter by some circumstance, however casual. It is to a time no more distant than this that I put off the soothing of every regret, the quieting of even the bitterest grief. As soon as you cease to observe yourself, the picture of sorrow which you have contemplated will fade away; at present you are keeping watch over your own suffering. But even while you keep watch it slips away from you, and the sharper it is, the more speedily it comes to an end.

Let us see to it that the recollection of those whom we have lost becomes a pleasant memory to us. No man reverts with pleasure to any subject which he will not be able to reflect upon without pain. So too it cannot but be that the names of those whom we have loved and lost come back to us with a sort of sting; but there is a pleasure even in this sting. For, as my friend Attalus* used to say: "The remembrance of lost friends is pleasant in the same way that certain fruits have an agreeably acid taste, or as in extremely old wines it is their very bitterness that pleases us. Indeed, after a certain lapse of time, every thought that gave pain is quenched, and the pleasure comes to us unalloyed." If we take the word of Attalus for it, "to think of friends who are alive and well is like enjoying a meal of cakes and honey; the recollection of friends who have passed away gives a pleasure that is not without a touch of bitterness. Yet who will deny that even these things, which are bitter and contain an element of sourness, do serve to arouse the stomach?" For my part, I do not agree with him. To me, the thought of my dead friends is sweet and appealing. For I have had

* The teacher of Seneca, often mentioned by him.

them as if I should one day lose them; I have lost them as if I have them still.

Therefore, Lucilius, act as befits your own serenity of mind, and cease to put a wrong interpretation on the gifts of Fortune. Fortune has taken away, but Fortune has given. Let us greedily enjoy our friends, because we do not know how long this privilege will be ours. Let us think how often we shall leave them when we go upon distant journeys, and how often we shall fail to see them when we tarry together in the same place; we shall thus understand that we have lost too much of their time while they were alive. But will you tolerate men who are most careless of their friends, and then mourn them most abjectly, and do not love anyone unless they have lost him? The reason why they lament too unrestrainedly at such times is that they are afraid lest men doubt whether they really have loved; all too late they seek for proofs of their emotions. If we have other friends, we surely deserve ill at their hands and think ill of them, if they are of so little account that they fail to console us for the loss of one. If, on the other hand, we have no other friends, we have injured ourselves more than Fortune has injured us; since Fortune has robbed us of one friend, but we have robbed ourselves of every friend whom we have failed to make. Again, he who has been unable to love more than one, has had none too much love even for that one.* If a man who has lost his one and only tunic through robbery chooses to bewail his plight rather than look about him for some way to escape the cold, or for something with which to cover his shoulders, would you not think him an utter fool?

You have buried one whom you loved; look about for someone to love. It is better to replace your friend than to weep for him. What I am about to add is, I know, a very hackneyed remark, but I shall not omit it simply because it is a common phrase: A man ends his grief by the mere passing of time, even if he has not ended it of his

---

* The reason is, as Lipsius observed, that friendship is essentially a social virtue, and is not confined to one object. The pretended friendship for one and only one is a form of self-love, and is not unselfish love.

own accord. But the most shameful cure for sorrow, in the case of a sensible man, is to grow weary of sorrowing. I should prefer you to abandon grief, rather than have grief abandon you; and you should stop grieving as soon as possible, since, even if you wish to do so, it is impossible to keep it up for a long time. Our forefathers* have enacted that, in the case of women, a year should be the limit for mourning; not that they needed to mourn for so long, but that they should mourn no longer. In the case of men, no rules are laid down, because to mourn at all is not regarded as honourable. For all that, what woman can you show me, of all the pathetic females that could scarcely be dragged away from the funeral-pile or torn from the corpse, whose tears have lasted a whole month? Nothing becomes offensive so quickly as grief; when fresh, it finds someone to console it and attracts one or another to itself; but after becoming chronic, it is ridiculed, and rightly. For it is either assumed or foolish.

He who writes these words to you is no other than I, who wept so excessively for my dear friend Annaeus Serenus† that, in spite of my wishes, I must be included among the examples of men who have been overcome by grief. Today, however, I condemn this act of mine, and I understand that the reason why I lamented so greatly was chiefly that I had never imagined it possible for his death to precede mine. The only thought which occurred to my mind was that he was the younger, and much younger, too,—as if the Fates kept to the order of our ages!

Therefore let us continually think as much about our own mortality as about that of all those we love. In former days I ought to have said: "My friend Serenus is younger than I; but what does that matter? He would naturally die after me, but he may precede me." It was just because I did not do this that I was unprepared when Fortune dealt me the sudden blow. Now is the time for you to reflect,

* According to tradition, from the time of Numa Pompilius.

† An intimate friend of Seneca, probably a relative, who died in the year 63 from eating poisoned mushrooms (Pliny, *N. H.* xxii. 96). Seneca dedicated to Serenus several of his philosophical essays.

not only that all things are mortal, but also that their mortality is subject to no fixed law. Whatever can happen at any time can happen today. Let us therefore reflect, my beloved Lucilius, that we shall soon come to the goal which this friend, to our own sorrow, has reached. And perhaps, if only the tale told by wise men is true* and there is a bourne to welcome us, then he whom we think we have lost has only been sent on ahead. Farewell.

* Cf. the closing chapter of the Agricola of Tacitus: *si, ut sapientibus placet, non cum corpore exstinguuntur magnae animae*, etc.

LETTER

LXV

ON THE FIRST CAUSE

I shared my time yesterday with ill health;* it claimed for itself all the period before noon; in the afternoon, however, it yielded to me. And so I first tested my spirit by reading; then, when reading was found to be possible, I dared to make more demands upon the spirit, or perhaps I should say, to make more concessions to it. I wrote a little, and indeed with more concentration than usual, for I am struggling with a difficult subject and do not wish to be downed. In the midst of this, some friends visited me, with the purpose of employing force and of restraining me, as if I were a sick man indulging in some excess. So conversation was substituted for writing; and from this conversation I shall communicate to you the topic which is still the subject of debate; for we have appointed you referee.† You have more of a task on your hands than you suppose, for the argument is threefold.

---

* For Seneca's troubles in this regard see also Epp. liv. and civ.

† The *arbiter* was a judge appointed to try a case according to *bona fides* (equity), as contrasted with the *iudex* proper, whose duty was defined by the magistrate.

Our Stoic philosophers, as you know, declare that there are two things in the universe which are the source of everything,—namely, cause and matter.* Matter lies sluggish, a substance ready for any use, but sure to remain unemployed if no one sets it in motion. Cause, however, by which we mean reason, moulds matter and turns it in whatever direction it will, producing thereby various concrete results. Accordingly, there must be, in the case of each thing, that from which it is made, and, next, an agent by which it is made. The former is its material, the latter its cause.

All art is but imitation of nature; therefore, let me apply these statements of general principles to the things which have to be made by man. A statue, for example, has afforded matter which was to undergo treatment at the hands of the artist, and has had an artist who was to give form to the matter. Hence, in the case of the statue, the material was bronze, the cause was the workman. And so it goes with all things,—they consist of that which is made, and of the maker. The Stoics believe in one cause only,—the maker; but Aristotle thinks that the word "cause" can be used in three ways: "The first cause," he says, "is the actual matter, without which nothing can be created. The second is the workman. The third is the form, which is impressed upon every work,—a statue, for example." This last is what Aristotle calls the *idos*.† "There is, too," says he, "a fourth,—the purpose of the work as a whole." Now I shall show you what this last means. Bronze is the "first cause" of the statue, for it could never have been made unless there had been something from which it could be cast and moulded. The "second cause" is the artist; for without the skilled hands of a workman that bronze could not have been shaped to the outlines of

---

* See Zeller's *Stoics* (translated by Reichel), pp. 139 ff.

† The statue figure is a frequent one in philosophy; cf. Ep. ix. 5. The "form" of Aristotle goes back to the "idea" of Plato. These four causes are the causes of Aristotle, matter (ὕλη), form (εἶδος), force (τὸ κινοῦν), and the end (τὸ τέλος); when they all concur, we pass from possibility to fact. Aristotle gives eight categories in *Phys.* 225 b 5; and ten in *Categ.* 1 b 25,—substance, quantity, quality, relation, place, time, situation, possession, action, passion. For a definition of εἶδος see Aristotle, *Phys* 190 b 20 γίγνεται πᾶν ἔκ τε τοῦ ὑποκειμένου καὶ τῆς μορφῆς (i.e. τοῦ εἴδους).

the statue. The "third cause" is the form, inasmuch as our statue could never be called The Lance-Bearer or The Boy Binding his Hair,[*] had not this special shape been stamped upon it. The "fourth cause" is the purpose of the work. For if this purpose had not existed, the statue would not have been made. Now what is this purpose? It is that which attracted the artist, which he followed when he made the statue. It may have been money, if he has made it for sale; or renown, if he has worked for reputation; or religion, if he has wrought it as a gift for a temple. Therefore this also is a cause contributing towards the making of the statue; or do you think that we should avoid including, among the causes of a thing which has been made, that element without which the thing in question would not have been made?

To these four Plato adds a fifth cause,—the pattern which he himself calls the "idea"; for it is this that the artist gazed upon[†] when he created the work which he had decided to carry out. Now it makes no difference whether he has his pattern outside himself, that he may direct his glance to it, or within himself, conceived and placed there by himself. God has within himself these patterns of all things, and his mind comprehends the harmonies and the measures of the whole totality of things which are to be carried out; he is filled with these shapes which Plato calls the "ideas,"—imperishable, unchangeable, not subject to decay. And therefore, though men die, humanity itself, or the idea of man, according to which man is moulded, lasts on, and though men toil and perish, it suffers no change. Accordingly, there are five causes, as Plato says:[‡] the material, the agent, the make-up, the model, and the end in view. Last comes the result of all these. Just as in the case of the statue,—to go back to the figure with which we began,—the material is the bronze, the agent is the artist, the make-up is the form

---

* Well-known works of Polyclitus, fifth century B.C.

† Explaining the derivation of the Greek word,—ἰδεῖν, "to behold." For a discussion of Plato's "ideas," those "independent, separate, self-existing, perfect, and eternal essences" (*Republic* vi. and vii.) see Adam, *The Republic of Plato*, ii. 168-179. According to Adam, Plato owes his theory of ideas to Socrates, the Eleatics, and the study of geometry; but his debt is not so great as his discovery.

‡ i.e., the four categories as established by Aristotle, plus the "idea" of Plato.

which is adapted to the material, the model is the pattern imitated by the agent, the end in view is the purpose in the maker's mind, and, finally, the result of all these is the statue itself. The universe also, in Plato's opinion, possesses all these elements. The agent is God; the source, matter; the form, the shape and the arrangement of the visible world. The pattern is doubtless the model according to which God has made this great and most beautiful creation. The purpose is his object in so doing. Do you ask what God's purpose is? It is goodness. Plato, at any rate, says: "What was God's reason for creating the world? God is good, and no good person is grudging of anything that is good. Therefore, God made it the best world possible." Hand down your opinion, then, O judge; state who seems to you to say what is truest, and not who says what is absolutely true. For to do that is as far beyond our ken as truth itself.

This throng of causes, defined by Aristotle and by Plato, embraces either too much or too little.* For if they regard as "causes" of an object that is to be made everything without which the object cannot be made, they have named too few. Time must be included among the causes; for nothing can be made without time. They must also include place; for if there be no place where a thing can be made, it will not be made. And motion too; nothing is either made or destroyed without motion. There is no art without motion, no change of any kind. Now, however, I am searching for the first, the general cause; this must be simple, inasmuch as matter, too, is simple. Do we ask what cause is? It is surely Creative Reason,†—in other words, God. For those elements to which you referred are not a great series of independent causes; they all hinge on one alone, and that will be the creative cause. Do you maintain that form is a cause? This is only what the artist stamps upon his work; it is part of a cause, but not the cause. Neither is the pattern a cause, but an

* The Stoic view (see § 2 of this letter), besides making the four categories of "substance," "form," "variety," and "variety of relation," regarded material things as the only things which possessed being. The Stoics thus differ from Aristotle and Plato in holding that nothing is real except matter; besides, they relate everything to one ultimate cause, the acting force or efficient cause.

† i.e., the λόγος σπερματικός, the creative force in nature, that is, Providence, or the will of Zeus.

indispensable tool of the cause. His pattern is as indispensable to the artist as the chisel or the file; without these, art can make no progress. But for all that, these things are neither parts of the art, nor causes of it. "Then," perhaps you will say, "the purpose of the artist, that which leads him to undertake to create something, is the cause." It may be a cause; it is not, however, the efficient cause, but only an accessory cause. But there are countless accessory causes; what we are discussing is the general cause. Now the statement of Plato and Aristotle is not in accord with their usual penetration, when they maintain that the whole universe, the perfectly wrought work, is a cause. For there is a great difference between a work and the cause of a work.

Either give your opinion, or, as is easier in cases of this kind, declare that the matter is not clear and call for another hearing.* But you will reply: "What pleasure do you get from wasting your time on these problems, which relieve you of none of your emotions, rout none of your desires?" So far as I am concerned, I treat and discuss them as matters which contribute greatly toward calming the spirit, and I search myself first, and then the world about me. And not even now am I, as you think, wasting my time. For all these questions, provided that they be not chopped up and torn apart into such unprofitable refinements, elevate and lighten the soul, which is weighted down by a heavy burden and desires to be freed and to return to the elements of which it was once a part. For this body of ours is a weight upon the soul and its penance; as the load presses down the soul is crushed and is in bondage, unless philosophy has come to its assistance and has bid it take fresh courage by contemplating the universe, and has turned it from things earthly to things divine. There it has its liberty, there it can roam abroad;† meantime it escapes the custody in which it

* i.e., restate the question and hear the evidence again.

† According to the Stoics the soul, which consisted of fire or breath and was a part of the divine essence, rose at death into the ether and became one with the stars. Seneca elsewhere (*Consolatio ad Marciam*) states that the soul went through a sort of purifying process,—a view which may have had some influence on Christian thought. The souls of the good, the Stoics maintained, were destined to last until the end of the world, the souls of the bad to be extinguished before that time.

is bound, and renews its life in heaven. Just as skilled workmen, who have been engaged upon some delicate piece of work which wearies their eyes with straining, if the light which they have is niggardly or uncertain, go forth into the open air and in some park devoted to the people's recreation delight their eyes in the generous light of day; so the soul, imprisoned as it has been in this gloomy and darkened house, seeks the open sky whenever it can, and in the contemplation of the universe finds rest.

The wise man, the seeker after wisdom, is bound closely, indeed, to his body, but he is an absentee so far as his better self is concerned, and he concentrates his thoughts upon lofty things. Bound, so to speak, to his oath of allegiance, he regards the period of life as his term of service. He is so trained that he neither loves nor hates life; he endures a mortal lot, although he knows that an ampler lot is in store for him. Do you forbid me to contemplate the universe? Do you compel me to withdraw from the whole and restrict me to a part? May I not ask what are the beginnings of all things, who moulded the universe, who took the confused and conglomerate mass of sluggish matter, and separated it into its parts? May I not inquire who is the Master-Builder of this universe, how the mighty bulk was brought under the control of law and order, who gathered together the scattered atoms, who separated the disordered elements and assigned an outward form to elements that lay in one vast shapelessness? Or whence came all the expanse of light? And whether is it fire, or something even brighter than fire?* Am I not to ask these questions? Must I be ignorant of the heights whence I have descended? Whether I am to see this world but once, or to be born many times? What is my destination afterwards? What abode awaits my soul on its release from the laws of slavery among men? Do you forbid me to have a share in heaven? In other words, do you bid me live with my head bowed down? No, I am above

* The sequence of elements from the earth outwards and upwards was earth, water, air, and fire. The upper fire was ether. Zeno (quoted by Cicero, *Acad.* i. 11. 39) refused to acknowledge a fifth essence: *statuebat enim ignem esse ipsam naturam, quae quaeque gigneret, et mentem et sensus.*

such an existence; I was born to a greater destiny than to be a mere chattel of my body, and I regard this body as nothing but a chain[*] which manacles my freedom. Therefore, I offer it as a sort of buffer to fortune, and shall allow no wound to penetrate through to my soul. For my body is the only part of me which can suffer injury. In this dwelling, which is exposed to peril, my soul lives free. Never shall this flesh drive me to feel fear, or to assume any pretence that is unworthy of a good man. Never shall I lie in order to honour this petty body. When it seems proper, I shall sever my connexion with it. And at present, while we are bound together, our alliance shall nevertheless not be one of equality; the soul shall bring all quarrels before its own tribunal. To despise our bodies is sure freedom.

To return to our subject; this freedom will be greatly helped by the contemplation of which we were just speaking. All things are made up of matter and of God;[†] God controls matter, which encompasses him and follows him as its guide and leader. And that which creates, in other words, God, is more powerful and precious than matter, which is acted upon by God. God's place in the universe corresponds to the soul's relation to man. World-matter corresponds to our mortal body; therefore let the lower serve the higher. Let us be brave in the face of hazards. Let us not fear wrongs, or wounds, or bonds, or poverty. And what is death? It is either the end, or a process of change. I have no fear of ceasing to exist; it is the same as not having begun. Nor do I shrink from changing into another state, because I shall, under no conditions, be as cramped as I am now. Farewell.

* The "prison of the body" is a frequent figure in Stoic as in all philosophy. See, for example, § 16 of this letter, "the soul in bondage."

† A restatement of the previous remark made in this letter; see note on § 11.

VOLUME 2

LETTER

LXXVII

ON TAKING ONE'S OWN LIFE

Suddenly there came into our view today the "Alexandrian" ships,—I mean those which are usually sent ahead to announce the coming of the fleet; they are called "mail-boats." The Campanians are glad to see them; all the rabble of Puteoli* stand on the docks, and can recognize the "Alexandrian" boats, no matter how great the crowd of vessels, by the very trim of their sails. For they alone may keep spread their topsails, which all ships use when out at sea, because nothing sends a ship along so well as its upper canvas; that is where most of the speed is obtained. So when the breeze has stiffened and becomes stronger than is comfortable, they set their yards lower; for the wind has less force near the surface of the water. Accordingly, when they have made Capreae and the headland whence

> Tall Pallas watches on the stormy peak,†

* Puteoli, in the bay of Naples, was the head-quarters in Italy of the important grain-trade with Egypt, on which the Roman magistrates relied to feed the populace.

† Author unknown.

all other vessels are bidden to be content with the mainsail, and the topsail stands out conspicuously on the "Alexandrian" mail-boats.

While everybody was bustling about and hurrying to the waterfront, I felt great pleasure in my laziness, because, although I was soon to receive letters from my friends, I was in no hurry to know how my affairs were progressing abroad, or what news the letters were bringing; for some time now I have had no losses, nor gains either. Even if I were not an old man, I could not have helped feeling pleasure at this; but as it is, my pleasure was far greater. For, however small my possessions might be, I should still have left over more travelling-money than journey to travel, especially since this journey upon which we have set out is one which need not be followed to the end. An expedition will be incomplete if one stops half-way, or anywhere on this side of one's destination; but life is not incomplete if it is honourable. At whatever point you leave off living, provided you leave off nobly, your life is a whole.* Often, however, one must leave off bravely, and our reasons therefore need not be momentous; for neither are the reasons momentous which hold us here.

Tullius Marcellinus,† a man whom you knew very well, who in youth was a quiet soul and became old prematurely, fell ill of a disease which was by no means hopeless; but it was protracted and troublesome, and it demanded much attention; hence he began to think about dying. He called many of his friends together. Each one of them gave Marcellinus advice,—the timid friend urging him to do what he had made up his mind to do; the flattering and wheedling friend giving counsel which he supposed would be more pleasing to Marcellinus when he came to think the matter over; but our Stoic friend, a rare man, and, to praise him in language which he deserves, a man of courage and vigour‡ admonished

* This thought, found in Ep. xii. 6 and often elsewhere, is a favourite with Seneca.

† It is not likely that this Marcellinus is the same person as the Marcellinus Ep. xxix., because of their different views on philosophy (Summers). But there is no definite evidence for or against.

‡ A Roman compliment; the Greeks would have used καλὸς κἀγαθός; cf. Horace, *Ep.* i. 7. 46

Strenuus et fortis causisque Philippus agendis Clarus.

him best of all, as it seems to me. For he began as follows: "Do not torment yourself, my dear Marcellinus, as if the question which you are weighing were a matter of importance. It is not an important matter to live; all your slaves live, and so do all animals; but it is important to die honourably, sensibly, bravely. Reflect how long you have been doing the same thing: food, sleep, lust,—this is one's daily round. The desire to die may be felt, not only by the sensible man or the brave or unhappy man, but even by the man who is merely surfeited."

Marcellinus did not need someone to urge him, but rather someone to help him; his slaves refused to do his bidding. The Stoic therefore removed their fears, showing them that there was no risk involved for the household except when it was uncertain whether the master's death was self-sought or not; besides, it was as bad a practice to kill one's master as it was to prevent him forcibly from killing himself. Then he suggested to Marcellinus himself that it would be a kindly act to distribute gifts to those who had attended him throughout his whole life, when that life was finished, just as, when a banquet is finished,* the remaining portion is divided among the attendants who stand about the table. Marcellinus was of a compliant and generous disposition, even when it was a question of his own property; so he distributed little sums among his sorrowing slaves, and comforted them besides. No need had he of sword or of bloodshed; for three days he fasted and had a tent put up in his very bedroom.† Then a tub was brought in; he lay in it for a long time, and, as the hot water was continually poured over him, he gradually passed away, not without a feeling of pleasure, as he himself remarked,—such a feeling as a slow dissolution is wont to give. Those of us who have ever fainted know from experience what this feeling is.

This little anecdote into which I have digressed will not be displeasing to you. For you will see that your friend departed neither with difficulty nor with suffering. Though he committed suicide, yet

---

* For this frequent "banquet of life" simile see Ep. xcviii. 15 *ipse vitae plenus est*, etc.

† So that the steam might not escape. One thinks of Seneca's last hours: Tac. *Ann.* xv. 64 *stagnum calidae aquae introiit . . . exin balneo inlatus et vapore eius exanimatus.*

he withdrew most gently, gliding out of life. The anecdote may also be of some use; for often a crisis demands just such examples. There are times when we ought to die and are unwilling; sometimes we die and are unwilling. No one is so ignorant as not to know that we must at some time die; nevertheless, when one draws near death, one turns to flight, trembles, and laments. Would you not think him an utter fool who wept because he was not alive a thousand years ago? And is he not just as much of a fool who weeps because he will not be alive a thousand years from now? It is all the same; you will not be, and you were not. Neither of these periods of time belongs to you. You have been cast upon this point of time;* if you would make it longer, how much longer shall you make it? Why weep? Why pray? You are taking pains to no purpose.

Give over thinking that your prayers can bend
Divine decrees from their predestined end.†

These decrees are unalterable and fixed; they are governed by a mighty and everlasting compulsion. Your goal will be the goal of all things. What is there strange in this to you? You were born to be subject to this law; this fate befell your father, your mother, your ancestors, all who came before you; and it will befall all who shall come after you. A sequence which cannot be broken or altered by any power binds all things together and draws all things in its course. Think of the multitudes of men doomed to death who will come after you, of the multitudes who will go with you! You would die more bravely, I suppose, in the company of many thousands; and yet there are many thousands, both of men and of animals, who at this very moment, while you are irresolute about death, are breathing their last, in their several ways. But you,—did you believe that you would not some day reach the goal towards which you have always been travelling? No journey but has its end.

* For the same thought cf. Ep. xlix. 3 *punctum est quod vivimus et adhuc puncto minus.*

† Vergil, *Aeneid*, vi. 376.

You think, I suppose, that it is now in order for me to cite some examples of great men. No, I shall cite rather the case of a boy. The story of the Spartan lad has been preserved: taken captive while still a stripling, he kept crying in his Doric dialect, "I will not be a slave!" and he made good his word; for the very first time he was ordered to perform a menial and degrading service,—and the command was to fetch a chamber-pot,—he dashed out his brains against the wall.* So near at hand is freedom, and is anyone still a slave? Would you not rather have your own son die thus than reach old age by weakly yielding? Why therefore are you distressed, when even a boy can die so bravely? Suppose that you refuse to follow him; you will be led. Take into your own control that which is now under the control of another. Will you not borrow that boy's courage, and say: "I am no slave!"? Unhappy fellow, you are a slave to men, you are a slave to your business, you are a slave to life. For life, if courage to die be lacking, is slavery.

Have you anything worth waiting for? Your very pleasures, which cause you to tarry and hold you back, have already been exhausted by you. None of them is a novelty to you, and there is none that has not already become hateful because you are cloyed with it. You know the taste of wine and cordials. It makes no difference whether a hundred or a thousand measures† pass through your bladder; you are nothing but a wine-strainer.‡ You are a connoisseur in the flavour of the oyster and of the mullet;§ your luxury has not left you anything untasted for the years that are to come; and yet these are the things from which you are torn away unwillingly. What else is there which you would regret to have taken from you? Friends? But who can be a friend to you? Country? What? Do you think enough of your country to be late to dinner? The light of the sun? You would extinguish it, if you

* See Plutarch, *Mor.* 234 b, for a similar act of the Spartan boy captured by King Antigonus. Hense (*Rhein. Mus.* xlvii. pp. 220 f.) thinks that this story may be taken from Bion, the third-century satirist and moral philosopher.

† About 5¾ gallons.

‡ Cf. Pliny, xiv. 22 *quin immo ut plus capiamus, sacco frangimus vires*. Strained wine could be drunk in greater quantities without intoxication.

§ Cf. Dio Cassius, xl. 54, for the exiled Milo's enjoyment of the mullets of Marseilles.

could; for what have you ever done that was fit to be seen in the light? Confess the truth; it is not because you long for the senate chamber or the forum, or even for the world of nature, that you would fain put off dying; it is because you are loth to leave the fish-market, though you have exhausted its stores.*

You are afraid of death; but how can you scorn it in the midst of a mushroom supper?† You wish to live; well, do you know how to live? You are afraid to die. But come now: is this life of yours anything but death? Gaius Caesar was passing along the Via Latina, when a man stepped out from the ranks of the prisoners, his grey beard hanging down even to his breast, and begged to be put to death. "What!" said Caesar, "are you alive now?" That is the answer which should be given to men to whom death would come as a relief. "You are afraid to die; what! are you alive now?" "But," says one, "I wish to live, for I am engaged in many honourable pursuits. I am loth to leave life's duties, which I am fulfilling with loyalty and zeal." Surely you are aware that dying is also one of life's duties? You are deserting no duty; for there is no definite number established which you are bound to complete. There is no life that is not short. Compared with the world of nature, even Nestor's life was a short one, or Sattia's,‡ the woman who bade carve on her tombstone that she had lived ninety and nine years. Some persons, you see, boast of their long lives; but who could have endured the old lady if she had had the luck to complete her hundredth year? It is with life as it is with a play,—it matters not how long the action is spun out, but how good the acting is. It makes no difference at what point you stop. Stop whenever you choose; only see to it that the closing period is well turned.§ Farewell.

* Probably the strong tone of disapproval used in this paragraph is directed against the Roman in general rather than against the industrious Lucilius. It is characteristic of the diatribe.

† Seneca may be recalling the death of the Emperor Claudius.

‡ A traditional example of old age, mentioned by Martial and the elder Pliny.

§ Compare the last words of the Emperor Augustus: *amicos percontatus ecquid iis videretur mimum vitae commode transegisse* (Suet. *Aug.* 99).

LETTER

LXXVIII

ON THE HEALING POWER OF THE MIND

That you are frequently troubled by the snuffling of catarrh and by short attacks of fever which follow after long and chronic catarrhal seizures, I am sorry to hear; particularly because I have experienced this sort of illness myself, and scorned it in its early stages. For when I was still young, I could put up with hardships and show a bold front to illness. But I finally succumbed, and arrived at such a state that I could do nothing but snuffle, reduced as I was to the extremity of thinness.* I often entertained the impulse of ending my life then and there; but the thought of my kind old father kept me back. For I reflected, not how bravely I had the power to die, but how little power he had to bear bravely the loss of me. And so I commanded myself to live. For sometimes it is an act of bravery even to live.

---

* To such a degree that Seneca's enemy Caligula refrained from executing him, on the ground that he would soon die.

Now I shall tell you what consoled me during those days, stating at the outset that these very aids to my peace of mind were as efficacious as medicine. Honourable consolation results in a cure; and whatever has uplifted the soul helps the body also. My studies were my salvation. I place it to the credit of philosophy that I recovered and regained my strength. I owe my life to philosophy, and that is the least of my obligations! My friends, too, helped me greatly toward good health; I used to be comforted by their cheering words, by the hours they spent at my bedside, and by their conversation. Nothing, my excellent Lucilius, refreshes and aids a sick man so much as the affection of his friends; nothing so steals away the expectation and the fear of death. In fact, I could not believe that, if they survived me, I should be dying at all. Yes, I repeat, it seemed to me that I should continue to live, not with them, but through them. I imagined myself not to be yielding up my soul, but to be making it over to them.

All these things gave me the inclination to succour myself and to endure any torture; besides, it is a most miserable state to have lost one's zest for dying, and to have no zest in living. These, then, are the remedies to which you should have recourse. The physician will prescribe your walks and your exercise; he will warn you not to become addicted to idleness, as is the tendency of the inactive invalid; he will order you to read in a louder voice and to exercise your lungs* the passages and cavity of which are affected; or to sail and shake up your bowels by a little mild motion; he will recommend the proper food, and the suitable time for aiding your strength with wine or refraining from it in order to keep your cough from being irritated and hacking. But as for me, my counsel to you is this,—and it is a cure, not merely of this disease of yours, but of your whole life,—"Despise death." There is no sorrow in the world, when we have escaped from the fear of death. There are these three serious elements in every disease: fear of death, bodily pain, and interruption of pleasures. Concerning death enough has been said, and I shall add only a word: this fear is not a fear of disease, but a fear

---

* Cf. Ep. xv. 7 f.

of nature. Disease has often postponed death, and a vision of dying has been many a man's salvation.* You will die, not because you are ill, but because you are alive; even when you have been cured, the same end awaits you; when you have recovered, it will be not death, but ill-health, that you have escaped.

Let us now return to the consideration of the characteristic disadvantage of disease: it is accompanied by great suffering. The suffering, however, is rendered endurable by interruptions; for the strain of extreme pain must come to an end.† No man can suffer both severely and for a long time; Nature, who loves us most tenderly, has so constituted us as to make pain either endurable or short.‡ The severest pains have their seat in the most slender parts of our body; nerves, joints, and any other of the narrow passages, hurt most cruelly when they have developed trouble within their contracted spaces. But these parts soon become numb, and by reason of the pain itself lose the sensation of pain, whether because the life-force, when checked in its natural course and changed for the worse, loses the peculiar power through which it thrives and through which it warns us, or because the diseased humours of the body, when they cease to have a place into which they may flow, are thrown back upon themselves, and deprive of sensation the parts where they have caused congestion. So gout, both in the feet and in the hands, and all pain in the vertebrae and in the nerves, have their intervals of rest at the times when they have dulled the parts which they before had tortured; the first twinges,§ in all such cases, are what cause the distress, and their onset is checked by lapse of time, so that there is an end of pain when numbness has set in. Pain in the teeth, eyes, and ears is most acute for the very reason that it begins among the narrow spaces of the body,—no less acute, indeed, than in the head itself. But if it is more violent than usual, it

* i.e., men have become healthier after passing through serious illness.

† Cf. Epicurus, Frag. 446 Usener.

‡ Compare, from among many parallels, Ep. xxiv. 14 *(dolor) levis es, si ferre possum, brevis es, si ferre non possum.*

§ See also Ep. xcv. 17. The word literally means "maggots," "bots," in horses or cattle.

turns to delirium and stupor. This is, accordingly, a consolation for excessive pain,—that you cannot help ceasing to feel it if you feel it to excess. The reason, however, why the inexperienced are impatient when their bodies suffer is, that they have not accustomed themselves to be contented in spirit. They have been closely associated with the body. Therefore a high-minded and sensible man divorces soul from body, and dwells much with the better or divine part, and only as far as he must with this complaining and frail portion.

"But it is a hardship," men say, "to do without our customary pleasures,—to fast, to feel thirst and hunger." These are indeed serious when one first abstains from them. Later the desire dies down, because the appetites themselves which lead to desire are wearied and forsake us; then the stomach becomes petulant, then the food which we craved before becomes hateful. Our very wants die away. But there is no bitterness in doing without that which you have ceased to desire. Moreover, every pain sometimes stops, or at any rate slackens; moreover, one may take precautions against its return, and, when it threatens, may check it by means of remedies. Every variety of pain has its premonitory symptoms; this is true, at any rate, of pain that is habitual and recurrent. One can endure the suffering which disease entails, if one has come to regard its results with scorn. But do not of your own accord make your troubles heavier to bear and burden yourself with complaining. Pain is slight if opinion has added nothing to it; but if, on the other hand, you begin to encourage yourself and say, "It is nothing,—a trifling matter at most; keep a stout heart and it will soon cease"; then in thinking it slight, you will make it slight. Everything depends on opinion; ambition, luxury, greed, hark back to opinion. It is according to opinion that we suffer. A man is as wretched as he has convinced himself that he is. I hold that we should do away with complaint about past sufferings and with all language like this: "None has ever been worse off than I. What sufferings, what evils have I endured! No one has thought that I shall recover. How often have my family bewailed me, and the physicians given me over! Men who are placed on the rack are not torn asunder with such agony!" However, even if all this is true, it is over and gone. What benefit is there in reviewing past sufferings, and in being unhappy, just because once you were unhappy? Besides, every one adds much to his own ills, and tells lies to himself. And that which was bitter to bear is pleasant to have borne; it is natural to rejoice at the ending of one's ills.

Two elements must therefore be rooted out once for all,—the fear of future suffering, and the recollection of past suffering; since the latter no longer concerns me, and the former concerns me not yet. But when set in the very midst of troubles one should say:

> Perchance some day the memory of this sorrow
> Will even bring delight.*

Let such a man fight against them with all his might: if he once gives way, he will be vanquished; but if he strives against his sufferings, he will conquer. As it is, however, what most men do is to drag down upon their own heads a falling ruin which they ought to try to support. If you begin to withdraw your support from that which thrusts toward you and totters and is ready to plunge, it will follow you and lean more heavily upon you; but if you hold your ground and make up your mind to push against it, it will be forced back. What blows do athletes receive on their faces and all over their bodies! Nevertheless, through their desire for fame they endure every torture, and they undergo these things not only because they are fighting but in order to be able to fight. Their very training means torture. So let us also win the way to victory in all our struggles,—for the reward is not a garland or a palm or a trumpeter who calls for silence at the proclamation of our names, but rather virtue, steadfastness of soul, and a peace that is won for all time, if fortune has once been utterly vanquished in any combat. You say, "I feel severe pain." What then; are you relieved from feeling it, if you endure it like a woman? Just as an enemy is more dangerous

---

* Vergil, *Aeneid*, i. 203.

to a retreating army, so every trouble that fortune brings attacks us all the harder if we yield and turn our backs. "But the trouble is serious." What? Is it for this purpose that we are strong,—that we may have light burdens to bear? Would you have your illness long-drawn-out, or would you have it quick and short? If it is long, it means a respite, allows you a period for resting yourself, bestows upon you the boon of time in plenty; as it arises, so it must also subside. A short and rapid illness will do one of two things: it will quench or be quenched. And what difference does it make whether it is not or I am not? In either case there is an end of pain.

This, too, will help—to turn the mind aside to thoughts of other things and thus to depart from pain. Call to mind what honourable or brave deeds you have done; consider the good side of your own life.* Run over in your memory those things which you have particularly admired. Then think of all the brave men who have conquered pain: of him who continued to read his book as he allowed the cutting out of varicose veins; of him who did not cease to smile, though that very smile so enraged his torturers that they tried upon him every instrument of their cruelty. If pain can be conquered by a smile, will it not be conquered by reason? You may tell me now of whatever you like—of colds, hard coughing-spells that bring up parts of our entrails, fever that parches our very vitals, thirst, limbs so twisted that the joints protrude in different directions; yet worse than these are the stake, the rack, the red-hot plates, the instrument that reopens wounds while the wounds themselves are still swollen and that drives their imprint still deeper.† Nevertheless there have been men who have not uttered a moan amid these tortures. "More yet!" says the torturer; but the victim has not begged for release. "More yet!" he says again; but no answer has come. "More yet!" the victim has smiled, and heartily, too. Can you not bring yourself, after an example like this, to make a mock at pain?

---

* Literally, perhaps, "the noble rôles which you have played." Summers compares Ep. xiv. 13 *ultimas partes Catonis*—"the closing scenes of Cato's life."

† Cf. Ep. xiv. 4 f. and the *crucibus adfixi, flamma usti*, etc., of Tac. *Ann.* xv. 44.

"But," you object, "my illness does not allow me to be doing anything; it has withdrawn me from all my duties." It is your body that is hampered by ill-health, and not your soul as well. It is for this reason that it clogs the feet of the runner and will hinder the handiwork of the cobbler or the artisan; but if your soul be habitually in practice, you will plead and teach, listen and learn, investigate and meditate. What more is necessary? Do you think that you are doing nothing if you possess self-control in your illness? You will be showing that a disease can be overcome, or at any rate endured. There is, I assure you, a place for virtue even upon a bed of sickness. It is not only the sword and the battle-line that prove the soul alert and unconquered by fear; a man can display bravery even when wrapped in his bed-clothes. You have something to do: wrestle bravely with disease. If it shall compel you to nothing, beguile you to nothing, it is a notable example that you display. O what ample matter were there for renown, if we could have spectators of our sickness! Be your own spectator; seek your own applause.

Again, there are two kinds of pleasures. Disease checks the pleasures of the body, but does not do away with them. Nay, if the truth is to be considered, it serves to excite them; for the thirstier a man is, the more he enjoys a drink; the hungrier he is, the more pleasure he takes in food. Whatever falls to one's lot after a period of abstinence is welcomed with greater zest. The other kind, however, the pleasures of the mind, which are higher and less uncertain, no physician can refuse to the sick man. Whoever seeks these and knows well what they are, scorns all the blandishments of the senses. Men say, "Poor sick fellow!" But why? Is it because he does not mix snow with his wine, or because he does not revive the chill of his drink—mixed as it is in a good-sized bowl—by chipping ice into it? Or because he does not have Lucrine* oysters opened fresh at his table? Or because there is no din of cooks about his dining-hall, as they bring in their very cooking apparatus along with their viands? For luxury has already

* The *lacus Lucrinus* was a salt-water lagoon, near Baiae in Campania.

devised this fashion—of having the kitchen accompany the dinner, so that the food may not grow luke-warm, or fail to be hot enough for a palate which has already become hardened. "Poor sick fellow!"—he will eat as much as he can digest. There will be no boar lying before his eyes,* banished from the table as if it were a common meat; and on his sideboard there will be heaped together no breast-meat of birds, because it sickens him to see birds served whole. But what evil has been done to you? You will dine like a sick man, nay, sometimes like a sound man.†

All these things, however, can be easily endured—gruel, warm water, and anything else that seems insupportable to a fastidious man, to one who is wallowing in luxury, sick in soul rather than in body—if only we cease to shudder at death. And we shall cease, if once we have gained a knowledge of the limits of good and evil; then, and then only, life will not weary us, neither will death make us afraid. For surfeit of self can never seize upon a life that surveys all the things which are manifold, great, divine; only idle leisure is wont to make men hate their lives. To one who roams‡ through the universe, the truth can never pall; it will be the untruths that will cloy. And, on the other hand, if death comes near with its summons, even though it be untimely in its arrival, though it cut one off in one's prime, a man has had a taste of all that the longest life can give. Such a man has in great measure come to understand the universe. He knows that honourable things do not depend on time for their growth; but any life must seem short to those who measure its length by pleasures which are empty and for that reason unbounded.

Refresh yourself with such thoughts as these, and meanwhile reserve some hours for our letters. There will come a time when we shall be united again and brought together; however short this time may be, we shall make it long by knowing how to employ it. For, as

---

* i.e., to be looked at; there are better dainties on the table.

† *Sanus* is used as signifying "sound in body" and as the opposite of *insanus*.

‡ Perhaps a reminiscence of Lucretius i. 74 *omne immensum peragravit mente animoque*.

Posidonius says:* "A single day among the learned lasts longer than the longest life of the ignorant." Meanwhile, hold fast to this thought, and grip it close: yield not to adversity; trust not to prosperity; keep before your eyes the full scope of Fortune's power, as if she would surely do whatever is in her power to do. That which has been long expected comes more gently. Farewell.

* Seneca often quotes Posidonius, as does Cicero also. These words may have been taken from his Προτρεπτικά (or Λόγοι προτρεπτικοί), *Exhortations*, a work in which he maintained that men should make a close study of philosophy, in spite of the varying opinions of its expositors.

LETTER

LXXXIII

ON DRUNKENNESS

You bid me give you an account of each separate day, and of the whole day too; so you must have a good opinion of me if you think that in these days of mine there is nothing to hide. At any rate, it is thus that we should live,—as if we lived in plain sight of all men; and it is thus that we should think,—as if there were someone who could look into our inmost souls; and there is one who can so look. For what avails it that something is hidden from man? Nothing is shut off from the sight of God. He is witness of our souls,* and he comes into the very midst of our thoughts—comes into them, I say, as one who may at any time depart. I shall therefore do as you bid, and shall gladly inform you by letter what I am doing, and in what sequence. I shall keep watching myself continually, and—a most useful habit—shall review each day.†

* Cf. Ep. xli. 2 *sacer intra nos spiritus, . . . malorum bonorumque nostrorum observator et custos.*

† Cf. Ep. i. 4 *ratio constat inpensae* (referring to his attempt to employ his time profitably).

For this is what makes us wicked: that no one of us looks back over his own life. Our thoughts are devoted only to what we are about to do. And yet our plans for the future always depend on the past.

Today has been unbroken; no one has filched the slightest part of it from me. The whole time has been divided between rest and reading. A brief space has been given over to bodily exercise, and on this ground I can thank old age—my exercise costs very little effort; as soon as I stir, I am tired. And weariness is the aim and end of exercise, no matter how strong one is. Do you ask who are my pacemakers? One is enough for me,—the slave Pharius, a pleasant fellow, as you know; but I shall exchange him for another. At my time of life I need one who is of still more tender years. Pharius, at any rate, says that he and I are at the same period of life; for we are both losing our teeth.[*] Yet even now I can scarcely follow his pace as he runs, and within a very short time I shall not be able to follow him at all; so you see what profit we get from daily exercise. Very soon does a wide interval open between two persons who travel different ways. My slave is climbing up at the very moment when I am coming down, and you surely know how much quicker the latter is. Nay, I was wrong; for now my life is not coming down; it is falling outright. Do you ask, for all that, how our race resulted today? We raced to a tie,[†]—something which rarely happens in a running contest. After tiring myself out in this way (for I cannot call it exercise), I took a cold bath; this, at my house, means just short of hot. I, the former cold-water enthusiast, who used to celebrate the new year by taking a plunge into the canal, who, just as naturally as I would set out to do some reading or writing, or to compose a speech, used to inaugurate the first of the year with a plunge into the Virgo aqueduct,[‡] have changed my allegiance, first to the Tiber, and then to my favourite tank, which is warmed only by the sun, at times when I am most robust and when there is not a flaw in my bodily processes. I

---

* See Ep. xii. 3 for a similar witticism.

† *Hieran* (*coronam*), as Lipsius thinks, when the result was doubtful, the garland was offered to the gods. From the Greek ἱερός, sacred.

‡ Constructed by Marcus Agrippa; now the fountain of Trevi.

have very little energy left for bathing. After the bath, some stale bread and breakfast without a table; no need to wash the hands after such a meal. Then comes a very short nap. You know my habit; I avail myself of a scanty bit of sleep,—unharnessing, as it were.* For I am satisfied if I can just stop staying awake. Sometimes I know that I have slept; at other times, I have a mere suspicion.

Lo, now the din of the Races sounds about me! My ears are smitten with sudden and general cheering. But this does not upset my thoughts or even break their continuity. I can endure an uproar with complete resignation. The medley of voices blended in one note sounds to me like the dashing of waves,† or like the wind that lashes the tree-tops, or like any other sound which conveys no meaning.

What is it, then, you ask, to which I have been giving my attention? I will tell you. A thought sticks in my mind, left over from yesterday,—namely, what men of the greatest sagacity have meant when they have offered the most trifling and intricate proofs for problems of the greatest importance,—proofs which may be true, but none the less resemble fallacies. Zeno, that greatest of men, the revered founder of our brave and holy school of philosophy, wishes to discourage us from drunkenness. Listen, then, to his arguments proving that the good man will not get drunk: "No one entrusts a secret to a drunken man; but one will entrust a secret to a good man; therefore, the good man will not get drunk."‡ Mark how ridiculous Zeno is made when we set up a similar syllogism in contrast with his. There are many, but one will be enough: "No one entrusts a secret to a man when he is asleep; but one entrusts a secret to a good man; therefore, the good man does not go to sleep."§ Posidonius pleads the cause of our master Zeno in the only possible way; but it cannot, I

* The same word is used by Seneca in *De Tranq. An.* xvii. 7 *quidam medio die interiunxerunt et in postmeridianas horas aliquid levioris operae distulerunt.*

† Cf. Ep. lvi. 3 *istum fremitum non magis curo quam fluctum aut deiectum aquae.*

‡ Zeno, Frag. 229 von Arnim,—quoting also Philo's εἰ τῷ μεθύοντι οὐκ ἄν τις εὐλόγως λόγον ἀπόρρητον παρακατάθοιτο . . . οὐκ ἄρα μεθύει ὁ ἀστεῖος.

§ Cf. Ep. xlix. 8 *quod non perdidisti, habes; cornua autem non perdidisti; cornua ergo habes,*—and the syllogisms given in Ep. xlviii.

hold, be pleaded even in this way. For Posidonius maintains that the word "drunken" is used in two ways,—in the one case of a man who is loaded with wine and has no control over himself; in the other, of a man who is accustomed to get drunk, and is a slave to the habit. Zeno, he says, meant the latter,—the man who is accustomed to get drunk, not the man who is drunk; and no one would entrust to this person any secret, for it might be blabbed out when the man was in his cups. This is a fallacy. For the first syllogism refers to him who is actually drunk and not to him who is about to get drunk. You will surely admit that there is a great difference between a man who is drunk and a drunkard. He who is actually drunk may be in this state for the first time and may not have the habit, while the drunkard is often free from drunkenness. I therefore interpret the word in its usual meaning, especially since the syllogism is set up by a man who makes a business of the careful use of words, and who weighs his language. Moreover, if this is what Zeno meant, and what he wished it to mean to us, he was trying to avail himself of an equivocal word in order to work in a fallacy; and no man ought to do this when truth is the object of inquiry.

But let us admit, indeed, that he meant what Posidonius says; even so, the conclusion is false,—that secrets are not entrusted to an habitual drunkard. Think how many soldiers who are not always sober have been entrusted by a general or a captain or a centurion with messages which might not be divulged! With regard to the notorious plot to murder Gaius Caesar,—I mean the Caesar who conquered Pompey and got control of the state,—Tillius Cimber was trusted with it no less than Gaius Cassius. Now Cassius throughout his life drank water; while Tillius Cimber was a sot as well as a brawler. Cimber himself alluded to this fact, saying: "*I* carry a master? I cannot carry my liquor!" So let each one call to mind those who, to his knowledge, can be ill trusted with wine, but well trusted with the spoken word; and yet one case occurs to my mind, which I shall relate, lest it fall into oblivion. For life should be provided with conspicuous illustrations. Let us not always be harking back to the dim past.

Lucius Piso, the Director of Public Safety at Rome, was drunk from the very time of his appointment. He used to spend the greater part of the night at banquets, and would sleep until noon. That was the way he spent his morning hours. Nevertheless, he applied himself most diligently to his official duties, which included the guardianship of the city. Even the sainted Augustus trusted him with secret orders when he placed him in command of Thrace.* Piso conquered that country. Tiberius, too, trusted him when he took his holiday in Campania, leaving behind him in the city many a critical matter that aroused both suspicion and hatred. I fancy that it was because Piso's drunkenness turned out well for the Emperor that he appointed to the office of city prefect Cossus, a man of authority and balance, but so soaked and steeped in drink that once, at a meeting of the Senate, whither he had come after banqueting, he was overcome by a slumber from which he could not be roused, and had to be carried home. It was to this man that Tiberius sent many orders, written in his own hand,—orders which he believed he ought not to trust even to the officials of his household. Cossus never let a single secret slip out, whether personal or public.

So let us abolish all such harangues as this: "No man in the bonds of drunkenness has power over his soul. As the very vats are burst by new wine, and as the dregs at the bottom are raised to the surface by the strength of the fermentation; so, when the wine effervesces, whatever lies hidden below is brought up and made visible. As a man overcome by liquor cannot keep down his food when he has over-indulged in wine, so he cannot keep back a secret either. He pours forth impartially both his own secrets and those of other persons." This, of course, is what commonly happens, but so does this,—that we take counsel on serious subjects with those whom we know to be in the habit of drinking freely. Therefore this proposition, which is laid down in the guise of a defence of Zeno's syllogism, is false,—that secrets are not entrusted to the habitual drunkard.

* In 11 B.C., when the Thracians were attacking Macedonia. The campaign lasted for three years, and Piso was rewarded with a triumph at its close.

How much better it is to arraign drunkenness frankly and to expose its vices! For even the middling good man avoids them, not to mention the perfect sage, who is satisfied with slaking his thirst; the sage, even if now and then he is led on by good cheer which, for a friend's sake, is carried somewhat too far, yet always stops short of drunkenness. We shall investigate later the question whether the mind of the sage is upset by too much wine and commits follies like those of the toper; but meanwhile, if you wish to prove that a good man ought not to get drunk, why work it out by logic? Show how base it is to pour down more liquor than one can carry, and not to know the capacity of one's own stomach; show how often the drunkard does things which make him blush when he is sober; state that drunkenness* is nothing but a condition of insanity purposely assumed. Prolong the drunkard's condition to several days; will you have any doubt about his madness? Even as it is, the madness is no less; it merely lasts a shorter time. Think of Alexander of Macedon,† who stabbed Clitus, his dearest and most loyal friend, at a banquet; after Alexander understood what he had done, he wished to die, and assuredly he ought to have died.

Drunkenness kindles and discloses every kind of vice, and removes the sense of shame that veils our evil undertakings.‡ For more men abstain from forbidden actions because they are ashamed of sinning than because their inclinations are good. When the strength of wine has become too great and has gained control over the mind, every lurking evil comes forth from its hiding-place. Drunkenness does not create vice, it merely brings it into view; at such times the lustful man does not wait even for the privacy of a bedroom, but without postponement gives free play to the demands of his passions; at such times the unchaste man proclaims and publishes his malady; at such times your cross-grained fellow does not restrain his tongue or his

* Like anger, which was interpreted by the ancients as "short-lived madness."

† For a dramatic account of the murder see Plutarch's *Alexander*, ch. 51.

‡ This is the firm conviction of Seneca, himself a most temperate man. §§ 14 and 15 admit that natural genius may triumph over drunkenness; § 17 may allow (with Chrysippus) a certain amount of hilarity; but the general conclusion is obvious.

hand. The haughty man increases his arrogance, the ruthless man his cruelty, the slanderer his spitefulness. Every vice is given free play and comes to the front. Besides, we forget who we are, we utter words that are halting and poorly enunciated, the glance is unsteady, the step falters, the head is dizzy, the very ceiling moves about as if a cyclone were whirling the whole house, and the stomach suffers torture when the wine generates gas and causes our very bowels to swell. However, at the time, these troubles can be endured, so long as the man retains his natural strength; but what can he do when sleep impairs his powers, and when that which was drunkenness becomes indigestion?

Think of the calamities caused by drunkenness in a nation! This evil has betrayed to their enemies the most spirited and warlike races; this evil has made breaches in walls defended by the stubborn warfare of many years; this evil has forced under alien sway peoples who were utterly unyielding and defiant of the yoke; this evil has conquered by the wine-cup those who in the field were invincible. Alexander, whom I have just mentioned, passed through his many marches, his many battles, his many winter campaigns (through which he worked his way by overcoming disadvantages of time or place), the many rivers which flowed from unknown sources, and the many seas, all in safety; it was intemperance in drinking that laid him low, and the famous death-dealing bowl of Hercules.*

What glory is there in carrying much liquor? When you have won the prize, and the other banqueters, sprawling asleep or vomiting, have declined your challenge to still other toasts; when you are the last survivor of the revels; when you have vanquished every one by your magnificent show of prowess and there is no man who has proved himself of so great capacity as you,—you are vanquished by the cask. Mark Antony was a great man, a man of distinguished ability; but what ruined him and drove him into foreign habits and un-Roman vices, if it was not

* Lipsius quotes Athenaeus as saying that Boeotian silver cups of large size were so called because the Boeotian Hercules drank from them; Servius, however, on Verg. *Aen.* viii. 278, declared that the name was derived from the large wooden bowl brought by Hercules to Italy and used for sacrificial purposes.

drunkenness and—no less potent than wine—love of Cleopatra? This it was that made him an enemy of the state; this it was that rendered him no match for his enemies; this it was that made him cruel, when as he sat at table the heads of the leaders of the state were brought in; when amid the most elaborate feasts and royal luxury he would identify the faces and hands of men whom he had proscribed;[*] when, though heavy with wine, he yet thirsted for blood. It was intolerable that he was getting drunk while he did such things; how much more intolerable that he did these things while actually drunk! Cruelty usually follows wine-bibbing; for a man's soundness of mind is corrupted and made savage. Just as a lingering illness makes men querulous and irritable and drives them wild at the least crossing of their desires, so continued bouts of drunkenness bestialize the soul. For when people are often beside themselves, the habit of madness lasts on, and the vices which liquor generated retain their power even when the liquor is gone.

Therefore you should state why the wise man ought not to get drunk. Explain by facts, and not by mere words, the hideousness of the thing, and its haunting evils. Do that which is easiest of all—namely, demonstrate that what men call pleasures are punishments as soon as they have exceeded due bounds. For if you try to prove that the wise man can souse himself with much wine and yet keep his course straight, even though he be in his cups, you may go on to infer by syllogisms that he will not die if he swallows poison, that he will not sleep if he takes a sleeping-potion, that he will not vomit and reject the matter which clogs his stomach when you give him hellebore.[†] But, when a man's feet totter and his tongue is unsteady, what reason have you for believing that he is half sober and half drunk? Farewell.

---

* "Antony gave orders to those that were to kill Cicero, to cut off his head and right hand . . . ; and, when they were brought before him, he regarded them joyfully, actually bursting out more than once into laughter, and when he had satiated himself with the sight of them, ordered them to be hung up . . . in the forum" (Clough's translation of Plutarch's *Antony*, p. 172).

† A plant which possessed cathartic properties and was widely used by the ancients. It was also applied in cases of mental derangement. The native Latin term is *veratrum*.

LETTER

LXXXVI

ON SCIPIO'S VILLA

I am resting at the country-house which once belonged to Scipio Africanus* himself; and I write to you after doing reverence to his spirit and to an altar which I am inclined to think is the tomb† of that great warrior. That his soul has indeed returned to the skies, whence it came, I am convinced, not because he commanded mighty armies—for Cambyses also had mighty armies, and Cambyses was a madman‡ who made successful use of his madness—but because he showed moderation and a sense of duty to a marvellous extent. I regard this trait in him as more admirable after his withdrawal from his native land than while he was defending her; for there was the alternative: Scipio should remain in Rome, or Rome should remain free. "It is my wish," said he, "not to infringe in the least upon our laws, or upon our customs; let all Roman citizens

---

* See Ep. li. 11.

† Cf. Livy xxxvii. 53 *morientem rure eo ipso loco sepeliri se iussisse ferunt monumentumque ibi aedificari.*

‡ Herodotus iii. 25 ἐμμανής τε ἐὼν καὶ οὐ φρενήρης.

have equal rights. O my country, make the most of the good that I have done, but without me. I have been the cause of your freedom, and I shall also be its proof; I go into exile, if it is true that I have grown beyond what is to your advantage!"

What can I do but admire this magnanimity, which led him to withdraw into voluntary exile and to relieve the state of its burden? Matters had gone so far that either liberty must work harm to Scipio, or Scipio to liberty. Either of these things was wrong in the sight of heaven. So he gave way to the laws and withdrew to Liternum, thinking to make the state a debtor for his own exile no less than for the exile of Hannibal.*

I have inspected the house, which is constructed of hewn stone; the wall which encloses a forest; the towers also, buttressed out on both sides for the purpose of defending the house; the well, concealed among buildings and shrubbery, large enough to keep a whole army supplied; and the small bath, buried in darkness according to the old style, for our ancestors did not think that one could have a hot bath except in darkness. It was therefore a great pleasure to me to contrast Scipio's ways with our own. Think, in this tiny recess the "terror of Carthage,"† to whom Rome should offer thanks because she was not captured more than once, used to bathe a body wearied with work in the fields! For he was accustomed to keep himself busy and to cultivate the soil with his own hands, as the good old Romans were wont to do. Beneath this dingy roof he stood; and this floor, mean as it is, bore his weight.

But who in these days could bear to bathe in such a fashion? We think ourselves poor and mean if our walls are not resplendent with large and costly mirrors; if our marbles from Alexandria‡ are not set off by mosaics of Numidian stone,§ if their borders are not faced

* Livy's account (see above) dwells more on the unwillingness of Scipio and his friends to permit the great conqueror to suffer the indignities of a trial.

† A phrase frequent in Roman literature; see Lucretius iii. 1034 *Scipiadas, belli fulmen, Carthaginis horror.*

‡ Porphyry, basalt, etc.

§ i.e., the so-called *giallo antico*, with red and yellow tints predominating.

over on all sides with difficult patterns, arranged in many colours like paintings; if our vaulted ceilings are not buried in glass; if our swimming-pools are not lined with Thasian marble,* once a rare and wonderful sight in any temple—pools into which we let down our bodies after they have been drained weak by abundant perspiration; and finally, if the water has not poured from silver spigots. I have so far been speaking of the ordinary bathing-establishments; what shall I say when I come to those of the freedmen? What a vast number of statues, of columns that support nothing, but are built for decoration, merely in order to spend money! And what masses of water that fall crashing from level to level! We have become so luxurious that we will have nothing but precious stones to walk upon.

In this bath of Scipio's there are tiny chinks—you cannot call them windows—cut out of the stone wall in such a way as to admit light without weakening the fortifications; nowadays, however, people regard baths as fit only for moths if they have not been so arranged that they receive the sun all day long through the widest of windows, if men cannot bathe and get a coat of tan at the same time, and if they cannot look out from their bath-tubs over stretches of land and sea.† So it goes; the establishments which had drawn crowds and had won admiration when they were first opened are avoided and put back in the category of venerable antiques as soon as luxury has worked out some new device, to her own ultimate undoing. In the early days, however, there were few baths, and they were not fitted out with any display. For why should men elaborately fit out that which, costs a penny only, and was invented for use, not merely for delight? The bathers of those days did not have water poured over them, nor did it always run fresh as if from a hot spring; and they did not believe that it mattered at all how perfectly pure was the water into which they were to leave their dirt. Ye gods, what a pleasure it is to enter that dark bath, covered with a common sort of roof, knowing that therein your hero Cato, as

* A white variety, from Thasos, an island off the Thracian coast.

† Cf. Pliny, *Ep.* ii. 17. 12 *piscina, ex qua natantes mare aspiciunt.*

aedile, or Fabius Maximus, or one of the Cornelia, has warmed the water with his own hands! For this also used to be the duty of the noblest aediles—to enter these places to which the populace resorted, and to demand that they be cleaned and warmed to a heat required by considerations of use and health, not the heat that men have recently made fashionable, as great as a conflagration—so much so, indeed, that a slave condemned for some criminal offence now ought to be *bathed* alive! It seems to me that nowadays there is no difference between "the bath is on fire," and "the bath is warm."

How some persons nowadays condemn Scipio as a boor because he did not let daylight into his perspiring-room through wide windows, or because he did not roast in the strong sunlight and dawdle about until he could stew in the hot water! "Poor fool," they say, "he did not know how to live! He did not bathe in filtered water; it was often turbid, and after heavy rains almost muddy!" But it did not matter much to Scipio if he had to bathe in that way; he went there to wash off sweat, not ointment. And how do you suppose certain persons will answer me? They will say: "I don't envy Scipio; that was truly an exile's life—to put up with baths like those!" Friend, if you were wiser, you would know that Scipio did not bathe every day. It is stated by those[*] who have reported to us the old-time ways of Rome that the Romans washed only their arms and legs daily—because those were the members which gathered dirt in their daily toil—and bathed all over only once a week. Here someone will retort: "Yes; pretty dirty fellows they evidently were! How they must have smelled!" But they smelled of the camp, the farm, and heroism. Now that spick-and-span bathing establishments have been devised, men are really fouler than of yore. What says Horatius Flaccus, when he wishes to describe a scoundrel, one who is notorious for his extreme luxury? He says: "Buccillus[†] smells of perfume." Show me a Buccillus in these days; his smell would be the veritable goat-smell—he would take the place of

* e.g., Varro, in the *Catus*: *balneum non cotidianum*.

† Horace calls him Rufillus (*Sat.* i. 2. 27): *pastillos Rufillus olet, Gargonius hircum.*

the Gargonius with whom Horace in the same passage contrasted him. It is nowadays not enough to use ointment, unless you put on a fresh coat two or three times a day, to keep it from evaporating on the body. But why should a man boast of this perfume as if it were his own?

If what I am saying shall seem to you too pessimistic, charge it up against Scipio's country-house, where I have learned a lesson from Aegialus, a most careful householder and now the owner of this estate; he taught me that a tree can be transplanted, no matter how far gone in years. We old men must learn this precept; for there is none of us who is not planting an olive-yard for his successor. I have seen them bearing fruit in due season after three or four years of unproductiveness.* And you too shall be shaded by the tree which

Is slow to grow, but bringeth shade to cheer
Your grandsons in the far-off years,†

as our poet Vergil says. Vergil sought, however, not what was nearest to the truth, but what was most appropriate, and aimed, not to teach the farmer, but to please the reader. For example, omitting all other errors of his, I will quote the passage in which it was incumbent upon me today to detect a fault:

In spring sow beans then, too, O clover plant,
Thou'rt welcomed by the crumbling furrows; and
The millet calls for yearly care.‡

You may judge by the following incident whether those plants should be set out at the same time, or whether both should be sowed in the spring. It is June at the present writing, and we are well on towards July; and I have seen on this very day farmers harvesting beans and sowing millet.

---

* This seems to be the general meaning of the passage.

† *Georgics*, ii. 58.

‡ *Georgics*, i. 215 f.

But to return to our olive-yard again. I saw it planted in two ways. If the trees were large, Aegialus took their trunks and cut off the branches to the length of one foot each; he then transplanted along with the ball, after cutting off the roots, leaving only the thick part from which the roots hang. He smeared this with manure, and inserted it in the hole, not only heaping up the earth about it, but stamping and pressing it down. There is nothing, he says, more effective than this packing process;* in other words, it keeps out the cold and the wind. Besides, the trunk is not shaken so much, and for this reason the packing makes it possible for the young roots to come out and get a hold in the soil. These are of necessity still soft; they have but a slight hold, and a very little shaking uproots them. This ball, moreover, Aegialus lops clean before he covers it up. For he maintains that new roots spring from all the parts which have been shorn. Moreover, the trunk itself should not stand more than three or four feet out of the ground. For there will thus be at once a thick growth from the bottom, nor will there be a large stump, all dry and withered, as is the case with old olive-yards. The second way of setting them out was the following: he set out in similar fashion branches that were strong and of soft bark, as those of young saplings are wont to be. These grow a little more slowly, but, since they spring from what is practically a cutting, there is no roughness or ugliness in them.

This too I have seen recently—an aged vine transplanted from its own plantation. In this case, the fibres also should be gathered together, if possible, and then you should cover up the vine-stem more generously, so that roots may spring up even from the stock. I have seen such plantings made not only in February, but at the very end of March; the plants take hold of and embrace alien elms. But all trees, he declares, which are, so to speak, "thick-stemmed,"† should be assisted with tank-water; if we have this help, we are our own rain-makers.

I do not intend to tell you any more of these precepts, lest, as Aegialus did with me, I may be training you up to be my competitor. Farewell.

---

* In Vitruvius vii. 1 G reads *pinsatione*, referring to the pounding of stones for flooring.

† An agricultural term not elsewhere found.

LETTER

LXXXVIII

ON LIBERAL AND VOCATIONAL STUDIES

You have been wishing to know my views with regard to liberal studies.* My answer is this: I respect no study, and deem no study good, which results in money-making. Such studies are profit-bringing occupations, useful only in so far as they give the mind a preparation and do not engage it permanently. One should linger upon them only so long as the mind can occupy itself with nothing greater; they are our apprenticeship, not our real work. Hence you see why "liberal studies" are so called; it is because they are studies worthy of a free-born gentleman. But there is only one really liberal study,—that which gives a man his liberty. It is the study of wisdom, and that is lofty, brave, and great-souled. All other

* The regular round of education, ἐγκύκλιος παιδεία, including grammar, music, geometry, arithmetic, astrology, and certain phases of rhetoric and dialectic, are in this letter contrasted with liberal studies—those which have for their object the pursuit of virtue. Seneca is thus interpreting *studia liberalia* in a higher sense than his contemporaries would expect. Compare J. R. Lowell's definition of a university, "a place where nothing useful is taught."

studies are puny and puerile. You surely do not believe that there is good in any of the subjects whose teachers are, as you see, men of the most ignoble and base stamp? We ought not to be learning such things; we should have done with learning them.

Certain persons have made up their minds that the point at issue with regard to the liberal studies is whether they make men good; but they do not even profess or aim at a knowledge of this particular subject. The scholar* busies himself with investigations into language, and if it be his desire to go farther afield, he works on history, or, if he would extend his range to the farthest limits, on poetry. But which of these paves the way to virtue? Pronouncing syllables, investigating words, memorizing plays, or making rules for the scansion of poetry,—what is there in all this that rids one of fear, roots out desire, or bridles the passions? The question is: do such men teach virtue, or not? If they do not teach it, then neither do they transmit it. If they do teach it, they are philosophers. Would you like to know how it happens that they have not taken the chair for the purpose of teaching virtue? See how unlike their subjects are; and yet their subjects would resemble each other if they taught the same thing.†

It may be, perhaps, that they make you believe that Homer was a philosopher,‡ although they disprove this by the very arguments through which they seek to prove it. For sometimes they make of him a Stoic, who approves nothing but virtue, avoids pleasures, and refuses to relinquish honour even at the price of immortality; sometimes they make him an Epicurean, praising the condition of a state in repose, which passes its days in feasting and song; sometimes a Peripatetic,

---

* *Grammaticus* in classical Greek means "one who is familiar with the alphabet"; in the Alexandrian age a "student of literature"; in the Roman age the equivalent of *litteratus*. Seneca means here a "specialist in linguistic science."

† i.e., philosophy (virtue).

‡ This theory was approved by Democritus, Hippias of Elis, and the allegorical interpreters; Xenophanes, Heraclitus, and Plato himself condemned Homer for his supposed unphilosophic fabrications.

classifying goodness in three ways;[*] sometimes an Academic, holding that all things are uncertain. It is clear, however, that no one of these doctrines is to be fathered upon Homer, just because they are all there; for they are irreconcilable with one another. We may admit to these men, indeed, that Homer was a philosopher; yet surely he became a wise man before he had any knowledge of poetry. So let us learn the particular things that made Homer wise.

It is no more to the point, of course, for me to investigate whether Homer or Hesiod was the older poet, than to know why Hecuba, although younger than Helen,[†] showed her years so lamentably. What, in your opinion, I say, would be the point in trying to determine the respective ages of Achilles and Patroclus? Do you raise the question, "Through what regions did Ulysses stray?" instead of trying to prevent ourselves from going astray at all times? We have no leisure to hear lectures on the question whether he was sea-tost between Italy and Sicily, or outside our known world (indeed, so long a wandering could not possibly have taken place within its narrow bounds); we ourselves encounter storms of the spirit, which toss us daily, and our depravity drives us into all the ills which troubled Ulysses. For us there is never lacking the beauty to tempt our eyes, or the enemy to assail us; on this side are savage monsters that delight in human blood, on that side the treacherous allurements of the ear, and yonder is shipwreck and all the varied category of misfortunes.[‡] Show me rather, by the example of Ulysses, how I am to love my country, my wife, my father, and how, even after suffering shipwreck, I am to sail toward these ends, honourable as they are. Why try to discover

---

* The *tria genera bonorum* of Cicero's *De Fin* v. 84. Cf. *ib.* 18, where the three proper objects of man's search are given as the desire for pleasure, the avoidance of pain, and the attainment of such natural goods as health, strength, and soundness of mind. The Stoics held that the good was absolute.

† Summers compares Lucian, *Gall.* 17. Seneca, however, does not take such gossip seriously.

‡ This sentence alludes to Calypso, Circe, the Cyclops, and the Sirens.

whether Penelope was a pattern of purity,* or whether she had the laugh on her contemporaries? Or whether she suspected that the man in her presence was Ulysses, before she knew it was he? Teach me rather what purity is, and how great a good we have in it, and whether it is situated in the body or in the soul.

Now I will transfer my attention to the musician. You, sir, are teaching me how the treble and the bass† are in accord with one another, and how, though the strings produce different notes, the result is a harmony; rather bring my soul into harmony with itself, and let not my purposes be out of tune. You are showing me what the doleful keys‡ are; show me rather how, in the midst of adversity, I may keep from uttering a doleful note. The mathematician teaches me how to lay out the dimensions of my estates; but I should rather be taught how to lay out what is enough for a man to own. He teaches me to count, and adapts my fingers to avarice; but I should prefer him to teach me that there is no point in such calculations, and that one is none the happier for tiring out the book-keepers with his possessions—or rather, how useless property is to any man who would find it the greatest misfortune if he should be required to reckon out, by his own wits, the amount of his holdings. What good is there for me in knowing how to parcel out a piece of land, if I know not how to share it with my brother? What good is there in working out to a nicety the dimensions of an acre, and in detecting the error if a piece has so much as escaped my measuring-rod, if I am embittered when an ill-tempered neighbour merely scrapes off a bit of my land? The mathematician teaches me how I may lose none of my boundaries; I, however, seek to learn how to lose them all with a light heart. "But," comes the reply, "I am being driven from the farm which my father and grandfather owned!" Well? Who owned the land before your grandfather? Can you explain what people (I will

* Unfavourable comment by Lycophron, and by Cicero, *De Nat. Deor.* iii. 22 *(Mercurius) ex quo et Penelopa Pana natum ferunt.*

† With *acutae* and *graves* supply *voces.*

‡ Perhaps the equivalent of a "minor."

not say what person) held it originally? You did not enter upon it as a master, but merely as a tenant. And whose tenant are you? If your claim is successful, you are tenant of the heir. The lawyers say that public property cannot be acquired privately by possession;* what you hold and call your own is public property—indeed, it belongs to mankind at large. O what marvellous skill! You know how to measure the circle; you find the square of any shape which is set before you; you compute the distances between the stars; there is nothing which does not come within the scope of your calculations. But if you are a real master of your profession, measure me the mind of man! Tell me how great it is, or how puny! You know what a straight line is; but how does it benefit you if you do not know what is straight in this life of ours?

I come next to the person who boasts his knowledge of the heavenly bodies, who knows

> Whither the chilling star of Saturn hides,
> And through what orbit Mercury doth stray.†

Of what benefit will it be to know this? That I shall be disturbed because Saturn and Mars are in opposition, or when Mercury sets at eventide in plain view of Saturn, rather than learn that those stars, wherever they are, are propitious,‡ and that they are not subject to change? They are driven along by an unending round of destiny, on a course from which they cannot swerve. They return at stated seasons; they either set in motion, or mark the intervals of the whole world's work. But if they are responsible for whatever happens, how will it

---

* i.e., for a certain term of years; see R. W. Leage, *Roman Private Law*, pp. 133 ff. Compare also Lucretius iii. 971, and Horace, *Ep.* ii. 2. 159.

† Vergil, *Georg.* i. 336 f.

‡ Saturn and Mars were regarded as unlucky stars. Astrology, which dates back beyond 3000 B.C. in Babylonia, was developed by the Greeks of the Alexandrian age and got a foothold in Rome by the second century B.C., flourished greatly under Tiberius. Cf. Horace, *Od.* i. 11. 1 f.; Juv. iii. 42 f., and F. Cumont, *Astrology and Religion among the Greeks and Romans* (trans.), esp. pp. 68 ff. and 84 ff.

help you to know the secrets of the immutable? Or if they merely give indications, what good is there in foreseeing what you cannot escape? Whether you know these things or not, they will take place.

Behold the fleeting sun,
The stars that follow in his train, and thou
Shalt never find the morrow play thee false,
Or be misled by nights without a cloud.*

It has, however, been sufficiently and fully ordained that I shall be safe from anything that may mislead me. "What," you say, "does the 'morrow never play me false'? Whatever happens without my knowledge plays me false." I, for my part, do not know what is to be, but I do know what may come to be. I shall have no misgivings in this matter; I await the future in its entirety; and if there is any abatement in its severity, I make the most of it. If the morrow treats me kindly, it is a sort of deception; but it does not deceive me even at that. For just as I know that all things can happen, so I know, too, that they will not happen in every case. I am ready for favourable events in every case, but I am prepared for evil.

In this discussion you must bear with me if I do not follow the regular course. For I do not consent to admit painting into the list of liberal arts, any more than sculpture, marble-working, and other helps toward luxury. I also debar from the liberal studies wrestling and all knowledge that is compounded of oil and mud;† otherwise, I should be compelled to admit perfumers also, and cooks, and all others who lend their wits to the service of our pleasures. For what "liberal" element is there in these ravenous takers of emetics, whose bodies are fed to fatness while their minds are thin and dull?‡ Or do we really believe that the training which they give is "liberal" for the young men of Rome, who used to be taught by our ancestors to stand

* Vergil, *Georg.* i. 424 ff.

† An allusion to the sand and oil of the wrestling-ring.

‡ Cf. Ep. xv. 3 *copia ciborum subtilitas inpeditur.*

straight and hurl a spear, to wield a pike, to guide a horse, and to handle weapons? Our ancestors used to teach their children nothing that could be learned while lying down. But neither the new system nor the old teaches or nourishes virtue. For what good does it do us to guide a horse and control his speed with the curb, and then find that our own passions, utterly uncurbed, bolt with us? Or to beat many opponents in wrestling or boxing, and then to find that we ourselves are beaten by anger?

"What then," you say, "do the liberal studies contribute nothing to our welfare?" Very much in other respects, but nothing at all as regards virtue. For even these arts of which I have spoken, though admittedly of a low grade—depending as they do upon handiwork—contribute greatly toward the equipment of life, but nevertheless have nothing to do with virtue. And if you inquire, "Why, then, do we educate our children in the liberal studies?"* it is not because they can bestow virtue, but because they prepare the soul for the reception of virtue. Just as that "primary course,"† as the ancients called it, in grammar, which gave boys their elementary training, does not teach them the liberal arts, but prepares the ground for their early acquisition of these arts, so the liberal arts do not conduct the soul all the way to virtue, but merely set it going in that direction.

Posidonius‡ divides the arts into four classes: first we have those which are common and low, then those which serve for amusement, then those which refer to the education of boys, and, finally, the liberal arts. The common sort belong to workmen and are mere hand-work; they are concerned with equipping life; there is in them no pretence to beauty or honour. The arts of amusement are those which aim to please the eye and the ear. To this class you may assign the stage-machinists, who invent scaffolding that goes aloft of its own accord, or

* In a strict sense; not, as in § 2, as Seneca thinks that the term should really be defined—the "liberal" study, i.e. the pursuit of wisdom.

† For the πρώτη ἀγωγή see Quintilian, ii. 1. 4.

‡ From what work of Posidonius Seneca is here quoting we do not know; it may be from the Προτρεπτικά, or *Exhortations*, indicating the training preliminary to philosophy.

floors that rise silently into the air, and many other surprising devices, as when objects that fit together then fall apart, or objects which are separate then join together automatically, or objects which stand erect then gradually collapse. The eye of the inexperienced is struck with amazement by these things; for such persons marvel at everything that takes place without warning, because they do not know the causes. The arts which belong to the education of boys, and are somewhat similar to the liberal arts, are those which the Greeks call the "cycle of studies,"* but which we Romans call the "liberal." However, those alone are really liberal—or rather, to give them a truer name, "free"—whose concern is virtue.

"But," one will say, "just as there is a part of philosophy which has to do with nature, and a part which has to do with ethics, and a part which has to do with reasoning, so this group of liberal arts also claims for itself a place in philosophy. When one approaches questions that deal with nature, a decision is reached by means of a word from the mathematician. Therefore mathematics is a department of that branch which it aids."† But many things aid us and yet are not parts of ourselves. Nay, if they were, they would not aid us. Food is an aid to the body, but is not a part of it. We get some help from the service which mathematics renders; and mathematics is as indispensable to philosophy as the carpenter is to the mathematician. But carpentering is not a part of mathematics, nor is mathematics a part of philosophy. Moreover, each has its own limits; for the wise man investigates and learns the causes of natural phenomena, while the mathematician follows up and computes their numbers and their measurements.‡ The wise man knows the laws by which the heavenly bodies persist, what powers belong to them, and what attributes; the astronomer merely notes their comings and goings, the rules which govern their

---

* See § 1 note.

† i.e., mathematics is a department of *philosophia naturalis.*

‡ This line of argument inversely resembles the criticism by Seneca of Posidonius in Ep. xc.—that the inventions of early science cannot be properly termed a part of philosophy.

settings and their risings, and the occasional periods during which they seem to stand still, although as a matter of fact no heavenly body can stand still. The wise man will know what causes the reflection in a mirror; but, the mathematician can merely tell you how far the body should be from the reflection, and what shape of mirror will produce a given reflection.* The philosopher will demonstrate that the sun is a large body, while the astronomer will compute just how large, progressing in knowledge by his method of trial and experiment; but in order to progress, he must summon to his aid certain principles. No art, however, is sufficient unto itself, if the foundation upon which it rests depends upon mere favour. Now philosophy asks no favours from any other source; it builds everything on its own soil; but the science of numbers is, so to speak, a structure built on another man's land—it builds on alien soil.† It accepts first principles, and by their favour arrives at further conclusions. If it could march unassisted to the truth, if it were able to understand the nature of the universe, I should say that it would offer much assistance to our minds; for the mind grows by contact with things heavenly, and draws into itself something from on high. There is but one thing that brings the soul to perfection—the unalterable knowledge of good and evil. But there is no other art‡ which investigates good and evil.

I should like to pass in review the several virtues. Bravery is a scorner of things which inspire fear; it looks down upon, challenges, and crushes the powers of terror and all that would drive our freedom under the yoke. But do "liberal studies"§ strengthen this virtue? Loyalty is the holiest good in the human heart; it is forced into betrayal by no constraint, and it is bribed by no rewards. Loyalty cries: "Burn me, slay me, kill me! I shall not betray my trust; and the more urgently torture shall seek to find my secret, the deeper in my heart will I bury it!" Can the "liberal arts" produce such a spirit within us? Temperance controls

---

* See *N. Q.* i. 4 ff.

† According to Roman law, *superficies solo cedit*, "the building goes with the ground."

‡ Except philosophy.

§ i.e., in the more commonly accepted sense of the term.

our desires; some it hates and routs, others it regulates and restores to a healthy measure, nor does it ever approach our desires for their own sake. Temperance knows that the best measure of the appetites is not what you want to take, but what you ought to take. Kindliness forbids you to be over-bearing towards your associates, and it forbids you to be grasping. In words and in deeds and in feelings it shows itself gentle and courteous to all men. It counts no evil as another's solely. And the reason why it loves its own good is chiefly because it will some day be the good of another. Do "liberal studies" teach a man such character as this? No; no more than they teach simplicity, moderation and self-restraint, thrift and economy, and that kindliness which spares a neighbour's life as if it were one's own and knows that it is not for man to make wasteful use of his fellow-man.

"But," one says, "since you declare that virtue cannot be attained without the 'liberal studies,' how is it that you deny that they offer any assistance to virtue?"* Because you cannot attain virtue without food, either; and yet food has nothing to do with virtue. Wood does not offer assistance to a ship, although a ship cannot be built except of wood. There is no reason, I say, why you should think that anything is made by the assistance of that without which it cannot be made. We might even make the statement that it is possible to attain wisdom without the "liberal studies"; for although virtue is a thing that must be learned, yet it is not learned by means of these studies.

What reason have I, however, for supposing that one who is ignorant of letters will never be a wise man, since wisdom is not to be found in letters? Wisdom communicates facts† and not words; and it may be true that the memory is more to be depended upon when it has no support outside itself. Wisdom is a large and spacious thing. It needs plenty of free room. One must learn about things divine and human, the past and the future, the ephemeral and the eternal; and

* This usage is a not infrequent one in Latin; cf. Petronius, *Sat.* 42 *neminem nihil boni facere oportet*; *id. ib.* 58; Verg. *Ecl.* v. 25, etc. See Draeger, *Hist. Syn.* ii. 75, and Roby, ii. 2246 ff.

† Cf. Epp. xxxi. 6 and lxxxi. 29 *aestimare res, de quibus . . . cum rerum natura deliberandum est.*

one must learn about Time.* See how many questions arise concerning time alone: in the first place, whether it is anything in and by itself; in the second place, whether anything exists prior to time and without time; and again, did time begin along with the universe, or, because there was something even before the universe began, did time also exist then? There are countless questions concerning the soul alone: whence it comes, what is its nature, when it begins to exist, and how long it exists; whether it passes from one place to another and changes its habitation, being transferred successively from one animal shape to another, or whether it is a slave but once, roaming the universe after it is set free; whether it is corporeal or not; what will become of it when it ceases to use us as its medium; how it will employ its freedom when it has escaped from this present prison; whether it will forget all its past, and at that moment begin to know itself when, released from the body, it has withdrawn to the skies.

Thus, whatever phase of things human and divine you have apprehended, you will be wearied by the vast number of things to be answered and things to be learned. And in order that these manifold and mighty subjects may have free entertainment in your soul, you must remove therefrom all superfluous things. Virtue will not surrender herself to these narrow bounds of ours; a great subject needs wide space in which to move. Let all other things be driven out, and let the breast be emptied to receive virtue.

"But it is a pleasure to be acquainted with many arts." Therefore let us keep only as much of them as is essential. Do you regard that man as blameworthy who puts superfluous things on the same footing with useful things, and in his house makes a lavish display of costly objects, but do not deem him blameworthy who has allowed himself to become engrossed with the useless furniture of learning? This desire to know more than is sufficient is a sort of intemperance.

---

* The ancient Stoics defined Time as "extension of the world's motion." The seasons were said to be "alive" because they depended on material conditions. But the Stoics really acknowledged Time to be immaterial. The same problem of corporeality was discussed with regard to the "good."

Why? Because this unseemly pursuit of the liberal arts makes men troublesome, wordy, tactless, self-satisfied bores, who fail to learn the essentials just because they have learned the non-essentials. Didymus the scholar wrote four thousand books. I should feel pity for him if he had only read the same number of superfluous volumes. In these books he investigates Homer's birthplace,* who was really the mother of Aeneas, whether Anacreon was more of a rake or more of a drunkard, whether Sappho was a bad lot,† and other problems the answers to which, if found, were forthwith to be forgotten. Come now, do not tell me that life is long! Nay, when you come to consider our own countrymen also, I can show you many works which ought to be cut down with the axe.

It is at the cost of a vast outlay of time and of vast discomfort to the ears of others that we win such praise as this: "What a learned man you are!" Let us be content with this recommendation, less citified though it be: "What a good man you are!" Do I mean this? Well, would you have me unroll the annals of the world's history and try to find out who first wrote poetry? Or, in the absence of written records, shall I make an estimate of the number of years which lie between Orpheus and Homer? Or shall I make a study of the absurd writings of Aristarchus, wherein he branded the text‡ of other men's verses, and wear my life away upon syllables? Shall I then wallow in the geometrician's dust?§

* Compare the schoolmaster of Juvenal (vii. 234 ff.), who must know
Nutricem Anchisae, nomen patriamque novercae
Anchemoli, dicat quot Acestes vixerit annis, etc.,
and Friedländer's note.

† A tradition, probably begun by the Greek comic-writers, and explained by Professor Smyth (*Greek Melic Poets*, pp. 227 f.) as due to the more independent position of women among the Aeolians. *Transcriber's note: Gummere has euphemistically translated Seneca here. The Latin is "in his an Sappho publica fuerit", and the feminine noun "publica" means "public woman", i.e. a courtesan or prostitute. So Gummere's translation "whether Sappho was a bad lot" is more accurately rendered as "whether Sappho was a prostitute."*

‡ Marking supposedly spurious lines by the *obelus*, and using other signs to indicate variations, repetitions, and interpolations. He paid special attention to Homer, Pindar, Hesiod, and the tragedians.

§ The geometricians drew their figures in the dust or sand.

Have I so far forgotten that useful saw "Save your time"? Must I know these things? And what may I choose not to know?

Apion, the scholar, who drew crowds to his lectures all over Greece in the days of Gaius Caesar and was acclaimed a Homerid* by every state, used to maintain that Homer, when he had finished his two poems, the *Iliad* and the *Odyssey*, added a preliminary poem to his work, wherein he embraced the whole Trojan war.† The argument which Apion adduced to prove this statement was that Homer had purposely inserted in the opening line two letters which contained a key to the number of his books. A man who wishes to know many things must know such things as these, and must take no thought of all the time which one loses by ill-health, public duties, private duties, daily duties, and sleep. Apply the measure to the years of your life; they have no room for all these things.

I have been speaking so far of liberal studies; but think how much superfluous and unpractical matter the philosophers contain! Of their own accord they also have descended to establishing nice divisions of syllables, to determining the true meaning of conjunctions and prepositions; they have been envious of the scholars, envious of the mathematicians. They have taken over into their own art all the superfluities of these other arts; the result is that they know more about careful speaking than about careful living. Let me tell you what evils are due to over-nice exactness, and what an enemy it is of truth! Protagoras declares that one can take either side on any question and debate it with equal success—even on this very question, whether every subject can be debated from either point of view. Nausiphanes holds that in things which seem to exist, there is no difference between existence and non-existence. Parmenides maintains that nothing exists of all this which seems to exist, except the universe

* Originally, rhapsodists who recited from Homer; in general, "interpreters and admirers—in short, the whole 'spiritual kindred'—of Homer" (D. B. Monro)

† An ancient explanation of the (now disproved) authorship by Homer of such poems as the *Cypria*, *Little Iliad*, *Sack of Troy*, etc.

alone.* Zeno of Elea removed all the difficulties by removing one; for he declares that nothing exists. The Pyrrhonean, Megarian, Eretrian, and Academic schools are all engaged in practically the same task; they have introduced a new knowledge, non-knowledge. You may sweep all these theories in with the superfluous troops of "liberal" studies; the one class of men give me a knowledge that will be of no use to me, the other class do away with any hope of attaining knowledge. It is better, of course, to know useless things than to know nothing. One set of philosophers offers no light by which I may direct my gaze toward the truth; the other digs out my very eyes and leaves me blind. If I cleave to Protagoras, there is nothing in the scheme of nature that is not doubtful; if I hold with Nausiphanes, I am sure only of this—that everything is unsure; if with Parmenides, there is nothing except the One;† if with Zeno, there is not even the One.

What are we, then? What becomes of all these things that surround us, support us, sustain us? The whole universe is then a vain or deceptive shadow. I cannot readily say whether I am more vexed at those who would have it that we know nothing, or with those who would not leave us even this privilege. Farewell.

* In other words, the unchangeable, perfect Being of the universe is contrasted with the mutable Non-Being of opinion and unreality.

† i.e., the universe.

LETTER

XC

ON THE PART PLAYED BY PHILOSOPHY IN THE PROGRESS OF MAN

Who can doubt, my dear Lucilius, that life is the gift of the immortal gods, but that living well* is the gift of philosophy? Hence the idea that our debt to philosophy is greater than our debt to the gods, in proportion as a good life is more of a benefit than mere life, would be regarded as correct, were not philosophy itself a boon which the gods have bestowed upon us. They have given the knowledge thereof to none, but the faculty of acquiring it they have given to all. For if they had made philosophy also a general good, and if we were gifted with understanding at our birth, wisdom would have lost her best attribute—that she is not one of the gifts of fortune. For as it is, the precious and noble characteristic of wisdom is that she does not advance to

* Cf. Plato, *Crito* 48, "not life itself, but a good life, is chiefly to be desired."

meet us, that each man is indebted to himself for her, and that we do not seek her at the hands of others.

What would there be in philosophy worthy of your respect, if she were a thing that came by bounty? Her sole function is to discover the truth about things divine and things human. From her side religion never departs, nor duty, nor justice, nor any of the whole company of virtues which cling together in close-united fellowship. Philosophy has taught us to worship that which is divine, to love that which is human;* she has told us that with the gods lies dominion, and among men, fellowship. This fellowship remained unspoiled for a long time, until avarice tore the community asunder and became the cause of poverty, even in the case of those whom she herself had most enriched. For men cease to possess all things the moment they desire all things for their own.

But the first men and those who sprang from them, still unspoiled, followed nature, having one man as both their leader and their law, entrusting themselves to the control of one better than themselves. For nature has the habit of subjecting the weaker to the stronger. Even among the dumb animals those which are either biggest or fiercest hold sway. It is no weakling bull that leads the herd; it is one that has beaten the other males by his might and his muscle. In the case of elephants, the tallest goes first; among men, the best is regarded as the highest. That is why it was to the mind that a ruler was assigned; and for that reason the greatest happiness rested with those peoples among whom a man could not be the more powerful unless he were the better. For that man can safely accomplish what he will who thinks he can do nothing except what he ought to do.

* Compare the "knowledge of things divine and things human" of lxxxix. 5.

Accordingly, in that age which is maintained to be the golden age,* Posidonius† holds that the government was under the jurisdiction of the wise. They kept their hands under control, and protected the weaker from the stronger. They gave advice, both to do and not to do; they showed what was useful and what was useless. Their forethought provided that their subjects should lack nothing; their bravery warded off dangers; their kindness enriched and adorned their subjects. For them ruling was a service, not an exercise of royalty. No ruler tried his power against those to whom he owed the beginnings of his power; and no one had the inclination, or the excuse, to do wrong, since the ruler ruled well and the subject obeyed well, and the king could utter no greater threat against disobedient subjects than that they should depart from the kingdom.

But when once vice stole in and kingdoms were transformed into tyrannies, a need arose for laws; and these very laws were in turn framed by the wise. Solon, who established Athens upon a firm basis by just laws, was one of the seven men renowned for their wisdom.‡ Had Lycurgus lived in the same period, an eighth would have been added to that hallowed number seven. The laws of Zaleucus and Charondas are praised; it was not in the forum or in the offices of skilled counsellors, but in the silent and holy retreat of Pythagoras, that these two men learned the principles of justice which they were to establish in Sicily (which at that time was prosperous) and throughout Grecian Italy.

---

* The "Golden Age" motif was a frequent one in Latin literature. Compare, e.g., Tibullus, i. 3. 35 ff., the passage beginning:

Quam bene Saturno vivebant rege, priusquam
Tellus in longas est patefacta vias!

Cf. § 46, summing up the message of Seneca's letter.

† While modern philosophy would probably side with Seneca rather than Posidonius, it is interesting to know the opinion of Macaulay, who holds (*Essay on Bacon*) that there is much in common between Posidonius and the English inductive philosopher, and thinks but little of Seneca's ideas on the subject. Cf. W. C. Summers, *Select letters of Seneca*, p. 312.

‡ Cleobulus of Rhodes, Periander of Corinth, Pittacus of Mitylene, Bias of Priene, Thales of Miletus, Chilon of Sparta, and Solon of Athens. For some of these substitutions are made in certain lists.

Up to this point I agree with Posidonius; but that philosophy discovered the arts of which life makes use in its daily round* I refuse to admit, nor will I ascribe to it an artisan's glory. Posidonius says: "When men were scattered over the earth, protected by caves or by the dug-out shelter of a cliff or by the trunk of a hollow tree, it was philosophy that taught them to build houses." But I, for my part, do not hold that philosophy devised these shrewdly-contrived dwellings of ours which rise story upon story, where city crowds against city, any more than that she invented the fish-preserves, which are enclosed for the purpose of saving men's gluttony from having to run the risk of storms, and in order that, no matter how wildly the sea is raging, luxury may have its safe harbours in which to fatten fancy breeds of fish. What! Was it philosophy that taught the use of keys and bolts? Nay, what was that except giving a hint to avarice? Was it philosophy that erected all these towering tenements, so dangerous to the persons who dwell in them? Was it not enough for man to provide himself a roof of any chance covering, and to contrive for himself some natural retreat without the help of art and without trouble? Believe me, that was a happy age, before the days of architects, before the days of builders! All this sort of thing was born when luxury was being born,—this matter of cutting timbers square and cleaving a beam with unerring hand as the saw made its way over the marked-out line.

The primal man with wedges split his wood.†

For they were not preparing a roof for a future banquet-ball; for no such use did they carry the pine-trees or the firs along the trembling streets‡ with a long row of drays—merely to fasten thereon panelled

---

* Cf. Ep. lxxxviii. 20 *ad alia multum, ad virtutem nihil.*

† Vergil, *Georg.* i. 144.

‡ Cf. Juvenal, iii. 254 ff.:

Longa coruscat
Serraco veniente abies, atque altera pinum
Plaustra vehunt, nutant alte populoque minantur.

Compare also the "towering tenements" of § 8.

ceilings heavy with gold. Forked poles erected at either end propped up their houses. With close-packed branches and with leaves heaped up and laid sloping they contrived a drainage for even the heaviest rains. Beneath such dwellings, they lived, but they lived in peace. A thatched roof once covered free men; under marble and gold dwells slavery.

On another point also I differ from Posidonius, when he holds that mechanical tools were the invention of wise men. For on that basis one might maintain that those were wise who taught the arts

> Of setting traps for game, and liming twigs
> For birds, and girdling mighty woods with dogs.*

It was man's ingenuity, not his wisdom, that discovered all these devices. And I also differ from him when he says that wise men discovered our mines of iron and copper, "when the earth, scorched by forest fires, melted the veins of ore which lay near the surface and caused the metal to gush forth."† Nay, the sort of men who discover such things are the sort of men who are busied with them. Nor do I consider this question so subtle as Posidonius thinks, namely, whether the hammer or the tongs came first into use. They were both invented by some man whose mind was nimble and keen, but not great or exalted; and the same holds true of any other discovery which can only be made by means of a bent body and of a mind whose gaze is upon the ground.

The wise man was easy-going in his way of living. And why not? Even in our own times he would prefer to be as little cumbered as possible. How, I ask, can you consistently admire both Diogenes and Daedalus? Which of these two seems to you a wise man—the one who devised the saw, or the one who, on seeing a boy drink water from the hollow of his hand, forthwith took his cup from his wallet

---

* Vergil, *Georg.* i. 139 f.

† Cf. T. Rice Holmes, *Ancient Britain*, pp. 121 f., who concludes that the discovery of ore-smelting was accidental.

and broke it, upbraiding himself with these words:* "Fool that I am, to have been carrying superfluous baggage all this time!" and then curled himself up in his tub and lay down to sleep? In these our own times, which man, pray, do you deem the wiser—the one who invents a process for spraying saffron perfumes to a tremendous height from hidden pipes, who fills or empties canals by a sudden rush of waters, who so cleverly constructs a dining room with a ceiling of movable panels that it presents one pattern after another, the roof changing as often as the courses,†—or the one who proves to others, as well as to himself, that nature has laid upon us no stern and difficult law when she tells us that we can live without the marble-cutter and the engineer, that we can clothe ourselves without traffic in silk fabrics, that we can have everything that is indispensable to our use, provided only that we are content with what the earth has placed on its surface? If mankind were willing to listen to this sage, they would know that the cook is as superfluous to them as the soldier. Those were wise men, or at any rate like the wise, who found the care of the body a problem easy to solve. The things that are indispensable require no elaborate pains for their acquisition; it is only the luxuries that call for labour. Follow nature, and you will need no skilled craftsmen.

Nature did not wish us to be harassed. For whatever she forced upon us, she equipped us. "But cold cannot be endured by the naked body." What then? Are there not the skins of wild beasts and other animals, which can protect us well enough, and more than enough, from the cold? Do not many tribes cover their bodies with the bark of trees? Are not the feathers of birds sewn together to serve for clothing? Even at the present day does not a large portion of the Scythian tribe garb itself in the skins of foxes and mice, soft to the touch and impervious to the winds? "For all that, men must have

* Cf. Diog. Laert. vi. 37 θεασάμενός ποτε παιδίον ταῖς χερσὶ ἐξέῤῥιψε τῆς πήρας τὴν κοτύλην, εἰπών, Παιδίον με νενίκηκεν εὐτελεία.

† Compare the halls of Nero which Seneca may easily have had in mind: (Suet. *Nero* 31) *cenationes laqueatae tabulis eburneis versatilibus . . . praecipua cenationum rotunda, quae perpetuo diebus ac noctibus vice mundi circumageretur.*

some thicker protection than the skin, in order to keep off the heat of the sun in summer." What then? Has not antiquity produced many retreats which, hollowed out either by the damage wrought by time or by any other occurrence you will, have opened into caverns? What then? Did not the very first-comers take twigs* and weave them by hand into wicker mats, smear them with common mud, and then with stubble and other wild grasses construct a roof, and thus pass their winters secure, the rains carried off by means of the sloping gables? What then? Do not the peoples on the edge of the Syrtes dwell in dug-out houses—and indeed all the tribes who, because of the too fierce blaze of the sun, possess no protection sufficient to keep off the heat except the parched soil itself?

Nature was not so hostile to man that, when she gave all the other animals an easy rôle in life, she made it impossible for him alone to live without all these artifices. None of these was imposed upon us by her; none of them had to be painfully sought out that our lives might be prolonged. All things were ready for us at our birth; it is we that have made everything difficult for ourselves, through our disdain for what is easy. Houses, shelter, creature comforts, food, and all that has now become the source of vast trouble, were ready at hand, free to all, and obtainable for trifling pains. For the limit everywhere corresponded to the need; it is we that have made all those things valuable, we that have made them admired, we that have caused them to be sought for by extensive and manifold devices. Nature suffices for what she demands. Luxury has turned her back upon nature; each day she expands herself, in all the ages she has been gathering strength, and by her wit promoting the vices. At first, luxury began to lust for what nature regarded as superfluous, then for that which was contrary to nature; and finally she made the soul a bondsman to the body, and

* Cf. Ovid, *Met.* i. 121 f.:

Domus antra fuerunt

Et densi frutices et vinctae cortice virgae.

Among many accounts by Roman writers of early man, compare this passage of Ovid, and that in the fifth book of Lucretius.

bade it be an utter slave to the body's lusts. All these crafts by which the city is patrolled—or shall I say kept in uproar—are but engaged in the body's business; time was when all things were offered to the body as to a slave, but now they are made ready for it as for a master. Accordingly, hence have come the workshops of the weavers and the carpenters; hence the savoury smells of the professional cooks; hence the wantonness of those who teach wanton postures, and wanton and affected singing. For that moderation which nature prescribes, which limits our desires by resources restricted to our needs, has abandoned the field; it has now come to this—that to want only what is enough is a sign both of boorishness and of utter destitution.

It is hard to believe, my dear Lucilius, how easily the charm of eloquence wins even great men away from the truth. Take, for example, Posidonius—who, in my estimation, is of the number of those who have contributed most to philosophy—when he wishes to describe the art of weaving. He tells how, first, some threads are twisted and some drawn out from the soft, loose mass of wool; next, how the upright warp keeps the threads stretched by means of hanging weights; then, how the inserted thread of the woof, which softens the hard texture of the web which holds it fast on either side, is forced by the batten to make a compact union with the warp. He maintains that even the weaver's art was discovered by wise men, forgetting that the more complicated art which he describes was invented in later days—the art wherein

The web is bound to frame; asunder now
The reed doth part the warp. Between the threads
Is shot the woof by pointed shuttles borne;
The broad comb's well-notched teeth then drive it home.*

Suppose he had had the opportunity of seeing the weaving of our own day, which produces the clothing that will conceal nothing, the

* Ovid, *Met.* vi. 55 ff.

clothing which affords—I will not say no protection to the body, but none even to modesty!

Posidonius then passes on to the farmer. With no less eloquence he describes the ground which is broken up and crossed again by the plough, so that the earth, thus loosened, may allow freer play to the roots; then the seed is sown, and the weeds plucked out by hand, lest any chance growth or wild plant spring up and spoil the crop. This trade also, he declares, is the creation of the wise,—just as if cultivators of the soil were not even at the present day discovering countless new methods of increasing the soil's fertility! Furthermore, not confining his attention to these arts, he even degrades the wise man by sending him to the mill. For he tells us how the sage, by imitating the processes of nature, began to make bread. "The grain,"* he says, "once taken into the mouth, is crushed by the flinty teeth, which meet in hostile encounter, and whatever grain slips out the tongue turns back to the selfsame teeth. Then it is blended into a mass, that it may the more easily pass down the slippery throat. When this has reached the stomach, it is digested by the stomach's equable heat; then, and not till then, it is assimilated with the body. Following this pattern," he goes on, "someone placed two rough stones, the one above the other, in imitation of the teeth, one set of which is stationary and awaits the motion of the other set. Then, by the rubbing of the one stone against the other, the grain is crushed and brought back again and again, until by frequent rubbing it is reduced to powder. Then this man sprinkled the meal with water, and by continued manipulation subdued the mass and moulded the loaf. This loaf was, at first, baked by hot ashes or by an earthen vessel glowing hot; later on ovens were gradually discovered and the other devices whose heat will render obedience to the sage's will." Posidonius came very near declaring that even the cobbler's trade was the discovery of the wise man.

---

* Professor Summers calls attention to the similarity of this passage and Cicero, *De Nat. Deor.* ii. 134 ff. *dentibus manditur . . . a lingua adiuvari videtur . . . in alvo . . . calore . . . in reliquum corpus dividantur.*

Reason did indeed devise all these things, but it was not right reason. It was man, but not the wise man, that discovered them; just as they invented ships, in which we cross rivers and seas—ships fitted with sails for the purpose of catching the force of the winds, ships with rudders added at the stern in order to turn the vessel's course in one direction or another. The model followed was the fish, which steers itself by its tail, and by its slightest motion on this side or on that bends its swift course. "But," says Posidonius, "the wise man did indeed discover all these things; they were, however, too petty for him to deal with himself and so he entrusted them to his meaner assistants." Not so; these early inventions were thought out by no other class of men than those who have them in charge today. We know that certain devices have come to light only within our own memory—such as the use of windows which admit the clear light through transparent tiles,* and such as the vaulted baths, with pipes let into their walls for the purpose of diffusing the heat which maintains an even temperature in their lowest as well as in their highest spaces. Why need I mention the marble with which our temples and our private houses are resplendent? Or the rounded and polished masses of stone by means of which we erect colonnades and buildings roomy enough for nations? Or our signs† for whole words, which enable us to take down a speech, however rapidly uttered, matching speed of tongue by speed of hand? All this sort of thing has been devised by the lowest grade of slaves. Wisdom's seat is higher; she trains not the hands, but is mistress of our minds.

Would you know what wisdom has brought forth to light, what she has accomplished? It is not the graceful poses of the body, or the varied notes produced by horn and flute, whereby the breath is

---

* Besides *lapis specularis* (window-glass) the Romans used alabaster, mica, and shells for this purpose.

† Suetonius tells us that a certain Ennius, a grammarian of the Augustan age, was the first to develop shorthand on a scientific basis, and that Tiro, Cicero's freedman, had invented the process. He also mentions Seneca as the most scientific and encyclopaedic authority on the subject.

received and, as it passes out or through, is transformed into voice. It is not wisdom that contrives arms, or walls, or instruments useful in war; nay, her voice is for peace, and she summons all mankind to concord. It is not she, I maintain, who is the artisan of our indispensable implements of daily use. Why do you assign to her such petty things? You see in her the skilled artisan of life. The other arts, it is true, wisdom has under her control; for he whom life serves is also served by the things which equip life. But wisdom's course is toward the state of happiness; thither she guides us, thither she opens the way for us. She shows us what things are evil and what things are seemingly evil; she strips our minds of vain illusion. She bestows upon us a greatness which is substantial, but she represses the greatness which is inflated, and showy but filled with emptiness; and she does not permit us to be ignorant of the difference between what is great and what is but swollen; nay, she delivers to us the knowledge of the whole of nature and of her own nature. She discloses to us what the gods are and of what sort they are; what are the nether gods, the household deities, and the protecting spirits; what are the souls which have been endowed with lasting life and have been admitted to the second class of divinities,* where is their abode and what their activities, powers, and will.

Such are wisdom's rites of initiation, by means of which is unlocked, not a village shrine, but the vast temple of all the gods—the universe itself, whose true apparitions and true aspects she offers to the gaze of our minds. For the vision of our eyes is too dull for sights so great. Then she goes back to the beginnings of things, to the eternal Reason† which was imparted to the whole, and to the force which inheres in all the seeds of things, giving them the power to fashion each thing according to its kind. Then wisdom begins to inquire about the soul, whence it comes, where it dwells, how long it abides, into how many divisions it falls. Finally, she has turned

---

* Possibly either the *manes* or the *indigitamenta* of the early Roman religion.

† i.e., λόγος.

her attention from the corporeal to the incorporeal, and has closely examined truth and the marks whereby truth is known, inquiring next how that which is equivocal can be distinguished from the truth, whether in life or in language; for in both are elements of the false mingled with the true.

It is my opinion that the wise man has not withdrawn himself, as Posidonius thinks, from those arts which we were discussing, but that he never took them up at all.* For he would have judged that nothing was worth discovering that he would not afterwards judge to be worth using always. He would not take up things which would have to be laid aside.

"But Anacharsis," says Posidonius, "invented the potter's wheel, whose whirling gives shape to vessels."† Then because the potter's wheel is mentioned in Homer, people prefer to believe that Homer's verses are false rather than the story of Posidonius! But I maintain that Anacharsis was not the creator of this wheel; and even if he was, although he was a wise man when he invented it, yet he did not invent it *qua* "wise man"—just as there are a great many things which wise men do as men, not as wise men. Suppose, for example, that a wise man is exceedingly fleet of foot; he will outstrip all the runners in the race by virtue of being fleet, not by virtue of his wisdom. I should like to show Posidonius some glass-blower who by his breath moulds the glass into manifold shapes which could scarcely be fashioned by the most skilful hand. Nay, these discoveries have been made since we men have ceased to discover wisdom.

---

* Seneca, himself one of the keenest scientific observers in history (witness *Nat. Quaest.*, Epp. lvii., lxxix., etc.), is pushing his argument very far in this letter. His message is clear enough; but the modern combination of natural science, psychology, and philosophy shows that Posidonius had some justification for his theories. Cf. also Lucretius, v. 1105-7 ff.

† This Scythian prince and friend of Solon, who visited Athens in the sixth century B.C., is also said to have invented the bellows and the anchor. Cf., however, *Iliad* xviii. 600 f. ὡς ὅτε τις τροχὸν ἄρμενον ἐν παλάμῃσιν ἑζόμενος κεραμεὺς πειρήσεται, and Leaf's comment: "The potter's wheel was known in pre-Mycenean times, and was a very ancient invention to the oldest Epic poets." Seneca is right.

But Posidonius again remarks: "Democritus is said to have discovered the arch,* whose effect was that the curving line of stones, which gradually lean toward each other, is bound together by the keystone." I am inclined to pronounce this statement false. For there must have been, before Democritus, bridges and gateways in which the curvature did not begin until about the top. It seems to have quite slipped your memory that this same Democritus discovered how ivory could be softened, how, by boiling, a pebble could be transformed into an emerald,†—the same process used even today for colouring stones which are found to be amenable to this treatment! It may have been a wise man who discovered all such things, but he did not discover them by virtue of being a wise man; for he does many things which we see done just as well, or even more skilfully and dexterously, by men who are utterly lacking in sagacity.

Do you ask what, then, the wise man has found out and what he has brought to light? First of all there is truth, and nature; and nature he has not followed as the other animals do, with eyes too dull to perceive the divine in it. In the second place, there is the law of life, and life he has made to conform to universal principles; and he has taught us, not merely to know the gods, but to follow them, and to welcome the gifts of chance precisely as if they were divine commands. He has forbidden us to give heed to false opinions, and has weighed the value of each thing by a true standard of appraisement. He has condemned those pleasures with which remorse is intermingled, and has praised those goods which will always satisfy; and he has published the truth abroad that he is most

* Seneca (see next sentence) is right again. The arch was known in Chaldaea and in Egypt before 3000 B.C. Greek bee-hive tombs, Etruscan gateways, and early Roman remains, testify to its immemorial use.

† The ancients judged precious stones merely by their colour; their *smaragdus* included also malachite, jade, and several kinds of quartz. Exposure to heat alters the colour of some stones; and the alchemists believed that the "angelic stone" changed common flints into diamonds, rubies, emeralds, etc. See G. F. Kunz, *The Magic of Jewels and Charms*, p. 16. It was also an ancient superstition that emeralds were produced from jasper.

happy who has no need of happiness, and that he is most powerful who has power over himself.

I am not speaking of that philosophy which has placed the citizen outside his country and the gods outside the universe, and which has bestowed virtue upon pleasure,* but rather of that philosophy which counts nothing good except what is honourable,—one which cannot be cajoled by the gifts either of man or of fortune, one whose value is that it cannot be bought for any value. That this philosophy existed in such a rude age, when the arts and crafts were still unknown and when useful things could only be learned by use,—this I refuse to believe.

Next there came the fortune-favoured period when the bounties of nature lay open to all, for men's indiscriminate use, before avarice and luxury had broken the bonds which held mortals together, and they, abandoning their communal existence, had separated and turned to plunder. The men of the second age were not wise men, even though they did what wise men should do.† Indeed, there is no other condition of the human race that anyone would regard more highly; and if God should commission a man to fashion earthly creatures and to bestow institutions upon peoples, this man would approve of no other system than that which obtained among the men of that age, when

> No ploughman tilled the soil, nor was it right
> To portion off or bound one's property.
> Men shared their gains, and earth more freely gave
> Her riches to her sons who sought them not.‡

What race of men was ever more blest than that race? They enjoyed all nature in partnership. Nature sufficed for them, now the guardian, as before she was the parent, of all; and this her gift consisted of the assured possession by each man of the common resources. Why should

---

* i.e., the Epicureans, who withdraw from civil life and regarded the gods as taking no part in the affairs of men.

† i.e., live according to nature.

‡ Verg. *Georg.* i. 125 ff.

I not even call that race the richest among mortals, since you could not find a poor person among them?

But avarice broke in upon a condition so happily ordained, and, by its eagerness to lay something away and to turn it to its own private use, made all things the property of others, and reduced itself from boundless wealth to straitened need. It was avarice that introduced poverty and, by craving much, lost all. And so, although she now tries to make good her loss, although she adds one estate to another, evicting a neighbour either by buying him out or by wronging him, although she extends her country-seats to the size of provinces and defines ownership as meaning extensive travel through one's own property,—in spite of all these efforts of hers, no enlargement of our boundaries will bring us back to the condition from which we have departed.

When there is no more that we can do, we shall possess much; but we once possessed the whole world! The very soil was more productive when untilled, and yielded more than enough for peoples who refrained from despoiling one another. Whatever gift nature had produced, men found as much pleasure in revealing it to another as in having discovered it. It was possible for no man either to surpass another or to fall short of him; what there was, was divided among unquarrelling friends. Not yet had the stronger begun to lay hands upon the weaker; not yet had the miser, by hiding away what lay before him, begun to shut off his neighbour from even the necessities of life; each cared as much for his neighbour as for himself. Armour lay unused, and the hand, unstained by human blood, had turned all its hatred against wild beasts. The men of that day, who had found in some dense grove protection against the sun, and security against the severity of winter or of rain in their mean hiding-places, spent their lives under the branches of the trees and passed tranquil nights without a sigh. Care vexes us in our purple, and routs us from our beds with the sharpest of goads; but how soft was the sleep the hard earth bestowed upon the men of that day! No fretted and panelled ceilings hung over them, but as they lay beneath the open sky the stars glided quietly above them, and the firmament, night's noble pageant, marched swiftly by, conducting its mighty task in silence. For them by day, as well as by night, the visions of this most glorious abode were free and open. It was their joy to watch the constellations as they sank from mid-heaven, and others, again, as they rose from their hidden abodes. What else but joy could it be to wander among the marvels which dotted the heavens far and wide? But you of the present day shudder at every sound your houses make, and as you sit among your frescoes the slightest creak makes you shrink in terror. *They* had no houses as big as cities. The air, the breezes blowing free through the open spaces, the flitting shade of crag or tree, springs crystal-clear and streams not spoiled by man's work, whether by water-pipe* or by any confinement of the channel, but running at will, and meadows beautiful without the use of art,—amid such scenes were their rude homes, adorned with rustic hand. Such a dwelling was in accordance with nature; therein it was a joy to live, fearing neither the dwelling itself nor for its safety. In these days, however, our houses constitute a large portion of our dread.

But no matter how excellent and guileless was the life of the men of that age, they were not wise men; for that title is reserved for the highest achievement. Still, I would not deny that they were men of lofty spirit and—I may use the phrase—fresh from the gods. For there is no doubt that the world produced a better progeny before it was yet worn out. However, not all were endowed with mental faculties of highest perfection, though in all cases their native powers were more sturdy than ours and more fitted for toil. For nature does not bestow virtue; it is an art to become good. They, at least, searched not in the lowest dregs of the earth for gold, nor yet for silver or transparent stones; and they still were merciful even to the dumb animals—so far removed was that epoch from the custom of slaying man by man, not in anger or through fear, but just to make a show! They had as yet no embroidered garments nor did they weave cloth of gold; gold was not yet even mined.

---

* Cf. Horace, *Ep.* i. 10. 20 f.:

Purior in vicis aqua tendit rumpere plumbum
Quam quae per pronum trepidat cum murmure rivum?

What, then, is the conclusion of the matter? It was by reason of their ignorance of things that the men of those days were innocent; and it makes a great deal of difference whether one wills not to sin or has not the knowledge to sin.* Justice was unknown to them, unknown prudence, unknown also self-control and bravery; but their rude life possessed certain qualities akin to all these virtues. Virtue is not vouchsafed to a soul unless that soul has been trained and taught, and by unremitting practice brought to perfection. For the attainment of this boon, but not in the possession of it, were we born; and even in the best of men, before you refine them by instruction, there is but the stuff of virtue, not virtue itself. Farewell.

* Because virtue depends upon reason, and none but voluntary acts should meet with praise or blame.

LETTER

XCI

ON THE LESSON TO BE DRAWN FROM THE BURNING OF LYONS*

Our friend Liberalis† is now downcast; for he has just heard of the fire which has wiped out the colony of Lyons. Such a calamity might upset anyone at all, not to speak of a man who dearly loves his country. But this incident has served to make him inquire about the strength of his own character, which he has trained, I suppose, just to meet situations that he thought might cause him fear. I do not wonder, however, that he was free from apprehension touching an evil so unexpected and practically unheard of as this, since it is without precedent. For fire has damaged many a city, but has annihilated none. Even when fire has been hurled against

* In spite of the *centesimus annus* of § 14 (q.v.), the most probable date of this letter, based on Tac. *Ann.* xvi. 13 and other general evidence, is July-September 64 A.D. 58 A.D. would be too early for many reasons—among them that "peace all over the world" would not be a true statement until January of 62. (See the monograph of Jonas, O. Binder, Peiper, and Schultess.)

† Probably Aebutius Liberalis, to whom the treatise De Beneficiis was dedicated.

the walls by the hand of a foe, the flame dies out in many places, and although continually renewed, rarely devours so wholly as to leave nothing for the sword. Even an earthquake has scarcely ever been so violent and destructive as to overthrow whole cities. Finally, no conflagration has ever before blazed forth so savagely in any town that nothing was left for a second. So many beautiful buildings, any single one of which would make a single town famous, were wrecked in one night. In time of such deep peace an event has taken place worse than men can possibly fear even in time of war. Who can believe it? When weapons are everywhere at rest, and when peace prevails throughout the world, Lyons, the pride of Gaul,* is missing!

Fortune has usually allowed all men, when she has assailed them collectively, to have a foreboding of that which they were destined to suffer. Every great creation has had granted to it a period of reprieve before its fall; but in this case, only a single night elapsed between the city at its greatest and the city non-existent. In short, it takes me longer to tell you it has perished than it took for the city to perish.

All this has affected our friend Liberalis, bending his will, which is usually so steadfast and erect in the face of his own trials. And not without reason has he been shaken; for it is the unexpected that puts the heaviest load upon us. Strangeness adds to the weight of calamities, and every mortal feels the greater pain as a result of that which also brings surprise.

Therefore, nothing ought to be unexpected by us. Our minds should be sent forward in advance to meet all problems, and we should consider, not what is wont to happen, but what can happen. For what is there in existence that Fortune, when she has so willed, does not drag down from the very height of its prosperity? And what is there that she does not the more violently assail the more brilliantly

* That Lyons, situated at the junction of the Arar and the Rhone, was of especial prominence in Gaul, may be also gathered from the fact that it boasted a government mint and the *Ara Augusti*—a shrine established for the annual worship of all the Gallic states. Moreover, the emperor Claudius delivered his famous address in that city (see Tac. *Ann.* xi. 23 f.).

it shines? What is laborious or difficult for her? She does not always attack in one way, or even with her full strength; at one time she summons our own hands against us; at another time, content with her own powers, she makes use of no agent in devising perils for us. No time is exempt; in the midst of our very pleasures there spring up causes of suffering. War arises in the midst of peace, and that which we depended upon for protection is transformed into a cause of fear; friend becomes enemy, ally becomes foeman. The summer calm is stirred into sudden storms, wilder than the storms of winter.* With no foe in sight we are victims of such fates as foes inflict, and if other causes of disaster fail, excessive good fortune finds them for itself. The most temperate are assailed by illness, the strongest by wasting disease, the most innocent by chastisement, the most secluded by the noisy mob.

Chance chooses some new weapon by which to bring her strength to bear against us, thinking we have forgotten her. Whatever structure has been reared by a long sequence of years, at the cost of great toil and through the great kindness of the gods, is scattered and dispersed by a single day. Nay, he who has said "a day" has granted too long a postponement to swift-coming misfortune; an hour, an instant of time, suffices for the overthrow of empires! It would be some consolation for the feebleness of our selves and our works, if all things should perish as slowly as they come into being; but as it is, increases are of sluggish growth, but the way to ruin is rapid. Nothing, whether public or private, is stable; the destinies of men, no less than those of cities, are in a whirl. Amid the greatest calm terror arises, and though no external agencies stir up commotion, yet evils burst forth from sources whence they were least expected. Thrones which have stood the shock of civil and foreign wars crash to the ground though no one sets them tottering. How few the states which have carried their good fortune through to the end!

---

* Cf. Ep. iv. 7, esp. the words *noli huic tranquillitati confidere; momento mare evertitur.*

We should therefore reflect upon all contingencies, and should fortify our minds against the evils which may possibly come. Exile, the torture of disease, wars, shipwreck,—we must think on these.* Chance may tear you from your country or your country from you, or may banish you to the desert; this very place, where throngs are stifling, may become a desert. Let us place before our eyes in its entirety the nature of man's lot, and if we would not be overwhelmed, or even dazed, by those unwonted evils, as if they were novel, let us summon to our minds beforehand, not as great an evil as oftentimes happens, but the very greatest evil that possibly can happen. We must reflect upon fortune fully and completely.

How often have cities in Asia, how often in Achaia, been laid low by a single shock of earthquake! How many towns in Syria, how many in Macedonia, have been swallowed up! How often has this kind of devastation laid Cyprus† in ruins! How often has Paphos collapsed! Not infrequently are tidings brought to us of the utter destruction of entire cities; yet how small a part of the world are we, to whom such tidings often come!

Let us rise, therefore, to confront the operations of Fortune, and whatever happens, let us have the assurance that it is not so great as rumour advertises it to be. A rich city has been laid in ashes, the jewel of the provinces, counted as one of them and yet not included with them;‡ rich though it was, nevertheless it was set upon a single hill,§ and that not very large in extent. But of all those cities, of whose

* The passage bears a striking resemblance to the words of Theseus in an unknown play of Euripides (Nauck. Frag. 964) quoted by Cicero, *Tusc.* iii. 14. 29, and by Plutarch, *Consolation to Apollonius*, 112d.

† Seneca (*N. Q.* vi. 26) speaks of Paphos (on the island of Cyprus) as having been more than once devastated. We know of two such accidents—one under Augustus and another under Vespasian. See the same passage for other earthquake shocks in various places.

‡ Lyons held an exceptional position in relation to the three Gallic provinces; it was a free town, belonging to none and yet their capital, much like the city of Washington in relation to the United States.

§ A fact mentioned merely to suggest Rome with her seven hills.

magnificence and grandeur you hear today, the very traces will be blotted out by time. Do you not see how, in Achaia, the foundations of the most famous cities have already crumbled to nothing, so that no trace is left to show that they ever even existed?* Not only does that which has been made with hands totter to the ground, not only is that which has been set in place by man's art and man's efforts overthrown by the passing days; nay, the peaks of mountains dissolve, whole tracts have settled, and places which once stood far from the sight of the sea are now covered by the waves. The mighty power of fires has eaten away the hills through whose sides they used to glow, and has levelled to the ground peaks which were once most lofty—the sailor's solace and his beacon. The works of nature herself are harassed; hence we ought to bear with untroubled minds the destruction of cities. They stand but to fall! This doom awaits them, one and all; it may be that some internal force, and blasts of violence which are tremendous because their way is blocked, will throw off the weight which holds then down; or that a whirlpool of raging currents, mightier because they are hidden in the bosom of the earth, will break through that which resists its power; or that the vehemence of flames will burst asunder the framework of the earth's crust; or that time, from which nothing is safe, will reduce them little by little; or that a pestilential climate will drive their inhabitants away and the mould will corrode their deserted walls. It would be tedious to recount all the ways by which fate may come; but this one thing I know: all the works of mortal man have been doomed to mortality, and in the midst of things which have been destined to die, we live!

Hence it is thoughts like these, and of this kind, which I am offering as consolation to our friend Liberalis, who burns with a love for his country that is beyond belief. Perhaps its destruction has been brought about only that it may be raised up again to a better destiny. Oftentimes a reverse has but made room for more prosperous fortune. Many structures have fallen only to rise to a greater height.

* For example, Mycenae and Tiryns.

Timagenes,[*] who had a grudge against Rome and her prosperity, used to say that the only reason he was grieved when conflagrations occurred in Rome was his knowledge that better buildings would arise than those which had gone down in the flames. And probably in this city of Lyons, too, all its citizens will earnestly strive that everything shall be rebuilt better in size and security than what they have lost. May it be built to endure and, under happier auspices, for a longer existence! This is indeed but the hundredth year since this colony was founded—not the limit even of a man's lifetime.[†] Led forth by Plancus, the natural advantages of its site have caused it to wax strong and reach the numbers which it contains today; and yet how many calamities of the greatest severity has it endured within the space of an old man's life!

Therefore let the mind be disciplined to understand and to endure its own lot, and let it have the knowledge that there is nothing which fortune does not dare—that she has the same jurisdiction over empires as over emperors, the same power over cities as over the citizens who dwell therein. We must not cry out at any of these calamities. Into such a world have we entered, and under such laws do we live. If you like it, obey; if not, depart whithersoever you wish. Cry out in anger if any unfair measures are taken with reference to you individually; but if this inevitable law is binding upon the highest and the lowest alike, be reconciled to fate, by which all things are dissolved. You should not estimate our worth by our funeral mounds or by these monuments of unequal size which line the road; their ashes level all men! We are unequal at birth, but are equal in death. What I say about cities I say also about their inhabitants: Ardea was

* Probably the writer, and intimate friend of Augustus, who began life in Rome as a captive from Egypt. Falling into disfavour with the Emperor, he took refuge with the malcontent Asinius Pollio at Tusculum, and subsequently died in the East. Cf. Seneca, *De Ira*, iii. 23.

† It was in 43 B.C. that Plancus led out the colonists who were chiefly Roman citizens driven from Vienna. Seneca would have been more accurate had he said "one hundred and eighth (or seventh)." Buecheler and Schultess would (unnecessarily) emend to read *centesimus septimus*. But Seneca was using round numbers.

captured as well as Rome.* The great founder of human law has not made distinctions between us on the basis of high lineage or of illustrious names, except while we live. When, however, we come to the end which awaits mortals, he says: "Depart, ambition! To all creatures that burden the earth let one and the same† law apply!" For enduring all things, we are equal; no one is more frail than another, no one more certain of his own life on the morrow.

Alexander, king of Macedon, began to study geometry;‡ unhappy man, because he would thereby learn how puny was that earth of which he had seized but a fraction! Unhappy man, I repeat, because he was bound to understand that he was bearing a false title. For who can be "great" in that which is puny? The lessons which were being taught him were intricate and could be learned only by assiduous application; they were not the kind to be comprehended by a madman, who let his thoughts range beyond the ocean.§ "Teach me something easy!" he cries; but his teacher answers: "These things are the same for all, as hard for one as for another." Imagine that nature is saying to us: "Those things of which you complain are the same for all. I cannot give anything easier to any man, but whoever wishes will make things easier for himself." In what way? By equanimity. You must suffer pain, and thirst, and hunger, and old age too, if a longer stay among men shall be granted you; you must be sick, and you must suffer loss and death. Nevertheless, you should not believe those whose noisy clamour surrounds you; none of these things is an evil, none is beyond your power to bear, or is burdensome. It is only

---

* Ardea, the earliest capital of Latium, and Rome, the present capital of the empire. Seneca probably refers to Ardea's capture and destruction by the Samnites in the fourth century; Rome was captured by the Celts in 390 B.C. The former greatness of Ardea was celebrated by Vergil, *Aeneid*, vii. 411 ff.:
et nunc magnum manet Ardea nomen,
Sed fortuna fuit.

† *Siremps* (or *sirempse*—Plaut. *Amph.* 73), an ancient legal term, is derived by Festus from *similis re ipsa*; but Corssen explains it as from *sic rem pse.*

‡ i.e., surveying. See Ep. lxxxviii. 10.

§ i.e., Ὠκεανός, the stream which encircles the earth.

by common opinion that there is anything formidable in them. Your fearing death is therefore like your fear of gossip. But what is more foolish than a man afraid of words? Our friend Demetrius* is wont to put it cleverly when he says: "For me the talk of ignorant men is like the rumblings which issue from the belly. For," he adds, "what difference does it make to me whether such rumblings come from above or from below?" What madness it is to be afraid of disrepute in the judgment of the disreputable! Just as you have had no cause for shrinking in terror from the talk of men, so you have no cause now to shrink from these things, which you would never fear had not their talk forced fear upon you. Does it do any harm to a good man to be besmirched by unjust gossip? Then let not this sort of thing damage death, either, in our estimation; death also is in bad odour. But no one of those who malign death has made trial of it.

Meanwhile it is foolhardy to condemn that of which you are ignorant. This one thing, however, you do know—that death is helpful to many, that it sets many free from tortures, want, ailments, sufferings, and weariness. We are in the power of nothing when once we have death in our own power! Farewell.

---

* This plain-living, plain-speaking philosopher appears also in Epp. xx. 9 and lxii. 3. Seneca refers to him as *seminudum, quanto minus quam stramentis incubantem.*

VOLUME
3

LETTER CIV

ON CARE OF HEALTH AND PEACE OF MIND

I have run off to my villa at Nomentum, for what purpose, do you suppose? To escape the city? No; to shake off a fever which was surely working its way into my system. It had already got a grip upon me. My physician kept insisting that when the circulation was upset and irregular, disturbing the natural poise, the disease was under way. I therefore ordered my carriage to be made ready at once, and insisted on departing, in spite of my wife Paulina's* efforts to stop me; for I remembered my master Gallio's† words, when he began to develop a fever in Achaia and took ship at once, insisting that the disease was not of the body but of the place. That is what I remarked to my dear Paulina, who always urges me to

* Pompeia Paulina, the second wife of Seneca; cf. Tac. *Ann.* xv. 60. Though much younger than her husband, she was a model of devotion, and remained loyal to him through all the Neronian persecution.

† Elder brother of Seneca, whose name before his adoption by Lucius Iunius Gallio was Annaeus Novatus. He was governor of Achaia from A.D. July 1, 51 to July 1, 52. See *Acts* xviii. 11 ff., and Duff, *Three Dialogues of Seneca*, p. xliii.

take care of my health. I know that her very life-breath comes and goes with my own, and I am beginning, in my solicitude for her, to be solicitous for myself. And although old age has made me braver to bear many things, I am gradually losing this boon that old age bestows. For it comes into my mind that in this old man there is a youth also, and youth needs tenderness. Therefore, since I cannot prevail upon her to love me any more heroically, she prevails upon me to cherish myself more carefully. For one must indulge genuine emotions; sometimes, even in spite of weighty reasons, the breath of life must be called back and kept at our very lips even at the price of great suffering, for the sake of those whom we hold dear; because the good man should not live as long as it pleases him, but as long as he ought. He who does not value his wife, or his friend, highly enough to linger longer in life—he who obstinately persists in dying—is a voluptuary.

The soul should also enforce this command upon itself whenever the needs of one's relatives require; it should pause and humour those near and dear, not only when it desires, but even when it has begun, to die. It gives proof of a great heart to return to life for the sake of others; and noble men have often done this. But this procedure also, I believe, indicates the highest type of kindness: that although the greatest advantage of old age is the opportunity to be more negligent regarding self-preservation and to use life more adventurously, one should watch over one's old age with still greater care if one knows that such action is pleasing, useful, or desirable in the eyes of a person whom one holds dear. This is also a source of no mean joy and profit; for what is sweeter than to be so valued by one's wife that one becomes more valuable to oneself for this reason? Hence my dear Paulina is able to make me responsible, not only for her fears, but also for my own.

So you are curious to know the outcome of this prescription of travel? As soon as I escaped from the oppressive atmosphere of the city, and from that awful odour of reeking kitchens which, when in use, pour forth a ruinous mess of steam and soot, I perceived at once that my health was mending. And how much stronger do you think I felt when I reached my vineyards! Being, so to speak, let out to pasture, I regularly walked into my meals! So I am my old self again, feeling now no wavering languor in my system, and no sluggishness in my brain. I am beginning to work with all my energy.

But the mere place avails little for this purpose, unless the mind is fully master of itself, and can, at its pleasure, find seclusion even in the midst of business; the man, however, who is always selecting resorts and hunting for leisure, will find something to distract his mind in every place. Socrates is reported to have replied, when a certain person complained of having received no benefit from his travels: "It serves you right! You travelled in your own company!"* O what a blessing it would be for some men to wander away from themselves! As it is, they cause themselves vexation, worry, demoralization, and fear! What profit is there in crossing the sea and in going from one city to another? If you would escape your troubles, you need not another place but another personality. Perhaps you have reached Athens, or perhaps Rhodes; choose any state you fancy, how does it matter what its character may be? You will be bringing to it your own.

Suppose that you hold wealth to be a good: poverty will then distress you, and,—which is most pitiable,—it will be an imaginary poverty. For you may be rich, and nevertheless, because your neighbour is richer, you suppose yourself to be poor exactly by the same amount in which you fall short of your neighbour. You may deem official position a good; you will be vexed at another's appointment or re-appointment to the consulship; you will be jealous whenever you see a name several times in the state records. Your ambition will be so frenzied that you will regard yourself last in the race if there is anyone in front of you. Or you may rate death as the worst of evils, although there is really no evil therein except that which precedes death's coming—fear. You will be frightened out of your wits, not only by

---

* Cf. Ep. x. 1 "*Mecum loquor.*" "*Cave, rogo, et diligenter adtende; cum homine malo loqueris.*"

real, but by fancied dangers, and will be tossed for ever on the sea of illusion. What benefit will it be to

> Have threaded all the towns of Argolis,
> A fugitive through midmost press of foes?*

For peace itself will furnish further apprehension. Even in the midst of safety you will have no confidence if your mind has once been given a shock; once it has acquired the habit of blind panic, it is incapable of providing even for its own safety. For it does not avoid danger, but runs away. Yet we are more exposed to danger when we turn our backs.

You may judge it the most grievous of ills to lose any of those you love; while all the same this would be no less foolish than weeping because the trees which charm your eye and adorn your home lose their foliage. Regard everything that pleases you as if it were a flourishing plant; make the most of it while it is in leaf, for different plants at different seasons must fall and die. But just as the loss of leaves is a light thing, because they are born afresh, so it is with the loss of those whom you love and regard as the delight of your life; for they can be replaced even though they cannot be born afresh. "New friends, however, will not be the same." No, nor will you yourself remain the same; you change with every day and every hour. But in other men you more readily see what time plunders; in your own case the change is hidden, because it will not take place visibly. Others are snatched from sight; we ourselves are being stealthily filched away from ourselves. You will not think about any of these problems, nor will you apply remedies to these wounds. You will of your own volition be sowing a crop of trouble by alternate hoping and despairing. If you are wise, mingle these two elements: do not hope without despair, or despair without hope.

What benefit has travel of itself ever been able to give anyone? No restraint upon pleasure, no bridling of desire, no checking of bad

* Vergil, *Aen.* iii. 282 f.

temper, no crushing of the wild assaults of passion, no opportunity to rid the soul of evil. Travelling cannot give us judgment, or shake off our errors; it merely holds our attention for a moment by a certain novelty, as children pause to wonder at something unfamiliar. Besides, it irritates us, through the wavering of a mind which is suffering from an acute attack of sickness; the very motion makes it more fitful and nervous. Hence the spots we had sought most eagerly we quit still more eagerly, like birds that flit and are off as soon as they have alighted. What travel will give is familiarity with other nations: it will reveal to you mountains of strange shape, or unfamiliar tracts of plain, or valleys that are watered by ever-flowing springs, or the characteristics of some river that comes to our attention. We observe how the Nile rises and swells in summer, or how the Tigris disappears, runs underground through hidden spaces, and then appears with unabated sweep; or how the Maeander,* that oft-rehearsed theme and plaything of the poets, turns in frequent bendings, and often in winding comes close to its own channel before resuming its course. But this sort of information will not make better or sounder men of us.†

We ought rather to spend our time in study, and to cultivate those who are masters of wisdom, learning something which has been investigated, but not settled; by this means the mind can be relieved of a most wretched serfdom, and won over to freedom. Indeed, as long as you are ignorant of what you should avoid or seek, or of what is necessary or superfluous, or of what is right or wrong, you will not be travelling, but merely wandering. There will be no benefit to you in this hurrying to and fro; for you are travelling with your emotions and are followed by your afflictions. Would that they were indeed following you! In that case, they would be farther away; as it is, you are carrying and not leading them. Hence they press about you on all sides, continually chafing and annoying you. It is medicine, not scenery, for which the sick man must go

* See Index of Proper Names.

† Although Seneca was deeply interested in such matters, as is proved by Ep. lxxix., the *Naturales Quaestiones*, and an early work on the geography of Egypt.

a-searching. Suppose that someone has broken a leg or dislocated a joint: he does not take carriage or ship for other regions, but he calls in the physician to set the fractured limb, or to move it back to its proper place in the socket. What then? When the spirit is broken or wrenched in so many places, do you think that change of place can heal it? The complaint is too deep-seated to be cured by a journey. Travel does not make a physician or an orator; no art is acquired by merely living in a certain place.

Where lies the truth, then? Can wisdom, the greatest of all the arts, be picked up on a journey? I assure you, travel as far as you like, you can never establish yourself beyond the reach of desire, beyond the reach of bad temper, or beyond the reach of fear; had it been so, the human race would long ago have banded together and made a pilgrimage to the spot. Such ills, as long as you carry with you their causes, will load you down and worry you to skin and bone in your wanderings over land and sea. Do you wonder that it is of no use to run away from them? That from which you are running, is within you. Accordingly, reform your own self, get the burden off your own shoulders, and keep within safe limits the cravings which ought to be removed. Wipe out from your soul all trace of sin. If you would enjoy your travels, make healthy the companion of your travels. As long as this companion is avaricious and mean, greed will stick to you; and while you consort with an overbearing man, your puffed-up ways will also stick close. Live with a hangman, and you will never be rid of your cruelty. If an adulterer be your club-mate, he will kindle the baser passions. If you would be stripped of your faults leave far behind you the patterns of the faults. The miser, the swindler, the bully, the cheat, who will do you much harm merely by being near you, are *within* you.

Change therefore to better associations: live with the Catos, with Laelius, with Tubero. Or, if you enjoy living with Greeks also, spend your time with Socrates and with Zeno: the former will show you how to die if it be necessary; the latter how to die before it is necessary. Live with Chrysippus, with Posidonius:[*] they will make you acquainted with things earthly and things heavenly; they will bid you work hard over something more than neat turns of language and phrases mouthed forth for the entertainment of listeners; they will bid you be stout of heart and rise superior to threats. The only harbour safe from the seething storms of this life is scorn of the future, a firm stand, a readiness to receive Fortune's missiles full in the breast, neither skulking nor turning the back. Nature has brought us forth brave of spirit, and, as she has implanted in certain animals a spirit of ferocity, in others craft, in others terror, so she has gifted us with an aspiring and lofty spirit, which prompts us to seek a life of the greatest honour, and not of the greatest security, that most resembles the soul of the universe, which it follows and imitates as far as our mortal steps permit. This spirit thrusts itself forward, confident of commendation and esteem. It is superior to all, monarch of all it surveys; hence it should be subservient to nothing, finding no task too heavy, and nothing strong enough to weigh down the shoulders of a man.

Shapes dread to look upon, of toil or death[†]

are not in the least dreadful, if one is able to look upon them with unflinching gaze, and is able to pierce the shadows. Many a sight that is held a terror in the night-time, is turned to ridicule by day. "Shapes dread to look upon, of toil or death": our Vergil has excellently said that these shapes are dread, not in reality, but only "to look upon"—in other words, they seem terrible, but are not. And in these visions what is there, I say, as fear-inspiring as rumour has proclaimed? Why, pray, my dear Lucilius, should a man fear toil, or a mortal death? Countless cases occur to my mind of men who think that what they

---

* These men are patterns or interpreters of the virtues. The first-named three represent courage, justice, and self-restraint respectively. Socrates is the ideal wise man, Zeno, Chrysippus, and Posidonus are in turn the founder, the classifier, and the modernizer of Stoicism.

† *Aeneid*, vi. 277.

themselves are unable to do is impossible, who maintain that we utter words which are too big for man's nature to carry out. But how much more highly do I think of these men! They can do these things, but decline to do them. To whom that ever tried have these tasks proved false? To what man did they not seem easier in the doing? Our lack of confidence is not the result of difficulty; the difficulty comes from our lack of confidence.

If, however, you desire a pattern, take Socrates, a long-suffering old man, who was sea-tossed amid every hardship and yet was unconquered both by poverty (which his troubles at home made more burdensome) and by toil, including the drudgery of military service. He was much tried at home, whether we think of his wife, a woman of rough manners and shrewish tongue, or of the children whose intractability showed them to be more like their mother than their father.[*] And if you consider the facts, he lived either in time of war, or under tyrants, or under a democracy, which is more cruel than wars and tyrants. The war lasted for twenty-seven years;[†] then the state became the victim of the Thirty Tyrants, of whom many were his personal enemies. At the last came that climax of condemnation under the gravest of charges: they accused him of disturbing the state religion and corrupting the youth,[‡] for they declared that he had influenced the youth to defy the gods, to defy the council, and to defy the state in general. Next came the prison, and the cup of poison.[§] But all these measures changed the soul of Socrates so little that they did not even change his features. What wonderful and rare distinction! He maintained this attitude up to the very end, and no man ever saw Socrates too much elated or too much depressed. Amid all the disturbance of Fortune, he was undisturbed.

---

* At first a sculptor, then an independent seeker after truth, whose wants were reduced to a minimum. Husband of the shrewish Xanthippe and father of the dull and worthless Lamprocles. Brave soldier at Potidaea, Delium, and Amphipolis.

† 431-404 B.C. (the Peloponnesian War).

‡ See Plato's *Apology*, 23 D. They had previously aimed at him a law forbidding the teaching of dialectic.

§ 399 B.C.

Do you desire another case? Take that of the younger Marcus Cato, with whom Fortune dealt in a more hostile and more persistent fashion. But he withstood her, on all occasions, and in his last moments, at the point of death, showed that a brave man can live in spite of Fortune, can die in spite of her. His whole life was passed either in civil warfare, or under a political regime which was soon to breed civil war. And you may say that he, just as much as Socrates, declared allegiance to liberty in the midst of slavery—unless perchance you think that Pompey, Caesar, and Crassus[*] were the allies of liberty! No one ever saw Cato change, no matter how often the state changed: he kept himself the same in all circumstances—in the praetorship,[†] in defeat, under accusation,[‡] in his province, on the platform, in the army, in death. Furthermore, when the republic was in a crisis of terror, when Caesar was on one side with ten embattled legions at his call, aided by so many foreign nations, and when Pompey was on the other, satisfied to stand alone against all comers, and when the citizens were leaning towards either Caesar or Pompey, Cato alone established a definite party for the Republic. If you would obtain a mental picture of that period, you may imagine on one side the people and the whole proletariat eager for revolution—on the other the senators and knights, the chosen and honoured men of the commonwealth; and there were left between them but these two—the Republic and Cato.

I tell you, you will marvel when you see

> Atreus' son, and Priam, and Achilles, wroth at both.[§]

Like Achilles, he scorns and disarms each faction. And this is the vote which he casts concerning them both: "If Caesar wins, I slay myself; if Pompey, I go into exile." What was there for a man to fear who,

---

* Triumvirs in 60 B.C. and rivals in acquiring unconstitutional power.

† 54 B.C.

‡ Perhaps a reference to his mission in Cyprus (58-56 B.C.), and his subsequent arraignment by Clodius.

§ Vergil, *Aen.* i. 458.

whether in defeat or in victory, had assigned to himself a doom which might have been assigned to him by his enemies in their utmost rage? So he died by his own decision.

You see that man can endure toil: Cato, on foot, led an army through African deserts. You see that thirst can be endured: he marched over sun-baked hills, dragging the remains of a beaten army and with no train of supplies, undergoing lack of water and wearing a heavy suit of armour; always the last to drink of the few springs which they chanced to find. You see that honour, and dishonour too, can be despised: for they report that on the very day when Cato was defeated at the elections, he played a game of ball. You see also that man can be free from fear of those above him in rank: for Cato attacked Caesar and Pompey simultaneously, at a time when none dared fall foul of the one without endeavouring to oblige the other. You see that death can be scorned as well as exile: Cato inflicted exile upon himself and finally death,* and war all the while.

And so, if only we are willing to withdraw our necks from the yoke, we can keep as stout a heart against such terrors as these. But first and foremost, we must reject pleasures; they render us weak and womanish; they make great demands upon us, and, moreover, cause us to make great demands upon Fortune. Second, we must spurn wealth: wealth is the diploma of slavery. Abandon gold and silver, and whatever else is a burden upon our richly-furnished homes; liberty cannot be gained for nothing. If you set a high value on liberty, you must set a low value on everything else. Farewell.

---

* At Utica, in 46 B.C.

LETTER CV

ON FACING THE WORLD WITH CONFIDENCE

I shall now tell you certain things to which you should pay attention in order to live more safely. Do you however,—such is my judgment,—hearken to my precepts just as if I were counselling you to keep safe your health in your country-place at Ardea.

Reflect on the things which goad man into destroying man: you will find that they are hope, envy, hatred, fear, and contempt. Now, of all these, contempt is the least harmful, so much so that many have skulked behind it as a sort of cure. When a man despises you, he works you injury, to be sure, but he passes on; and no one persistently or of set purpose does hurt to a person whom he despises. Even in battle, prostrate soldiers are neglected: men fight with those who stand their ground. And you can avoid the envious hopes of the wicked so long as you have nothing which can stir the evil desires of others, and so long as you possess nothing remarkable. For people crave even little things, if these catch the attention or are of rare occurrence.

You will escape envy if you do not force yourself upon the public view, if you do not boast your possessions, if you understand how to enjoy things privately. Hatred comes either from running foul of others: and this can be avoided by never provoking anyone; or else it is uncalled for: and common-sense* will keep you safe from it. Yet it has been dangerous to many; some people have been hated without having had an enemy. As to not being feared, a moderate fortune and an easy disposition will guarantee you that; men should know that you are the sort of person who can be offended without danger; and your reconciliation should be easy and sure. Moreover, it is as troublesome to be feared at home as abroad; it is as bad to be feared by a slave as by a gentleman. For every one has strength enough to do you some harm. Besides, he who is feared, fears also; no one has been able to arouse terror and live in peace of mind.

Contempt remains to be discussed. He who has made this quality an adjunct of his own personality, who is despised because he wishes to be despised and not because he *must* be despised, has the measure of contempt under his control. Any inconveniences in this respect can be dispelled by honourable occupations and by friendships with men who have influence with an influential person; with these men it will profit you to engage but not to entangle yourself, lest the cure may cost you more than the risk. Nothing, however, will help you so much as keeping still—talking very little with others, and as much as may be with yourself. For there is a sort of charm about conversation, something very subtle and coaxing, which, like intoxication or love, draws secrets from us. No man will keep to himself what he hears. No one will tell another only as much as he has heard. And he who tells tales will tell names, too. Everyone has someone to whom he entrusts exactly what has been entrusted to him. Though he checks his own garrulity, and is content with one hearer, he will bring about him a nation, if that which was a secret shortly before becomes common talk.

---

* i.e., tact.

The most important contribution to peace of mind is never to do wrong. Those who lack self-control lead disturbed and tumultuous lives; their crimes are balanced by their fears, and they are never at ease. For they tremble after the deed, and they are embarrassed; their consciences do not allow them to busy themselves with other matters, and continually compel them to give an answer. Whoever expects punishment, receives it, but whoever deserves it, expects it. Where there is an evil conscience something may bring safety, but nothing can bring ease; for a man imagines that, even if he is not under arrest, he may soon be arrested. His sleep is troubled; when he speaks of another man's crime, he reflects upon his own, which seems to him not sufficiently blotted out, not sufficiently hidden from view. A wrongdoer sometimes has the luck to escape notice but never the assurance thereof. Farewell.

LETTER

CVII

ON OBEDIENCE TO THE UNIVERSAL WILL

Where is that common-sense of yours? Where that deftness in examining things? That greatness of soul? Have you come to be tormented by a trifle? Your slaves regarded your absorption in business as an opportunity for them to run away. Well, if your friends deceived you (for by all means let them have the name which we mistakenly bestowed upon them, and so call them, that they may incur more shame by not being such friends)—if your friends, I repeat, deceived you, all your affairs would lack something; as it is, you merely lack men who damaged your own endeavours and considered you burdensome to your neighbours. None of these things is unusual or unexpected. It is as nonsensical to be put out by such events as to complain of being spattered in the street or at getting befouled in the mud. The programme of life is the same as that of a bathing establishment, a crowd, or a journey: sometimes things will be thrown at you, and sometimes they will strike you by accident. Life is not a dainty business. You have started on a long journey; you are bound to slip, collide, fall, become weary, and cry out: "O for Death!"—or in other words, tell lies. At one stage you will leave a comrade behind you, at another you will bury someone, at another you will be apprehensive. It is amid stumblings of this sort that you must travel out this rugged journey.

Does one wish to die? Let the mind be prepared to meet everything; let it know that it has reached the heights round which the thunder plays. Let it know that it has arrived where –

> Grief and avenging Care have set their couch,
> And pallid sickness dwells, and drear Old Age.*

With such messmates must you spend your days. Avoid them you cannot, but despise them you can. And you will despise them, if you often take thought and anticipate the future. Everyone approaches courageously a danger which he has prepared himself to meet long before, and withstands even hardships if he has previously practised how to meet them. But, contrariwise, the unprepared are panic-stricken even at the most trifling things. We must see to it that nothing shall come upon us unforeseen. And since things are all the more serious when they are unfamiliar, continual reflection will give you the power, no matter what the evil may be, not to play the unschooled boy.

"My slaves have run away from me!" Yes, other men have been robbed, blackmailed, slain, betrayed, stamped under foot, attacked by poison or by slander; no matter what trouble you mention, it has happened to many. Again, there are manifold kinds of missiles which are hurled at us. Some are planted in us, some are being brandished and at this very moment are on the way, some which were destined for other men graze us instead. We should not manifest surprise at any sort of condition into which we are born, and which should be lamented by no one, simply because it is equally ordained for all. Yes, I say, equally ordained; for a man might have experienced even that which he has escaped. And an equal law consists, not of that which

---

* Vergil, *Aen.* vi. 274 f.

all have experienced, but of that which is laid down for all. Be sure to prescribe for your mind this sense of equity; we should pay without complaint the tax of our mortality.

Winter brings on cold weather; and we must shiver. Summer returns, with its heat; and we must sweat. Unseasonable weather upsets the health; and we must fall ill. In certain places we may meet with wild beasts, or with men who are more destructive than any beasts. Floods, or fires, will cause us loss. And we cannot change this order of things; but what we can do is to acquire stout hearts, worthy of good men, thereby courageously enduring chance and placing ourselves in harmony with Nature. And Nature moderates this world-kingdom which you see, by her changing seasons: clear weather follows cloudy; after a calm, comes the storm; the winds blow by turns; day succeeds night; some of the heavenly bodies rise, and some set. Eternity consists of opposites.

It is to this law that our souls must adjust themselves, this they should follow, this they should obey. Whatever happens, assume that it was bound to happen, and do not be willing to rail at Nature. That which you cannot reform, it is best to endure, and to attend uncomplainingly upon the God under whose guidance everything progresses; for it is a bad soldier who grumbles when following his commander. For this reason we should welcome our orders with energy and vigour, nor should we cease to follow the natural course of this most beautiful universe, into which all our future sufferings are woven.

Let us address Jupiter, the pilot of this world-mass, as did our great Cleanthes in those most eloquent lines—lines which I shall allow myself to render in Latin, after the example of the eloquent Cicero. If you like them, make the most of them; if they displease you, you will understand that I have simply been following the practice of Cicero:

Lead me, O Master of the lofty heavens,
My Father, whithersoever thou shalt wish.

I shall not falter, but obey with speed.
And though I would not, I shall go, and suffer,
In sin and sorrow what I might have done
In noble virtue. Aye, the willing soul
Fate leads, but the unwilling drags along.*

Let us live thus, and speak thus; let Fate find us ready and alert. Here is your great soul—the man who has given himself over to Fate; on the other hand, that man is a weakling and a degenerate who struggles and maligns the order of the universe and would rather reform the gods than reform himself. Farewell.

* Cleanthes, Frag. 527 von Arnim. In Epictetus (*Ench.* 53) these verses are assigned to Cleanthes (omitting the last line); while St. Augustine (*Civ. Dei.* v. 8) quotes them as Seneca's: *Annaei Senecae sunt, nisi fallor, hi versus.* Wilamowitz and others follow the latter view.

LETTER

CVIII

ON THE APPROACHES TO PHILOSOPHY

The topic about which you ask me is one of those where our only concern with knowledge is to have the knowledge. Nevertheless, because it does so far concern us, you are in a hurry; you are not willing to wait for the books which I am at this moment arranging for you, and which embrace the whole department of moral philosophy.* I shall send you the books at once; but I shall, before doing that, write and tell you how this eagerness to learn, with which I see you are aflame, should be regulated, so that it may not get in its own way. Things are not to be gathered at random; nor should they be greedily attacked in the mass; one will arrive at a knowledge of the whole by studying the parts. The burden should be suited to your strength, nor should you tackle more than you can adequately handle. Absorb not all that you wish, but all that you can hold. Only be of a sound mind, and then

* Cf. Ep. cvi. 2 *scis enim me moralem philosophiam velle conplecti*, etc.

you will be able to hold all that you wish. For the more the mind receives, the more does it expand.

This was the advice, I remember, which Attalus* gave me in the days when I practically laid siege to his class-room, the first to arrive and the last to leave. Even as he paced up and down, I would challenge him to various discussions; for he not only kept himself accessible to his pupils, but met them half-way. His words were: "The same purpose should possess both master and scholar—an ambition in the one case to promote, and in the other to progress." He who studies with a philosopher should take away with him some one good thing every day: he should daily return home a sounder man, or in the way to become sounder. And he will thus return; for it is one of the functions of philosophy to help not only those who study her, but those also who associate with her. He that walks in the sun, though he walk not for that purpose, must needs become sunburned. He who frequents the perfumer's shop and lingers even for a short time, will carry with him the scent of the place. And he who follows a philosopher is bound to derive some benefit therefrom, which will help him even though he be remiss. Mark what I say: "remiss," not "recalcitrant."

"What then?" you say, "do we not know certain men who have sat for many years at the feet of a philosopher and yet have not acquired the slightest tinge of wisdom?" Of course I know such men. There are indeed persevering gentlemen who stick at it; I do not call them pupils of the wise, but merely "squatters."† Certain of them come to hear and not to learn, just as we are attracted to the theatre to satisfy the pleasures of the ear, whether by a speech, or by a song, or by a play. This class, as you will see, constitutes a large part of the listeners, who regard the philosopher's lecture-room merely as a sort of lounging-place for their leisure. They do not set about to lay aside any faults there, or to receive a rule of life, by which they may test their characters;

* Seneca's first and most convincing teacher of Stoicism, to whom this letter is a tribute. The ablest of contemporary philosophers, he was banished during the reign of Tiberius. See Index of Proper Names.

† Literally "tenants," "lodgers," of a temporary sort.

they merely wish to enjoy to the full the delights of the ear. And yet some arrive even with notebooks, not to take down the matter, but only the words,* that they may presently repeat them to others with as little profit to these as they themselves received when they heard them. A certain number are stirred by high-sounding phrases, and adapt themselves to the emotions of the speaker with lively change of face and mind—just like the emasculated Phrygian priests† who are wont to be roused by the sound of the flute and go mad to order. But the true hearer is ravished and stirred by the beauty of the subject matter, not by the jingle of empty words. When a bold word has been uttered in defiance of death, or a saucy fling in defiance of Fortune, we take delight in acting straightway upon that which we have heard. Men are impressed by such words, and become what they are bidden to be, should but the impression abide in the mind, and should the populace, who discourage honourable things, not immediately lie in wait to rob them of this noble impulse; only a few can carry home the mental attitude with which they were inspired. It is easy to rouse a listener so that he will crave righteousness; for Nature has laid the foundations and planted the seeds of virtue in us all. And we are all born to these general privileges; hence, when the stimulus is added, the good spirit is stirred as if it were freed from bonds. Have you not noticed how the theatre re-echoes whenever any words are spoken whose truth we appreciate generally and confirm unanimously?

The poor lack much; the greedy man lacks all.‡
A greedy man does good to none; he does
Most evil to himself.§

---

* Cf. the dangers of such *lusoria* (Ep. xlviii. 8) and *a rebus studium transferendum est ad verba* (Ep. xl. 14).

† i.e., mendicant Galli, worshippers of Cybele, the Magna Mater.

‡ *Syri Sententiae*, Frag. 236 Ribbeck.

§ *Ib.*, Frag. 234 R.

At such verses as these, your meanest miser claps applause and rejoices to hear his own sins reviled. How much more do you think this holds true, when such things are uttered by a philosopher, when he introduces verses among his wholesome precepts, that he may thus make those verses sink more effectively into the mind of the neophyte! Cleanthes used to say:* "As our breath produces a louder sound when it passes through the long and narrow opening of the trumpet and escapes by a hole which widens at the end, even so the fettering rules of poetry clarify our meaning." The very same words are more carelessly received and make less impression upon us, when they are spoken in prose; but when metre is added and when regular prosody has compressed a noble idea, then the selfsame thought comes, as it were, hurtling with a fuller fling. We talk much about despising money, and we give advice on this subject in the lengthiest of speeches, that mankind may believe true riches to exist in the mind and not in one's bank account, and that the man who adapts himself to his slender means and makes himself wealthy on a little sum, is the truly rich man; but our minds are struck more effectively when a verse like this is repeated:

He needs but little who desires but little.

or,

He hath his wish, whose wish includeth naught
Save that which is enough.†

When we hear such words as these, we are led towards a confession of the truth.

Even men in whose opinion nothing is enough, wonder and applaud when they hear such words, and swear eternal hatred against money. When you see them thus disposed, strike home, keep at

* Frag. 487 von Arnim.

† Pall. Incert. Fab. 65 and 66 Ribbeck.

them, and charge them with this duty, dropping all double meanings, syllogisms, hair-splitting, and the other side-shows of ineffective smartness. Preach against greed, preach against high living; and when you notice that you have made progress and impressed the minds of your hearers, lay on still harder. You cannot imagine how much progress can be brought about by an address of that nature, when you are bent on curing your hearers and are absolutely devoted to their best interests. For when the mind is young, it may most easily be won over to desire what is honourable and upright; truth, if she can obtain a suitable pleader, will lay strong hands upon those who can still be taught, those who have been but superficially spoiled.

At any rate, when I used to hear Attalus denouncing sin, error, and the evils of life, I often felt sorry for mankind and regarded Attalus as a noble and majestic being,—above our mortal heights. He called himself a king, but I thought him more than a king, because he was entitled to pass judgment on kings. And in truth, when he began to uphold poverty, and to show what a useless and dangerous burden was everything that passed the measure of our need, I often desired to leave his lecture-room a poor man. Whenever he castigated our pleasure-seeking lives, and extolled personal purity, moderation in diet, and a mind free from unnecessary, not to speak of unlawful, pleasures, the desire came upon me to limit my food and drink. And that is why some of these habits have stayed with me, Lucilius. For I had planned my whole life with great resolves. And later, when I returned to the duties of a citizen, I did indeed keep a few of these good resolutions. That is why I have forsaken oysters and mushrooms for ever: since they are not really food, but are relishes to bully the sated stomach into further eating, as is the fancy of gourmands and those who stuff themselves beyond their powers of digestion: down with it quickly, and up with it quickly! That is why I have also throughout my life avoided perfumes; because the best scent for the

---

* A characteristic Stoic paradox.

person is no scent at all.* That is why my stomach is unacquainted with wine. That is why throughout my life I have shunned the bath, and have believed that to emaciate the body and sweat it into thinness is at once unprofitable and effeminate. Other resolutions have been broken, but after all in such a way that, in cases where I ceased to practice abstinence, I have observed a limit which is indeed next door to abstinence; perhaps it is even a little more difficult, because it is easier for the will to cut off certain things utterly than to use them with restraint.

Inasmuch as I have begun to explain to you how much greater was my impulse to approach philosophy in my youth than to continue it in my old age, I shall not be ashamed to tell you what ardent zeal Pythagoras inspired in me. Sotion† used to tell me why Pythagoras abstained from animal food, and why, in later times, Sextius did also. In each case, the reason was different, but it was in each case a noble reason. Sextius believed that man had enough sustenance without resorting to blood, and that a habit of cruelty is formed whenever butchery is practised for pleasure. Moreover, he thought we should curtail the sources of our luxury; he argued that a varied diet was contrary to the laws of health, and was unsuited to our constitutions. Pythagoras, on the other hand, held that all beings were inter-related, and that there was a system of exchange between souls which transmigrated from one bodily shape into another. If one may believe him, no soul perishes or ceases from its functions at all, except for a tiny interval—when it is being poured from one body into another. We may question at what time and after what seasons of change the soul returns to man, when it has wandered through many a dwelling-place; but meantime, he made men fearful of guilt and parricide, since they might be, without knowing it, attacking the soul of a parent and injuring it with knife or with teeth—if, as is possible, the related spirit be dwelling temporarily in this bit of flesh! When Sotion had set forth this doctrine, supplementing it with his own

* An almost proverbial saying; cf. the *recte olet ubi nil olet* of Plautus (*Most.* 273), Cicero, and Martial.

† Pythagorean philosopher of the Augustine age, and one of Seneca's early teachers.

proofs, he would say: "You do not believe that souls are assigned, first to one body and then to another, and that our so-called death is merely a change of abode? You do not believe that in cattle, or in wild beasts, or in creatures of the deep, the soul of him who was once a man may linger? You do not believe that nothing on this earth is annihilated, but only changes its haunts? And that animals also have cycles of progress and, so to speak, an orbit for their souls, no less than the heavenly bodies, which revolve in fixed circuits? Great men have put faith in this idea; therefore, while holding to your own view, keep the whole question in abeyance in your mind. If the theory is true, it is a mark of purity to refrain from eating flesh; if it be false, it is economy. And what harm does it do to you to give such credence? I am merely depriving you of food which sustains lions and vultures."

I was imbued with this teaching, and began to abstain from animal food; at the end of a year the habit was as pleasant as it was easy. I was beginning to feel that my mind was more active; though I would not today positively state whether it really was or not. Do you ask how I came to abandon the practice? It was this way: The days of my youth coincided with the early part of the reign of Tiberius Caesar. Some foreign rites were at that time* being inaugurated, and abstinence from certain kinds of animal food was set down as a proof of interest in the strange cult. So at the request of my father, who did not fear prosecution, but who detested philosophy, I returned to my previous habits; and it was no very hard matter to induce me to dine more comfortably.

Attalus used to recommend a pillow which did not give in to the body; and now, old as I am, I use one so hard that it leaves no trace after pressure. I have mentioned all this in order to show you how zealous neophytes are with regard to their first impulses towards the highest ideals, provided that some one does his part in exhorting them and in kindling their ardour. There are indeed mistakes made, through the fault of our advisers, who teach us how to debate and not how to

* A.D. 19. Cf. Tacitus, *Ann.* ii. 85 *actum de sacris Aegyptiis Iudaicisque pellendis.*

live; there are also mistakes made by the pupils, who come to their teachers to develop, not their souls, but their wits. Thus the study of wisdom has become the study of words.

Now it makes a great deal of difference what you have in mind when you approach a given subject. If a man is to be a scholar,* and is examining the works of Vergil, he does not interpret the noble passage

Time flies away, and cannot be restored†

in the following sense: "We must wake up; unless we hasten, we shall be left behind. Time rolls swiftly ahead, and rolls us with it. We are hurried along ignorant of our destiny; we arrange all our plans for the future, and on the edge of a precipice are at our ease." Instead of this, he brings to our attention how often Vergil, in speaking of the rapidity of time, uses the word "flies" (*fugit*).

The choicest days of hapless human life
Fly first; disease and bitter eld succeed,
And toil, till harsh death rudely snatches all.‡

He who considers these lines in the spirit of a philosopher comments on the words in their proper sense: "Vergil never says, 'Time goes,' but 'Time flies,' because the latter is the quickest kind of movement, and in every case our best days are the first to be snatched away; why, then, do we hesitate to bestir ourselves so that we may be able to keep pace with this swiftest of all swift things?" The good flies past and the bad takes its place. Just as the purest wine flows from the top of the jar and the thickest dregs settle at the bottom; so in our human life, that which is best comes first. Shall we allow other men to quaff the best, and keep

* In this passage Seneca differs (as also in Ep. lxxxviii. § 3) from the earlier Roman idea of *grammaticus* as *poetarum interpres*: he is thinking of one who deals with verbal expressions and the meaning of words. Cf. Sandys, *Hist. Class. Schol.* i. 8 ff.

† *Georg.* iii. 284.

‡ *Georg.* iii. 66 ff.

the dregs for ourselves? Let this phrase cleave to your soul; you should be satisfied thereby as if it were uttered by an oracle:

Each choicest day of hapless human life
Flies first.

Why "choicest day"? Because what's to come is unsure. Why "choicest day"? Because in our youth we are able to learn; we can bend to nobler purposes minds that are ready and still pliable; because this is the time for work, the time for keeping our minds busied in study and in exercising our bodies with useful effort; for that which remains is more sluggish and lacking in spirit—nearer the end.

Let us therefore strive with all courage, omitting attractions by the way; let us struggle with a single purpose, lest, when we are left behind, we comprehend too late the speed of quick-flying time, whose course we cannot stay. Let every day, as soon as it comes, be welcome as being the choicest, and let it be made our own possession. We must catch that which flees. Now he who scans with a scholar's eye the lines I have just quoted, does not reflect that our first days are the best because disease is approaching and old age weighs upon us and hangs over our heads while we are still thinking about our youth. He thinks rather of Vergil's usual collocation of *disease and eld*; and indeed rightly. For old age is a disease which we cannot cure. "Besides," he says to himself, "think of the epithet that accompanies *eld*; Vergil calls it *bitter*,"—

Disease and bitter eld succeed.

And elsewhere Vergil says:

There dwelleth pale disease and bitter eld.*

There is no reason why you should marvel that each man can

---

* *Aen.* vi. 275.

collect from the same source suitable matter for his own studies; for in the same meadow the cow grazes, the dog hunts the hare, and the stork the lizard. When Cicero's book *On the State* is opened by a philologist, a scholar, or a follower of philosophy, each man pursues his investigation in his own way. The philosopher wonders that so much could have been said therein against justice. The philologist takes up the same book and comments on the text as follows: There were two Roman kings—one without a father and one without a mother. For we cannot settle who was Servius's mother, and Ancus, the grandson of Numa, has no father on record.[*] The philologist also notes that the officer whom we call dictator, and about whom we read in our histories under that title, was named in old times the *magister populi*; such is the name existing today in the augural records, proved by the fact that he whom the dictator chose as second in command was called *magister equitum*. He will remark, too, that Romulus met his end during an eclipse; that there was an appeal to the people even from the kings (this is so stated in the pontiffs' register and is the opinion of others, including Fenestella[†]). When the scholar unrolls this same volume, he puts down in his notebook the forms of words, noting that *reapse*, equivalent to *re ipsa*, is used by Cicero, and *sepse*[‡] just as frequently, which means *se ipse*. Then he turns his attention to changes in current usage. Cicero, for example, says: "Inasmuch as we are summoned back from the very calx by his interruption." Now the line in the circus which we call the *creta*[§] was called the calx by men of old time. Again, he puts together some verses by Ennius, especially those which referred to Africanus:

> A man to whom nor friend nor foe could give
> Due meed for all his efforts and his deed.[¶]

* Cicero, *De re publica*, ii. 18 *Numae Pompili nepos ex filia rex a populo est Ancus Marcius constitutus . . . siquidem istius regis matrem habemus, ignoramus patrem.*

† Fl. in the Augustan Age. *Provocatio* is defined by Greenidge (*Rom. Pub. Life*. p. 64) as "a challenge by an accused to a magistrate to appear before another tribunal."

‡ A suffix, probably related to the intensive *-pte*

§ Literally, the chalk-marked, or lime-marked, goal-line.

¶ Vahlen's *Ennius*, p. 215.

From this passage the scholar declares that he infers the word *opem* to have meant formerly not merely *assistance*, but *efforts*. For Ennius must mean that neither friend nor foe could pay Scipio a reward worthy of his efforts. Next, he congratulates himself on finding the source of Vergil's words:

> Over whose head the mighty gate of Heaven
> Thunders,*

remarking that Ennius stole the idea from Homer, and Vergil from Ennius. For there is a couplet by Ennius, preserved in this same book of Cicero's, *On the State*:†

> If it be right for a mortal to scale the regions of Heaven,
> Then the huge gate of the sky opens in glory to *me*.

But that I, too, while engaged upon another task, may not slip into the department of the philologist or the scholar, my advice is this—that all study of philosophy and all reading should be applied to the idea of living the happy life, that we should not hunt out archaic or far-fetched words and eccentric metaphors and figures of speech, but that we should seek precepts which will help us, utterances of courage and spirit which may at once be turned into facts. We should so learn them that words may become deeds. And I hold that no man has treated mankind worse than he who has studied philosophy as if it were some marketable trade, who lives in a different manner from that which he advises. For those who are liable to every fault which they castigate advertise themselves as patterns of useless training. A teacher like that can help me no more than a sea-sick pilot can be efficient in a storm. He must hold the tiller when the waves are tossing him; he must wrestle, as it were, with the sea; he must furl his

* *Georg.* iii. 260 f.

† Vahlen's *Ennius*, p. 216.

sails when the storm rages; what good is a frightened and vomiting steersman to *me*? And how much greater, think you, is the storm of life than that which tosses any ship! One must steer, not talk.

All the words that these men utter and juggle before a listening crowd, belong to others. They have been spoken by Plato, spoken by Zeno, spoken by Chrysippus or by Posidonius, and by a whole host of Stoics as numerous as excellent. I shall show you how men can prove their words to be their own: it is by doing what they have been talking about. Since therefore I have given you the message I wished to pass on to you, I shall now satisfy your craving and shall reserve for a new letter a complete answer to your summons; so that you may not approach in a condition of weariness a subject which is thorny and which should be followed with an attentive and painstaking ear. Farewell.

LETTER CXIV

ON STYLE AS A MIRROR OF CHARACTER

You have been asking me why, during certain periods, a degenerate style of speech comes to the fore, and how it is that men's wits have gone downhill into certain vices—in such a way that exposition at one time has taken on a kind of puffed-up strength, and at another has become mincing and modulated like the music of a concert piece. You wonder why sometimes bold ideas—bolder than one could believe—have been held in favour, and why at other times one meets with phrases that are disconnected and full of innuendo, into which one must read more meaning than was intended to meet the ear. Or why there have been epochs which maintained the right to a shameless use of metaphor. For answer, here is a phrase which you are wont to notice in the popular speech—one which the Greeks have made into a proverb: "Man's speech is just like his life."* Exactly as each

* οἷος ὁ βίος, τοιοῦτος καὶ ὁ λόγος. The saying is referred to Socrates by Cicero (*Tusc.* v. 47).

individual man's actions seem to speak, so people's style of speaking often reproduces the general character of the time, if the morale of the public has relaxed and has given itself over to effeminacy. Wantonness in speech is proof of public luxury, if it is popular and fashionable, and not confined to one or two individual instances. A man's ability* cannot possibly be of one sort and his soul of another. If his soul be wholesome, well-ordered, serious, and restrained, his ability also is sound and sober. Conversely, when the one degenerates, the other is also contaminated. Do you not see that if a man's soul has become sluggish, his limbs drag and his feet move indolently? If it is womanish, that one can detect the effeminacy by his very gait? That a keen and confident soul quickens the step? That madness in the soul, or anger (which resembles madness), hastens our bodily movements from walking to rushing?

And how much more do you think that this affects one's ability, which is entirely interwoven with the soul,—being moulded thereby, obeying its commands, and deriving therefrom its laws! How Maecenas lived is too well-known for present comment. We know how he walked, how effeminate he was, and how he desired to display himself; also, how unwilling he was that his vices should escape notice. What, then? Does not the looseness of his speech match his ungirt attire?† Are his habits, his attendants, his house, his wife,‡ any less clearly marked than his words? He would have been a man of great powers, had he set himself to his task by a straight path, had he not shrunk from making himself understood, had he not been so loose in his style of speech also. You will therefore see that his eloquence was that of an intoxicated man—twisting, turning, unlimited in its slackness.

* i.e., that inborn quality which is compounded of character and intelligence.

† Cf. Suetonius, *Aug.* 86, where the Emperor *Maecenatem suum, cuius "myrobrechis," ut ait, "cincinnos"* ("unguent-dripping curls" (Rolfe)) *usque quaque persequitur et imitando per iocum irridet.* Augustus here refers especially to the style of Maecenas as a writer.

‡ Terentia. For her charms see Horace, *Od.* ii. 12; for her faults see *De prov.* iii. 10, where Seneca calls her "petulant."

What is more unbecoming than the words:[*] "A stream and a bank covered with long-tressed woods"? And see how "men plough the channel with boats and, turning up the shallows, leave gardens behind them." Or, "He curls his lady-locks, and bills and coos, and starts a-sighing, like a forest lord who offers prayers with down-bent neck." Or, "An unregenerate crew, they search out people at feasts, and assail households with the wine-cup, and, by hope, exact death." Or, "A Genius could hardly bear witness to his own festival"; or "threads of tiny tapers and crackling meal"; "mothers or wives clothing the hearth."

Can you not at once imagine, on reading through these words, that this was the man who always paraded through the city with a flowing[†] tunic? For even if he was discharging the absent emperor's duties, he was always in undress when they asked him for the countersign. Or that this was the man who, as judge on the bench, or as an orator, or at any public function, appeared with his cloak wrapped about his head, leaving only the ears exposed,[‡] like the millionaire's runaway slaves in the farce? Or that this was the man who, at the very time when the state was embroiled in civil strife, when the city was in difficulties and under martial law, was attended in public by two eunuchs—both of them more men than himself? Or that this was the man who had but one wife, and yet was married countless times?[§] These words of his, put together so faultily, thrown off so carelessly, and arranged in such marked contrast to the usual practice, declare that the character of their writer was equally unusual, unsound, and eccentric. To be sure, we bestow upon him the highest praise for his humanity; he was sparing with the sword and refrained from bloodshed;[¶] and he made a show of his power only in the course of his loose living; but he spoiled, by such preposterous finickiness of style, this genuine praise, which was his

* Maecenas, Frag. 11 Lunderstedt.

† Instead of properly girt up—a mark of slackness.

‡ For a similar mark of slovenliness, in Pompey's freedman Demetrius, see Plutarch, *Pompey*, xl. 4.

§ i.e., often repulsed by his wife Terentia, and then restored to grace.

¶ i.e., the "ring" of onlookers, the "pit."

due. For it is evident that he was not really gentle, but effeminate, as is proved by his misleading word-order, his inverted expressions, and the surprising thoughts which frequently contain something great, but in finding expression have become nerveless. One would say that his head was turned by too great success.

This fault is due sometimes to the man, and sometimes to his epoch. When prosperity has spread luxury far and wide, men begin by paying closer attention to their personal appearance. Then they go crazy over furniture. Next, they devote attention to their houses—how to take up more space with them, as if they were country-houses, how to make the walls glitter with marble that has been imported over seas, how to adorn a roof with gold, so that it may match the brightness of the inlaid floors. After that, they transfer their exquisite taste to the dinner-table, attempting to court approval by novelty and by departures from the customary order of dishes, so that the courses which we are accustomed to serve at the end of the meal may be served first, and so that the departing guests may partake of the kind of food which in former days was set before them on their arrival.

When the mind has acquired the habit of scorning the usual things of life, and regarding as mean that which was once customary, it begins to hunt for novelties in speech also; now it summons and displays obsolete and old-fashioned words; now it coins even unknown words or misshapes them; and now a bold and frequent metaphorical usage is made a special feature of style, according to the fashion which has just become prevalent. Some cut the thoughts short, hoping to make a good impression by leaving the meaning in doubt and causing the hearer to suspect his own lack of wit. Some dwell upon them and lengthen them out. Others, too, approach just short of a fault—for a man must really do this if he hopes to attain an imposing effect—but actually love the fault for its own sake. In short, whenever you notice that a degenerate style pleases the critics, you may be sure that character also has deviated from the right standard.

Just as luxurious banquets and elaborate dress are indications of disease in the state, similarly a lax style, if it be popular, shows that the mind (which is the source of the word) has lost its balance. Indeed you ought not to wonder that corrupt speech is welcomed not merely by the more squalid mob[*] but also by our more cultured throng; for it is only in their dress and not in their judgments that they differ. You may rather wonder that not only the effects of vices, but even vices themselves, meet with approval. For it has ever been thus: no man's ability has ever been approved without something being pardoned. Show me any man, however famous; I can tell you what it was that his age forgave in him, and what it was that his age purposely overlooked. I can show you many men whose vices have caused them no harm, and not a few who have been even helped by these vices. Yes, I will show you persons of the highest reputation, set up as models for our admiration; and yet if you seek to correct their errors, you destroy them; for vices are so intertwined with virtues that they drag the virtues along with them. Moreover, style has no fixed laws; it is changed by the usage of the people, never the same for any length of time. Many orators hark back to earlier epochs for their vocabulary, speaking in the language of the Twelve Tables.[†] Gracchus, Crassus, and Curio, in their eyes, are too refined and too modern; so back to Appius and Coruncanius![‡] Conversely, certain men, in their endeavour to maintain nothing but well-worn and common usages, fall into a humdrum style. These two classes, each in its own way, are degenerate; and it is no less degenerate to use no words except those which are conspicuous, high-sounding, and poetical, avoiding what is familiar and in ordinary usage. One is, I believe, as faulty as the other: the one class are unreasonably elaborate, the other are unreasonably negligent; the former depilate the leg, the latter not even the armpit.[§]

Let us now turn to the arrangement of words. In this department,

---

* i.e., the "ring" of onlookers, the "pit."

† Fifth century B.C.

‡ i.e., from the second and first centuries B.C., back to the third century.

§ The latter a reasonable mark of good breeding, the former an ostentatious bit of effeminacy. Summers cites Ovid, *A. A.* i. 506 "don't rub your legs smooth with the tight-scraping pumice stone."

what countless varieties of fault I can show you! Some are all for abruptness and unevenness of style, purposely disarranging anything which seems to have a smooth flow of language. They would have jolts in all their transitions; they regard as strong and manly whatever makes an uneven impression on the ear. With some others it is not so much an "arrangement" of words as it is a setting to music; so wheedling and soft is their gliding style. And what shall I say of that arrangement in which words are put off and, after being long waited for, just manage to come in at the end of a period? Or again of that softly-concluding style, Cicero-fashion,[*] with a gradual and gently poised descent always the same and always with the customary arrangement of the rhythm! Nor is the fault only in the style of the sentences, if they are either petty and childish, or debasing, with more daring than modesty should allow, or if they are flowery and cloying, or if they end in emptiness, accomplishing mere sound and nothing more.

Some individual makes these vices fashionable—some person who controls the eloquence of the day; the rest follow his lead and communicate the habit to each other. Thus when Sallust[†] was in his glory, phrases were lopped off, words came to a close unexpectedly, and obscure conciseness was equivalent to elegance. L. Arruntius, a man of rare simplicity, author of a historical work on the Punic War, was a member and a strong supporter of the Sallust school. There is a phrase in Sallust: *exercitum argento fecit*,[‡] meaning thereby that he *recruited*[§] an army by means of money. Arruntius began to like this idea; he therefore inserted the verb *facio* all through his book. Hence, in one passage, *fugam nostris fecere*;[¶] in another, *Hiero, rex Syracusanorum, bellum*

* As Cicero (see Ep. xl. 11) was an example of the rhythmical in style, so Pollio is the representative of the "bumpy" (*salebrosa*) manner (Ep. c. 7).

† Flor. 40 B.C.

‡ For these Sallust fragments see the edition of Kritz, Nos. 33, *Jug.* 37. 4, and 42; for Arruntius see H. Peter, *Frag. Hist. Rom.* ii. pp. 41 f.

§ Literally, "created," "made."

¶ [(§) (§)] "Brought to pass flight for our men"; "Hiero, king of the Syracusans brought about war"; "The news brought the men of Panormus" (now Palermo, Sicily) "to the point of surrendering to the Romans."

fecit;[§] and in another, *quae audita Panhormitanos dedere Romanis fecere.*[§] I merely desired to give you a taste; his whole book is interwoven with such stuff as this. What Sallust reserved for occasional use, Arruntius makes into a frequent and almost continual habit—and there was a reason: for Sallust used the words as they occurred to his mind, while the other writer went afield in search of them. So you see the results of copying another man's vices. Again, Sallust said: *aquis hiemantibus.*[*] Arruntius, in his first book on the Punic War, uses the words: *repente hiemavit tempestas.*[*] And elsewhere, wishing to describe an exceptionally cold year, he says: *totus hiemavit annus.* [*] And in another passage: *inde sexaginta onerarias leves praeter militem et necessarios nautarum hiemante aquilone misit*;[*] and he continues to bolster many passages with this metaphor. In a certain place, Sallust gives the words: *inter arma civilia aequi bonique famas*[†] *petit*; and Arruntius cannot restrain himself from mentioning at once, in the first book, that there were extensive "reminders" concerning Regulus.

These and similar faults, which imitation stamps upon one's style, are not necessarily indications of loose standards or of debased mind; for they are bound to be personal and peculiar to the writer, enabling one to judge thereby of a particular author's temperament; just as an angry man will talk in an angry way, an excitable man in a flurried way, and an effeminate man in a style that is soft and unresisting. You note this tendency in those who pluck out, or thin out, their beards, or who closely shear and shave the upper lip while preserving the rest of the hair and allowing it to grow, or in those who wear cloaks of outlandish colours, who wear transparent togas, and who never deign to do anything which will escape general notice; they endeavour to excite and attract men's attention, and they put up even with censure, provided that they can advertise themselves. That is the

* [*] [*] [*] "Amid the wintry waters"; "The storm suddenly grew wintry"; "The whole year was like winter"; "Then he dispatched sixty transports of light draught besides the soldiers and the necessary sailors amid a wintry storm."

† The peculiarity here is the use of the plural instead of the singular form. "Amid civil war he seeks reminders of justice and virtue."

style of Maecenas and all the others who stray from the path, not by hazard, but consciously and voluntarily. This is the result of great evil in the soul. As in the case of drink, the tongue does not trip until the mind is overcome beneath its load and gives way or betrays itself; so that intoxication of style—for what else than this can I call it?—never gives trouble to anyone unless the soul begins to totter. Therefore, I say, take care of the soul; for from the soul issue our thoughts, from the soul our words, from the soul our dispositions, our expressions, and our very gait. When the soul is sound and strong, the style too is vigorous, energetic, manly; but if the soul lose its balance, down comes all the rest in ruins.

> If but the king be safe, your swarm will live
> Harmonious; if he die, the bees revolt.*

The soul is our king. If it be safe, the other functions remain on duty and serve with obedience; but the slightest lack of equilibrium in the soul causes them to waver along with it. And when the soul has yielded to pleasure, its functions and actions grow weak, and any undertaking comes from a nerveless and unsteady source. To persist in my use of this simile—our soul is at one time a king, at another a tyrant. The king, in that he respects things honourable, watches over the welfare of the body which is entrusted to his charge, and gives that body no base, no ignoble commands. But an uncontrolled, passionate, and effeminate soul changes kingship into that most dread and detestable quality—tyranny; then it becomes a prey to the uncontrolled emotions, which dog its steps, elated at first, to be sure, like a populace idly sated with a largess which will ultimately be its undoing, and spoiling what it cannot consume. But when the disease has gradually eaten away the strength, and luxurious habits have penetrated the marrow and the sinews, such a soul exults at the sight of limbs which, through its overindulgence, it has made useless;

* Vergil, *Georg.* iv. 212 f.

instead of its own pleasures, it views those of others; it becomes the go-between and witness of the passions which, as the result of self-gratification, it can no longer feel. Abundance of delights is not so pleasing a thing to that soul as it is bitter, because it cannot send all the dainties of yore down through the over-worked throat and stomach, because it can no longer whirl in the maze of eunuchs and mistresses, and it is melancholy because a great part of its happiness is shut off, through the limitations of the body.

Now is it not madness, Lucilius, for none of us to reflect that he is mortal? Or frail? Or again that he is but one individual? Look at our kitchens, and the cooks, who bustle about over so many fires; is it, think you, for a single belly that all this bustle and preparation of food takes place? Look at the old brands of wine and store-houses filled with the vintages of many ages; is it, think you, a single belly that is to receive the stored wine, sealed with the names of so many consuls, and gathered from so many vineyards? Look, and mark in how many regions men plough the earth, and how many thousands of farmers are tilling and digging; is it, think you, for a single belly that crops are planted in Sicily and Africa? We should be sensible, and our wants more reasonable, if each of us were to take stock of himself, and to measure his bodily needs also, and understand how little he can consume, and for how short a time! But nothing will give you so much help toward moderation as the frequent thought that life is short and uncertain here below; whatever you are doing, have regard to death. Farewell.

LETTER CXXI

ON INSTINCT IN ANIMALS

You will bring suit against me, I feel sure, when I set forth for you today's little problem, with which we have already fumbled long enough. You will cry out again: "What has this to do with character?" Cry out if you like, but let me first of all match you with other opponents,* against whom you may bring suit—such as Posidonius and Archidemus;† these men will stand trial. I shall then go on to say that whatever deals with character does not necessarily produce good character. Man needs one thing for his food, another for his exercise, another for his clothing, another for his instruction, and another for his pleasure. Everything, however, has reference to man's needs, although everything does not make him better. Character is affected by different things in different ways: some things serve to correct and regulate character, and others investigate its nature and origin.

---

* i.e., in addition to myself and confirming my statement.

† Frag. 17 von Arnim.

And when I seek the reason why Nature brought forth man, and why she set him above other animals, do you suppose that I have left character-study in the rear? No; that is wrong. For how are you to know what character is desirable, unless you have discovered what is best suited to man? Or unless you have studied his nature? You can find out what you should do and what you should avoid, only when you have learned what you owe to your own nature.

"I desire," you say, "to learn how I may crave less, and fear less. Rid me of my unreasoning beliefs. Prove to me that so-called felicity is fickle and empty, and that the word easily admits of a syllable's increase."* I shall fulfil your want, encouraging your virtues and lashing your vices. People may decide that I am too zealous and reckless in this particular; but I shall never cease to hound wickedness, to check the most unbridled emotions, to soften the force of pleasures which will result in pain, and to cry down men's prayers. Of course I shall do this; for it is the greatest evils that we have prayed for, and from that which has made us give thanks comes all that demands consolation.

Meanwhile, allow me to discuss thoroughly some points which may seem now to be rather remote from the present inquiry. We were once debating whether all animals had any feelings about their "constitution."† That this is the case is proved particularly by their making motions of such fitness and nimbleness that they seem to be trained for the purpose. Every being is clever in its own line. The skilled workman handles his tools with an ease born of experience; the pilot knows how to steer his ship skilfully; the artist can quickly lay on the colours which he has prepared in great variety for the purpose of rendering the likeness, and passes with ready eye and hand from palette to canvas. In the same way an animal is agile in all that pertains to the use of its body. We are apt to wonder at skilled dancers because their gestures are perfectly adapted to the meaning of the piece and its accompanying emotions, and their movements match

* i.e. *felicitas* becomes in*felicitas*.

† i.e., their physical make-up, the elements of their physical being.

the speed of the dialogue. But that which art gives to the craftsman, is given to the animal by nature. No animal handles its limbs with difficulty, no animal is at a loss how to use its body. This function they exercise immediately at birth. They come into the world with this knowledge; they are born full-trained.

But people reply: "The reason why animals are so dexterous in the use of their limbs is that if they move them unnaturally, they will feel pain. They are *compelled* to do thus, according to your school, and it is fear rather than will-power which moves them in the right direction." This idea is wrong. Bodies driven by a compelling force move slowly; but those which move of their own accord possess alertness. The proof that it is not fear of pain which prompts them thus, is, that even when pain checks them they struggle to carry out their natural motions. Thus the child who is trying to stand and is becoming used to carry his own weight, on beginning to test his strength, falls and rises again and again with tears until through painful effort he has trained himself to the demands of nature. And certain animals with hard shells, when turned on their backs, twist and grope with their feet and make motions sideways until they are restored to their proper position. The tortoise on his back feels no suffering; but he is restless because he misses his natural condition, and does not cease to shake himself about until he stands once more upon his feet.

So all these animals have a consciousness of their physical constitution, and for that reason can manage their limbs as readily as they do; nor have we any better proof that they come into being equipped with this knowledge than the fact that no animal is unskilled in the use of its body. But some object as follows: "According to your account, one's constitution consists of a ruling power* in the soul which has a certain relation towards the body. But how can a child comprehend this intricate and subtle principle, which I can scarcely

* i.e., the "soul of the world," of which each living soul is a part. The Stoics believed that it was situated in the heart. Zeno called it ἡγεμονικόν, "ruling power"; while the Romans used the term *principale* or *principatus*. The principle described above is ὁρμή (impulse) or τόνος (tension).

explain even to you? All living creatures should be born logicians, so as to understand a definition which is obscure to the majority of Roman citizens!" Your objection would be true if I spoke of living creatures as understanding "a definition of constitution," and not "their actual constitution." Nature is easier to understand than to explain; hence, the child of whom we were speaking does not understand what "constitution" is, but understands *its own* constitution. He does not know what "a living creature" is, but he feels that he is an animal. Moreover, that very constitution of his own he only understands confusedly, cursorily, and darkly. We also know that we possess souls, but we do not know the essence, the place, the quality, or the source, of the soul. Such as is the consciousness of our souls which we possess, ignorant as we are of their nature and position, even so all animals possess a consciousness of their own constitutions. For they must necessarily feel this, because it is the same agency by which they feel other things also; they must necessarily have a feeling of the principle which they obey and by which they are controlled. Everyone of us understands that there is something which stirs his impulses, but he does not know what it is. He knows that he has a sense of striving, although he does not know what it is or its source. Thus even children and animals have a consciousness of their primary element, but it is not very clearly outlined or portrayed.

"You maintain, do you," says the objector, "that every living thing is at the start adapted to its constitution, but that man's constitution is a reasoning one, and hence man is adapted to himself not merely as a living, but as a reasoning, being? For man is dear to himself in respect of that wherein he is a man. How, then, can a child, being not yet gifted with reason, adapt himself to a reasoning constitution?" But each age has its own constitution, different in the case of the child, the boy, and the old man; they are all adapted to the constitution wherein they find themselves. The child is toothless, and he is fitted to this condition. Then his teeth grow, and he is fitted to that condition also. Vegetation also, which will develop into grain and fruits, has a special constitution when young and scarcely peeping over the tops of the furrows, another when it is strengthened and stands upon a stalk which is soft but strong enough to bear its weight, and still another when the colour changes to yellow, prophesies threshing-time, and hardens in the ear—no matter what may be the constitution into which the plant comes, it keeps it, and conforms thereto. The periods of infancy, boyhood, youth, and old age, are different; but I, who have been infant, boy, and youth, am still the same. Thus, although each has at different times a different constitution, the adaptation of each to its constitution is the same. For nature does not consign boyhood or youth, or old age, to me; it consigns me to them. Therefore, the child is adapted to that constitution which is his at the present moment of childhood, not to that which will be his in youth. For even if there is in store for him any higher phase into which he must be changed, the state in which he is born is also according to nature. First of all, the living being is adapted to itself, for there must be a pattern to which all other things may be referred. I seek pleasure; for whom? For myself. I am therefore looking out for myself. I shrink from pain; on behalf of whom? Myself. Therefore, I am looking out for myself. Since I gauge all my actions with reference to my own welfare, I am looking out for myself before all else. This quality exists in all living beings—not engrafted but inborn.

Nature brings up her own offspring and does not cast them away; and because the most assured security is that which is nearest, every man has been entrusted to his own self. Therefore, as I have remarked in the course of my previous correspondence, even young animals, on issuing from the mother's womb or from the egg, know at once of their own accord what is harmful for them, and avoid death-dealing things.* They even shrink when they notice the shadow of birds of prey which flit overhead.

No animal, when it enters upon life, is free from the fear of death. People may ask: "How can an animal at birth have an understanding

* Seneca is both sound and modern in his account of animal "intelligence." It is instinct, due to sensory-motor reactions, and depending largely upon type heredity.

of things wholesome or destructive?" The first question, however, is *whether* it can have such understanding, and not *how* it can understand. And it is clear that they have such understanding from the fact that, even if you add understanding, they will act no more adequately than they did in the first place. Why should the hen show no fear of the peacock or the goose, and yet run from the hawk, which is a so much smaller animal not even familiar to the hen? Why should young chickens fear a cat and not a dog? These fowls clearly have a presentiment of harm—one not based on actual experiments; for they avoid a thing before they can possibly have experience of it. Furthermore, in order that you may not suppose this to be the result of chance, they do not shrink from certain other things which you would expect them to fear, nor do they ever forget vigilance and care in this regard; they all possess equally the faculty of avoiding what is destructive. Besides, their fear does not grow as their lives lengthen.

Hence indeed it is evident that these animals have not reached such a condition through experience; it is because of an inborn desire for self-preservation. The teachings of experience are slow and irregular; but whatever Nature communicates belongs equally to everyone, and comes immediately. If, however, you require an explanation, shall I tell you how it is that every living thing tries to understand that which is harmful? It feels that it is constructed of flesh; and so it perceives to what an extent flesh may be cut or burned or crushed, and what animals are equipped with the power of doing this damage; it is of animals of this sort that it derives an unfavourable and hostile idea. These tendencies are closely connected; for each animal at the same time consults its own safety, seeking that which helps it, and shrinks from that which will harm it. Impulses towards useful objects, and revulsion from the opposite, are according to nature; without any reflection to prompt the idea, and without any advice, whatever Nature has prescribed, is done.

Do you not see how skillful bees are in building their cells? How completely harmonious in sharing and enduring toil? Do you not see how the spider weaves a web so subtle that man's hand cannot imitate it; and what a task it is to arrange the threads, some directed straight towards the centre, for the sake of making the web solid, and others running in circles and lessening in thickness—for the purpose of tangling and catching in a sort of net the smaller insects for whose ruin the spider spreads the web? This art is born, not taught; and for this reason no animal is more skilled than any other. You will notice that all spider-webs are equally fine, and that the openings in all honeycomb cells are identical in shape. Whatever art communicates is uncertain and uneven; but Nature's assignments are always uniform. Nature has communicated nothing except the duty of taking care of themselves and the skill to do so; that is why living and learning begin at the same time. No wonder that living things are born with a gift whose absence would make birth useless. This is the first equipment that Nature granted them for the maintenance of their existence—the quality of adaptability and self-love. They could not survive except by desiring to do so. Nor would this desire alone have made them prosper, but without it nothing could have prospered. In no animal can you observe any low esteem, or even any carelessness, of self. Dumb beasts, sluggish in other respects, are clever at living. So you will see that creatures which are useless to others are alert for their own preservation.* Farewell.

* A theme developed by Cicero (*De fin.* iii. 16): *placet . . . simul atque natum sit animal . . . , ipsum sibi conciliari et commendari ad se conservandum.*

LETTER CXXII

ON DARKNESS AS A VEIL FOR WICKEDNESS

The day has already begun to lessen. It has shrunk considerably, but yet will still allow a goodly space of time if one rises, so to speak, with the day itself. We are more industrious, and we are better men if we anticipate the day and welcome the dawn; but we are base churls if we lie dozing when the sun is high in the heavens, or if we wake up only when noon arrives; and even then to many it seems not yet dawn. Some have reversed the functions of light and darkness; they open eyes sodden with yesterday's debauch only at the approach of night. It is just like the condition of those peoples whom, according to Vergil, Nature has hidden away and placed in an abode directly opposite to our own:

When in our face the Dawn with panting steeds
Breathes down, for them the ruddy evening kindles
Her late-lit fires.*

* Vergil, *Georg.* i. 250 ff.

It is not the country of these men, so much as it is their life, that is "directly opposite" to our own. There may be Antipodes dwelling in this same city of ours who, in Cato's words,* "have never seen the sun rise or set." Do you think that these men know *how* to live, if they do not know *when* to live? Do these men fear death, if they have buried themselves alive? They are as weird as the birds of night.† Although they pass their hours of darkness amid wine and perfumes, although they spend the whole extent of their unnatural waking hours in eating dinners—and those too cooked separately to make up many courses—they are not really banqueting; they are conducting their own funeral services. And the dead at least have their banquets by daylight.‡

But indeed to one who is active no day is long. So let us lengthen our lives; for the duty and the proof of life consist in action. Cut short the night; use some of it for the day's business. Birds that are being prepared for the banquet, that they may be easily fattened through lack of exercise, are kept in darkness; and similarly, if men vegetate without physical activity, their idle bodies are overwhelmed with flesh, and in their self-satisfied retirement the fat of indolence grows upon them. Moreover, the bodies of those who have sworn allegiance to the hours of darkness have a loathsome appearance. Their complexions are more alarming than those of anaemic invalids; they are lackadaisical and flabby with dropsy; though still alive, they are already carrion. But this, to my thinking, would be among the least of their evils. How much more darkness there is in their souls! Such a man is internally dazed; his vision is darkened; he envies the blind. And what man ever had eyes for the purpose of seeing in the dark?

You ask me how this depravity comes upon the soul—this habit of reversing the daylight and giving over one's whole existence to the night? All vices rebel against Nature; they all abandon the appointed order. It is the motto of luxury to enjoy what is unusual, and not only to

* Cato, Frag. p. 110 Jordan.

† i.e., owls, of ill omen.

‡ In connexion with the *Parentalia*, Feb. 13-21, and at other anniversary observations, the ceremonies were held in the daytime.

depart from that which is right, but to leave it as far behind as possible, and finally even take a stand in opposition thereto. Do you not believe that men live contrary to Nature who drink fasting,* who take wine into empty veins, and pass to their food in a state of intoxication? And yet this is one of youth's popular vices—to perfect their strength in order to drink on the very threshold of the bath, amid the unclad bathers; nay even to soak in wine and then immediately to rub off the sweat which they have promoted by many a hot glass of liquor! To them, a glass after lunch or one after dinner is *bourgeois*; it is what the country squires do, who are not connoisseurs in pleasure. This unmixed wine delights them just because there is no food to float in it, because it readily makes its way into their muscles; this boozing pleases them just because the stomach is empty.

Do you not believe that men live contrary to Nature who exchange the fashion of their attire with women?† Do not men live contrary to Nature who endeavour to look fresh and boyish at an age unsuitable for such an attempt? What could be more cruel or more wretched? Cannot time and man's estate ever carry such a person beyond an artificial boyhood?‡ Do not men live contrary to Nature who crave roses in winter, or seek to raise a spring flower like the lily by means of hot-water heaters and artificial changes of temperature? Do not men live contrary to Nature who grow fruit-trees on the top of a wall? Or raise waving forests upon the roofs and battlements of their houses—the roots starting at a point to which it would be outlandish for the tree-tops to reach? Do not men live contrary to Nature who lay the foundations of bathrooms in the sea and do not imagine that they can enjoy their swim unless the heated pool is lashed as with the waves of a storm?

---

* A vice which Seneca especially abhors; cf. Ep. xv. 3 *multum potionis altius ieiunio iturae.*

† By wearing silk gowns of transparent material.

‡ Not literally translated. For the same thought see Ep. xlvii. 7, etc. *Transcriber's note: The Latin which Gummere refused to translate literally is "Numquam vir erit, ut diu virum pati possit? Et cum illum contumeliae sexus eripuisse debuerat, non ne aetas quidem eripiet?" or roughly: "Will he never become a man, so that he can continue to be screwed by men? And though his sex ought to spare him this insult, won't even his age spare him?"*

When men have begun to desire all things in opposition to the ways of Nature, they end by entirely abandoning the ways of Nature. They cry: "It is daytime—let us go to sleep! It is the time when men rest: now for exercise, now for our drive, now for our lunch! Lo, the dawn approaches: it is dinner-time! We should not do as mankind do. It is low and mean to live in the usual and conventional way. Let us abandon the ordinary sort of day. Let us have a morning that is a special feature of ours, peculiar to ourselves!" Such men are, in my opinion, as good as dead. Are they not all but present at a funeral—and before their time too—when they live amid torches and tapers?* I remember that this sort of life was very fashionable at one time: among such men as Acilius Buta, a person of praetorian rank, who ran through a tremendous estate and on confessing his bankruptcy to Tiberius, received the answer: "You have waked up too late!" Julius Montanus was once reading a poem aloud; he was a middling good poet, noted for his friendship with Tiberius, as well as his fall from favour. He always used to fill his poems with a generous sprinkling of sunrises and sunsets. Hence, when a certain person was complaining that Montanus had read all day long, and declared that no man should attend any of his readings, Natta Pinarius† remarked: "I couldn't make a fairer bargain than this: I am ready to listen to him from sunrise to sunset!" Montanus was reading, and had reached the words:‡

'Gins the bright morning to spread forth his flames clear-burning; the red dawn
Scatters its light; and the sad-eyed swallow§ returns to her nestlings,
Bringing the chatterers' food, and with sweet bill sharing and serving.

---

* The symbols of a Roman funeral. For the same practice, purposely performed, see Ep. xii. 8 (and the note of W. C. Summers).

† Called by Tacitus, *Ann.* iv. 34, a *Seiani cliens.*

‡ Baehrens, *Frag. Poet. Rom.* p. 355.

§ i.e., Procne, in the well-known nightingale myth.

Then Varus, a Roman knight, the hanger-on of Marcus Vinicius,* and a sponger at elegant dinners which he earned by his degenerate wit, shouted: "Bed-time for Buta!" And later, when Montanus declaimed

> Lo, now the shepherds have folded their flocks, and the slow-moving darkness
> 'Gins to spread silence o'er lands that are drowsily lulled into slumber,

this same Varus remarked: "What? Night already? I'll go and pay my morning call on Buta!" You see, nothing was more notorious than Buta's upside-down manner of life. But this life, as I said, was fashionable at one time. And the reason why some men live thus is not because they think that night in itself offers any greater attractions, but because that which is normal gives them no particular pleasure; light being a bitter enemy of the evil conscience, and, when one craves or scorns all things in proportion as they have cost one much or little, illumination for which one does not pay is an object of contempt. Moreover, the luxurious person wishes to be an object of gossip his whole life; if people are silent about him, he thinks that he is wasting his time. Hence he is uncomfortable whenever any of his actions escape notoriety.

Many men eat up their property, and many men keep mistresses. If you would win a reputation among such persons, you must make your programme not only one of luxury but one of notoriety; for in such a busy community wickedness does not discover the ordinary sort of scandal. I heard Pedo Albinovanus, that most attractive story-teller, speaking of his residence above the town-house of Sextus Papinius. Papinius belonged to the tribe of those who shun the light. "About nine o'clock at night I hear the sound of whips. I ask what is going on, and they tell me that Papinius is going over his accounts.† About twelve there is a strenuous shouting; I ask what the matter is, and they say he is

* Son of the P. Vinicius ridiculed in Ep. xl. 9. He was husband of Julia, youngest daughter of Germanicus, and was poisoned by Messalina.

† i.e., is punishing his slaves for errors in the day's work.

exercising his voice. About two a.m. I ask the significance of the sound of wheels; they tell me that he is off for a drive. And at dawn there is a tremendous flurry-calling of slaves and butlers, and pandemonium among the cooks. I ask the meaning of this also, and they tell me that he has called for his cordial and his appetizer, after leaving the bath. His dinner," said Pedo, "never went beyond the day,* for he lived very sparingly; he was lavish with nothing but the night. Accordingly, if you believe those who call him tight-fisted and mean, you will call him also a 'slave of the lamp.'"†

You should not be surprised at finding so many special manifestations of the vices; for vices vary, and there are countless phases of them, nor can all their various kinds be classified. The method of maintaining righteousness is simple; the method of maintaining wickedness is complicated, and has infinite opportunity to swerve. And the same holds true of character; if you follow nature, character is easy to manage, free, and with very slight shades of difference; but the sort of person I have mentioned possesses badly warped character, out of harmony with all things, including himself. The chief cause, however, of this disease seems to me to be a squeamish revolt from the normal existence. Just as such persons mark themselves off from others in their dress, or in the elaborate arrangement of their dinners, or in the elegance of their carriages; even so they desire to make themselves peculiar by their way of dividing up the hours of their day. They are unwilling to be wicked in the conventional way, because notoriety is the reward of their sort of wickedness. Notoriety is what all such men seek—men who are, so to speak, *living backwards*.

For this reason, Lucilius, let us keep to the way which Nature has mapped out for us, and let us not swerve therefrom. If we follow Nature, all is easy and unobstructed; but if we combat Nature, our life differs not a whit from that of men who row against the current. Farewell.

---

* i.e., balancing the custom of the ordinary Roman, whose dinner never continued beyond nightfall.

† "'A liver by candle-light,' with a play on the word λίχνος, 'luxurious'" (Summers).

LETTER CXXIII

ON THE CONFLICT BETWEEN PLEASURE AND VIRTUE

Wearied with the discomfort rather than with the length of my journey, I have reached my Alban villa late at night, and I find nothing in readiness except myself. So I am getting rid of fatigue at my writing-table: I derive some good from this tardiness on the part of my cook and my baker. For I am communing with myself on this very topic—that nothing is heavy if one accepts it with a light heart, and that nothing need provoke one's anger if one does not add to one's pile of troubles by getting angry. My baker is out of bread; but the overseer, or the house-steward, or one of my tenants can supply me therewith. "Bad bread!" you say. But just wait for it; it will become good. Hunger will make even such bread delicate and of the finest flavour. For that reason I must not eat until hunger bids me; so I shall wait and shall not eat until I can either get good bread or else cease to be squeamish about it. It is necessary that one grow accustomed to slender fare: because there are many problems of time and place which will cross the path even of the rich man and one equipped for pleasure, and bring him up with a round turn. To have whatsoever he wishes is in no man's power; it is in his power not to wish for what he has not, but cheerfully to employ what comes to him. A great step towards independence is a good-humoured stomach, one that is willing to endure rough treatment.

You cannot imagine how much pleasure I derive from the fact that my weariness is becoming reconciled to itself; I am asking for no slaves to rub me down, no bath, and no other restorative except time. For that which toil has accumulated, rest can lighten. This repast, whatever it may be, will give me more pleasure than an inaugural banquet.* For I have made trial of my spirit on a sudden—a simpler and a truer test. Indeed, when a man has made preparations and given himself a formal summons to be patient, it is not equally clear just how much real strength of mind he possesses; the surest proofs are those which one exhibits off-hand, viewing one's own troubles not only fairly but calmly, not flying into fits of temper or wordy wranglings, supplying one's own needs by not craving something which was really due, and reflecting that our habits may be unsatisfied, but never our own real selves. How many things are superfluous we fail to realize until they begin to be wanting; we merely used them not because we needed them but because we had them. And how much do we acquire simply because our neighbours have acquired such things, or because most men possess them! Many of our troubles may be explained from the fact that we live according to a pattern, and, instead of arranging our lives according to reason, are led astray by convention.

There are things which, if done by the few, we should refuse to imitate; yet when the majority have begun to do them, we follow along—just as if anything were more honourable because it is more frequent! Furthermore, wrong views, when they have become prevalent, reach, in our eyes, the standard of righteousness. Everyone now travels with Numidian outriders preceding him, with a troop

* i.e., a dinner given by an official when he entered upon (*adeo*) his office.

of slave-runners to clear the way; we deem it disgraceful to have no attendants who will elbow crowds from the road, or will prove, by a great cloud of dust, that a high dignitary is approaching! Everyone now possesses mules that are laden with crystal and myrrhine cups carved by skilled artists of great renown; it is disgraceful for all your baggage to be made up of that which can be rattled along without danger. Everyone has pages who ride along with ointment-covered faces, so that the heat or the cold will not harm their tender complexions; it is disgraceful that none of your attendant slave-boys should show a healthy cheek, not covered with cosmetics.

You should avoid conversation with all such persons: they are the sort that communicate and engraft their bad habits from one to another. We used to think that the very worst variety of these men were those who vaunted their words; but there are certain men who vaunt their wickedness. Their talk is very harmful; for even though it is not at once convincing, yet they leave the seeds of trouble in the soul, and the evil which is sure to spring into new strength follows us about even when we have parted from them. Just as those who have attended a concert* carry about in their heads the melodies and the charm of the songs they have heard—a proceeding which interferes with their thinking and does not allow them to concentrate upon serious subjects,—even so the speech of flatterers and enthusiasts over that which is depraved sticks in our minds long after we have heard them talk. It is not easy to rid the memory of a catching tune; it stays with us, lasts on, and comes back from time to time. Accordingly, you should close your ears against evil talk, and right at the outset, too; for when such talk has gained an entrance and the words are admitted and are in our minds, they become more shameless. And then we begin to speak as follows: "Virtue, Philosophy, Justice—this is a jargon of empty words. The only way to be happy is to do yourself well. To eat, drink, and spend

* For *symphonia* see Ep. li. 4 and note. Compare also the *commissiones*, orchestral exhibitions, composed of many voices, flutes, and brass instruments, Ep. lxxxiv. 10.

your money is the only real life, the only way to remind yourself that you are mortal. Our days flow on, and life—which we cannot restore—hastens away from us. Why hesitate to come to our senses? This life of ours will not always admit pleasures; meantime, while it can do so, while it clamours for them, what profit lies in imposing thereupon frugality? Therefore get ahead of death, and let anything that death will filch from you be squandered now upon yourself. You have no mistress, no favourite slave to make your mistress envious; you are sober when you make your daily appearance in public; you dine as if you had to show your account-book to 'Papa'; but *that* is not living, it is merely going shares in someone else's existence. And what madness it is to be looking out for the interests of your heir, and to deny yourself everything, with the result that you turn friends into enemies by the vast amount of the fortune you intend to leave! For the more the heir is to get from you, the more he will rejoice in your taking-off! All those sour fellows who criticize other men's lives in a spirit of priggishness and are real enemies to their own lives, playing schoolmaster to the world—you should not consider them as worth a farthing, nor should you hesitate to prefer good living to a good reputation."

These are voices which you ought to shun just as Ulysses did; he would not sail past them until he was lashed to the mast. They are no less potent; they lure men from country, parents, friends, and virtuous ways; and by a hope that, if not base, is ill-starred, they wreck them upon a life of baseness. How much better to follow a straight course and attain a goal where the words "pleasant" and "honourable" have the same meaning!* This end will be possible for us if we understand that there are two classes of objects which either attract us or repel us. We are attracted by such things as riches, pleasures, beauty, ambition, and other such coaxing and pleasing objects; we are repelled by toil, death, pain, disgrace, or lives of greater frugality. We ought therefore to train ourselves so that we

* i.e., to live by Stoicism rather than by Epicureanism.

may avoid a fear of the one or a desire for the other. Let us fight in the opposite fashion: let us retreat from the objects that allure, and rouse ourselves to meet the objects that attack.

Do you not see how different is the method of descending a mountain from that employed in climbing upwards? Men coming down a slope bend backwards; men ascending a steep place lean forward. For, my dear Lucilius, to allow yourself to put your body's weight ahead when coming down, or, when climbing up, to throw it backward is to comply with vice. The pleasures take one down hill but one must work upwards toward that which is rough and hard to climb; in the one case let us throw our bodies forward, in the others let us put the check-rein on them.

Do you believe me to be stating now that only those men bring ruin to our ears, who praise pleasure, who inspire us with fear of pain—that element which is in itself provocative of fear? I believe that we are also in injured by those who masquerade under the disguise of the Stoic school and at the same time urge us on into vice. They boast that only the wise man and the learned is a lover.* "He alone has wisdom in this art; the wise man too is best skilled in drinking and feasting. Our study ought to be this alone: up to what age the bloom of love can endure!" All this may be regarded as a concession to the ways of Greece; we ourselves should preferably turn our attention to words like these: "No man is good by chance. Virtue is something which must be learned. Pleasure is low, petty, to be deemed worthless, shared even by dumb animals—the tiniest and meanest of whom fly towards pleasure. Glory is an empty and fleeting thing, lighter than air. Poverty is an evil to no man unless he kick against the goads.† Death is not an evil; why need you ask? Death alone is the equal privilege of mankind. Superstition is the misguided idea of a lunatic;

* Meaning, in line with the Stoic paradoxes, that only the sage knows how to be rightly in love.

† *Transcriber's note: The Latin is "Paupertas nulli malum est nisi repugnanti," i.e. "Poverty is an evil to noone unless they resist." Gummere's odd phrase "kick against the goads" is actually from the Bible (Acts 26:14)*

it fears those whom it ought to love; it is an outrage upon those whom it worships. For what difference is there between denying the gods and dishonouring them?"

You should learn such principles as these, nay rather you should learn them by heart; philosophy ought not to try to explain away vice. For a sick man, when his physician bids him live recklessly, is doomed beyond recall. Farewell.

LETTER

CXXIV

ON THE TRUE GOOD AS ATTAINED BY REASON

Full many an ancient precept could I give,
Didst thou not shrink, and feel it shame to learn
Such lowly duties.*

But you do not shrink, nor are you deterred by any subtleties of study. For your cultivated mind is not wont to investigate such important subjects in a free-and-easy manner. I approve your method in that you make everything count towards a certain degree of progress, and in that you are disgruntled only when nothing can be accomplished by the greatest degree of subtlety. And I shall take pains to show that this is the case now also. Our question is, whether the Good is grasped by the senses or by the understanding; and the corollary thereto is that it does not exist in dumb animals or little children.

* Vergil, *Georg.* i. 176 f.

Those who rate pleasure as the supreme ideal hold that the Good is a matter of the senses; but we Stoics maintain that it is a matter of the understanding, and we assign it to the mind. If the senses were to pass judgment on what is good, we should never reject any pleasure; for there is no pleasure that does not attract, no pleasure that does not please. Conversely, we should undergo no pain voluntarily; for there is no pain that does not clash with the senses. Besides, those who are too fond of pleasure and those who fear pain to the greatest degree would in that case not deserve reproof. But we condemn men who are slaves to their appetites and their lusts, and we scorn men who, through fear of pain, will dare no manly deed. But what wrong could such men be committing if they looked merely to the senses as arbiters of good and evil? For it is to the senses that you and yours have entrusted the test of things to be sought and things to be avoided!

Reason, however, is surely the governing element in such a matter as this; as reason has made the decision concerning the happy life, and concerning virtue and honour also, so she has made the decision with regard to good and evil. For with them* the vilest part is allowed to give sentence about the better, so that the senses—dense as they are, and dull, and even more sluggish in man than in the other animals,—pass judgment on the Good. Just suppose that one should desire to distinguish tiny objects by the touch rather than by the eyesight! There is no special faculty more subtle and acute than the eye, that would enable us to distinguish between good and evil. You see, therefore, in what ignorance of truth a man spends his days and how abjectly he has overthrown lofty and divine ideals, if he thinks that the sense of touch can pass judgment upon the nature of the Supreme Good and the Supreme Evil! He† says: "Just as every science and every art should possess an element that is palpable and capable of being grasped by the senses (their source of origin and growth), even so the happy life derives its foundation and

* i.e., the Epicureans.

† i.e., the advocate of the "touch" theory.

its beginnings from things that are palpable, and from that which falls within the scope of the senses. Surely you admit that the happy life takes its beginnings from things palpable to the senses." But we define as "happy" those things that are in accord with Nature. And that which is in accord with Nature is obvious and can be seen at once—just as easily as that which is complete. That which is according to Nature, that which is given us as a gift immediately at our birth, is, I maintain, not a Good, but the beginning of a Good. You, however, assign the Supreme Good, pleasure, to mere babies, so that the child at its birth begins at the point whither the perfected man arrives. You are placing the tree-top where the root ought to be. If anyone should say that the child, hidden in its mother's womb, of unknown sex too, delicate, unformed, and shapeless—if one should say that this child is already in a state of goodness, he would clearly seem to be astray in his ideas. And yet how little difference is there between one who has just lately received the gift of life, and one who is still a hidden burden in the bowels of the mother! They are equally developed, as far as their understanding of good or evil is concerned; and a child is as yet no more capable of comprehending the Good than is a tree or any dumb beast.

But why is the Good non-existent in a tree or in a dumb beast? Because there is no reason there, either. For the same cause, then, the Good is non-existent in a child, for the child also has no reason; the child will reach the Good only when he reaches reason.[*] There are animals without reason, there are animals not yet endowed with reason, and there are animals who possess reason, but only incompletely;[†] in none of these does the Good exist, for it is reason that brings the Good in its company. What, then, is the distinction between the classes which I have mentioned? In that which does not possess reason, the Good will never exist. In that which is not

---

* According to the Stoics (and other schools also), the "innate notions," or groundwork of knowledge, begin to be subject to reason after the attainment of a child's seventh year.

† i.e., they are limited to "practical judgment."

yet endowed with reason, the Good cannot be existent at the time. And in that which possesses reason but only incompletely, the Good is capable of existing, but does not yet exist. This is what I mean, Lucilius: the Good cannot be discovered in any random person, or at any random age; and it is as far removed from infancy as last is from first, or as that which is complete from that which has just sprung into being. Therefore, it cannot exist in the delicate body, when the little frame has only just begun to knit together. Of course not—no more than in the seed. Granting the truth of this, we understand that there is a certain kind of Good of a tree or in a plant; but this is not true of its first growth, when the plant has just begun to spring forth out of the ground. There is a certain Good of wheat: it is not yet existent, however, in the swelling stalk, nor when the soft ear is pushing itself out of the husk, but only when summer days and its appointed maturity have ripened the wheat. Just as Nature in general does not produce her Good until she is brought to perfection, even so man's Good does not exist in man until both reason and man are perfected. And what is this Good? I shall tell you: it is a free mind, an upright mind, subjecting other things to itself and itself to nothing. So far is infancy from admitting this Good that boyhood has no hope of it, and even young manhood cherishes the hope without justification; even our old age is very fortunate if it has reached this Good after long and concentrated study. If this, then, is the Good, the good is a matter of the understanding.

"But," comes the retort, "you admitted that there is a certain Good of trees and of grass; then surely there can be a certain Good of a child also." But the true Good is not found in trees or in dumb animals the Good which exists in them is called "good" only by courtesy.* "Then what is it?" you say. Simply that which is in accord with the nature of each. The real Good cannot find a place in dumb animals—not by any means; its nature is more blest and is of a higher

* Just as Academic and Peripatetic philosophers sometimes defined as "goods" what the Stoics called "advantages."

class. And where there is no place for reason, the Good does not exist. There are four natures which we should mention here: of the tree, animal, man, and God. The last two, having reasoning power, are of the same nature, distinct only by virtue of the immortality of the one and the mortality of the other. Of one of these, then—to wit God—it is Nature that perfects the Good; of the other—to wit man—pains and study do so. All other things are perfect only in their particular nature, and not truly perfect, since they lack reason.

Indeed, to sum up, that alone is perfect which is perfect according to nature as a whole, and nature as a whole is possessed of reason. Other things can be perfect according to their kind. That which cannot contain the happy life cannot contain that which produces the happy life; and the happy life is produced by Goods alone. In dumb animals there is not a trace of the happy life, nor of the means whereby the happy life is produced; in dumb animals the Good does not exist. The dumb animal comprehends the present world about him through his senses alone. He remembers the past only by meeting with something which reminds his senses; a horse, for example, remembers the right road only when he is placed at the starting-point. In his stall, however, he has no memory of the road, no matter how often he may have stepped along it. The third state—the future—does not come within the ken of dumb beasts.

How, then, can we regard as perfect the nature of those who have no experience of time in its perfection? For time is three-fold,—past, present, and future. Animals perceive only the time which is of greatest moment to them within the limits of their coming and going—the present. Rarely do they recollect the past—and that only when they are confronted with present reminders. Therefore the Good of a perfect nature cannot exist in an imperfect nature; for if the latter sort of nature should possess the Good, so also would mere vegetation. I do not indeed deny that dumb animals have strong and swift impulses toward actions which seem according to nature, but such impulses are confused and disordered. The Good however, is never confused or disordered.

"What!" you say, "do dumb animals move in disturbed and ill-ordered fashion?" I should say that they moved in disturbed and ill-ordered fashion, if their nature admitted of order; as it is, they move in accordance with their nature. For that is said to be "disturbed" which can also at some other time be "not disturbed"; so, too, that is said to be in a state of trouble which can be in a state of peace. No man is vicious except one who has the capacity of virtue; in the case of dumb animals their motion is such as results from their nature. But, not to weary you, a certain sort of good will be found in a dumb animal, and a certain sort of virtue, and a certain sort of perfection—but neither the Good, nor virtue, nor perfection in the absolute sense. For this is the privilege of reasoning beings alone, who are permitted to know the cause, the degree, and the means. Therefore, good can exist only in that which possesses reason.

Do you ask now whither our argument is tending, and of what benefit it will be to your mind? I will tell you: it exercises and sharpens the mind, and ensures, by occupying it honourably, that it will accomplish some sort of good. And even that is beneficial which holds men back when they are hurrying into wickedness. However, I will say this also: I can be of no greater benefit to you than by revealing the Good that is rightly yours, by taking you out of the class of dumb animals, and by placing you on a level with God. Why, pray, do you foster and practise your bodily strength? Nature has granted strength in greater degree to cattle and wild beasts. Why cultivate your beauty? After all your efforts, dumb animals surpass you in comeliness. Why dress your hair with such unending attention? Though you let it down in Parthian fashion, or tie it up in the German style, or, as the Scythians do, let it flow wild—yet you will see a mane of greater thickness tossing upon any horse you choose, and a mane of greater beauty bristling upon the neck of any lion. And even after training yourself for speed, you will be no match for the hare. Are you not willing to abandon all these details—wherein you must acknowledge defeat, striving as you are for something that is not your own—and come back to the Good that is really yours?

And what is this Good? It is a clear and flawless mind, which rivals that of God,* raised far above mortal concerns, and counting nothing of its own to be outside itself. You are a reasoning animal. What Good, then, lies within you? Perfect reason. Are you willing to develop this to its farthest limits—to its greatest degree of increase? Only consider yourself happy when all your joys are born of reason, and when—having marked all the objects which men clutch at, or pray for, or watch over—you find nothing which you will desire; mind, I do not say *prefer*. Here is a short rule by which to measure yourself, and by the test of which you may feel that you have reached perfection: "You will come to your own when you shall understand that those whom the world calls fortunate are really the most unfortunate of all." Farewell.

* One of the most conspicuous Stoic paradoxes maintained that "the wise man is a God."